Irvine Welsh

NEW BRITISH FICTION

Series editors:
Philip Tew
Rod Mengham

Published
Bradley Buchanan: Hanif Kureishi
Robert Morace: Irvine Welsh

Forthcoming
Sonya Andermahr: **Jeanette Winterson**
Frederick M. Holmes: **Julian Barnes**
Rod Mengham: **Jonathan Coe**
Kaye Mitchell: **A. L. Kennedy**
Stephen Morton: **Salman Rushdie**
Mark Rawlinson: **Pat Barker**
Philip Tew: **Zadie Smith**
Lynn Wells: **Ian McEwan**
Wendy Wheeler: **A. S. Byatt**

New British Fiction Series
Series Standing Order

ISBN 1–4039–4274-9 hardback
ISBN 1–4039–4275-7 paperback
(*outside North America only*)

You can receive future titles in this series as they are published by placing a standing order. Please contact your bookseller or, in the case of difficulty, write to us at the address below with your name and address, the title of the series and the ISBN quoted above.

Customer Services Department, Palgrave Ltd
Houndmills, Basingstoke, Hampshire RG21 6XS, England

NEW BRITISH FICTION

Irvine Welsh

Robert A. Morace

First published 2007 by
PALGRAVE MACMILLAN
Houndmills, Basingstoke, Hampshire RG21 6XS and
175 Fifth Avenue, New York, N.Y. 10010
Companies and representatives throughout the world

PALGRAVE MACMILLAN is the global academic imprint of the Palgrave Macmillan division of St. Martin's Press, LLC and of Palgrave Macmillan Ltd. Macmillan® is a registered trademark in the United States, United Kingdom and other countries. Palgrave is a registered trademark in the European Union and other countries.

ISBN-13: 978–1–4039–9675–6   hardback
ISBN-10: 1–4039–9675–X   hardback
ISBN-13: 978–1–4039–9676–3   paperback
ISBN-10: 1–4039–9676–8   paperback

This book is printed on paper suitable for recycling and made from fully managed and sustained forest sources. Logging, pulping and manufacturing processes are expected to conform to the environmental regulations of the country of origin.

A catalogue record for this book is available from the British Library.

A catalog record for this book is available from the Library of Congress.

10   9   8   7   6   5   4   3   2   1
16 15 14 13 12 11 10 09 08 07

Printed and bound in China

To Neela, again

CONTENTS

CONTENTS

GENERAL EDITORS' PREFACE

This series highlights with its very title two crucial elements in the nature of contemporary British fiction, especially as a field for academic research and study. The first term indicates the originality and freshness of such writing expressed in a huge formal diversity. The second evokes the cultural identity of the authors included, who nevertheless represent through their diversity a challenge to any hegemonic or narrow view of Britishness. As regards the fiction, many of the writers featured in this series continue to draw from and adapt long traditions of cultural and aesthetic practice. Such aesthetic continuities contrast starkly with the conditions of knowledge at the end of the twentieth century and the beginning of the twenty-first, a period that has been characterized by an apprehension of radical presentness, a sense of unprecedented forms of experience and an obsession with new modes of self-awareness. This stage of the survival of the novel may perhaps be best remembered as a millennial and post-millennial moment, a time of fluctuating reading practices and of historical events whose impact is largely still unresolved. The new fiction of these times reflects a rapidly changing cultural and ideological reality, as well as a renewal of the commitment of both writers and readers to both the relevance and utility of narrative forms of knowledge.

Each volume in this series will serve as an introductory guide to an individual author chosen from a list of those whose work has proved to be of general interest to reviewers, academics, students and the general reading public. Each volume will offer information concerning the life, work and literary and cultural contexts appropriate to the chosen subject of each book; individual volumes will share the same overall structure with a largely common organization of materials. The result is intended to be suitable for both academic and general readers: putting accessibility at a premium, without compromising an ambitious series of readings of today's most vitally interesting British novelists, interpreting their work, assessing their influences, and exploring their relationship to the times in which they live.

Philip Tew and Rod Mengham

ACKNOWLEDGEMENTS

Writing this book would not have been possible without the help and encouragement of Daemen College's Faculty Research and Faculty Travel Committees; Shirley Peterson, Chair of the Daemen College English Department; and Ed Clausen, Daemen College's Vice-President for Academic Affairs. Friends who kept asking how the book was progressing – Sheila and Arindam, Frank and Helene, Michael and Milind, and Marie – helped keep me honest and on schedule. My parents, for doing the same and for letting me make my own mistakes. My sons, Robin and Arun at home and Jason from afar, for giving me both the time to work and a reason to believe that the work may be useful. Neela, for being here the past twenty years rather than half a world away. And Irvine Welsh, whose *Trainspotting* arrived at just the right time for this American reader who finds its mix of angry cynicism and joyous excess just as relevant now as it was then.

PART I
Introduction

TIMELINE

1960   PM Harold Macmillan's 'Winds of Change' speech, Cape Town, South Africa
John F. Kennedy elected as US President
Aged six, Kazuo Ishiguro arrives in Britain

1961   Adolf Eichmann on trial in Israel for role in Holocaust
Bay of Pigs: attempted invasion of Cuba
Berlin Wall constructed
Yuri Gagarin first person in Space
Silicon chip patented
Private Eye magazine begins publication
Muriel Spark, *The Prime of Miss Jean Brodie*
Jonathan Coe born

1962   Cuban Missile Crisis
Marilyn Monroe dies
Independence for Uganda; followed this decade by Kenya (1963), Northern Rhodesia (1964), Southern Rhodesia (1965), Barbados (1966)

1

1963   John F. Kennedy assassinated in Dallas
Martin Luther King Jr delivers 'I Have a Dream' speech
Profumo Affair

1964   Nelson Mandela sentenced to life imprisonment
Commercial pirate radio challenges BBC monopoly

1965   State funeral of Winston Churchill
US sends troops to Vietnam
A. L. Kennedy born in Dundee, Scotland

1966   Ian Brady and Myra Hindley sentenced to life imprison-
ment for Moors Murders
England beats West Germany 4–2 at Wembley to win
Football World Cup
Star Trek series debut on NBC television
Jean Rhys, *The Wide Sargasso Sea*

1967   Six-Day War in the Middle East
World's first heart transplant
Abortion Act legalizes termination of pregnancy in UK
Sergeant Pepper's Lonely Hearts Club Band album released by
The Beatles
Flann O'Brien, *The Third Policeman*
The last of the great Clyde-built ocean liners, *The Queen
Elizabeth II*, is launched

1968   Anti-Vietnam War protestors attempt to storm American
Embassy in Grosvenor Square
Martin Luther King Jr assassinated
Robert F. Kennedy assassinated
Student protests and riots in France
Lord Chamberlain's role as censor of plays in the UK is
abolished
Lindsay Anderson, *If…*

1969 Civil rights march in Northern Ireland attacked by Protestants

Apollo 11 lands on the Moon with Neil Armstrong's famous first steps

Rock concert at Woodstock

Yasser Arafat becomes leader of PLO

Booker Prize first awarded; winner P. H. Newby, *Something to Answer for*

Open University founded in the UK

John Fowles, *The French Lieutenant's Woman*

1970 Popular Front for the Liberation of Palestine (PFLP) hijacks five planes

Students activists and bystanders shot in anti-Vietnam War protest at Kent State University, Ohio, four killed, nine wounded

UK voting age reduced from 21 years to 18

1971 Decimal currency introduced in the UK

Internment without trial of terrorist suspects in Northern Ireland begins

India and Pakistan in conflict after Bangladesh declares independence

Sixty-six people die at Ibrox Stadium in Scotland's worst football disaster (2 January)

1972 Miners' strike

Bloody Sunday in Londonderry, 14 protestors killed outright or fatally wounded by British troops

Aldershot barracks bomb initiates IRA campaign with seven dead

Britain enters Common Market

Massacre of Israeli athletes at Munich Olympics

Watergate scandal

Anthony Burgess, *A Clockwork Orange*

Samuel Beckett, *Not I*

1973 US troops leave Vietnam

Arab-Israeli 15-day Yom Kippur War

PM Edward Heath introduces three-day working week
Martin Amis, *The Rachel Papers*

1974 Miners' strike
IRA bombings in Guildford (five dead) and Birmingham
(21 dead)

1975 Microsoft founded
Sex Discrimination Act
Zadie Smith born in North London
Malcolm Bradbury, *The History Man*
Scotland's 34 counties are reorganized into 12 regions

1976 Weak economy forces UK government loan from the
International Monetary Fund (IMF)
Ian McEwan, *First Love, Last Rites*

1977 *Star Wars* released
UK unemployment tops 1,600,000
Nintendo begins to sell computer games
The Sex Pistols 'Anarchy In the UK' tour

1978 Soviet troops occupy Afghanistan
First test-tube baby born in Oldham, England

1979 Iranian Revolution establishes Islamic theocracy
Margaret Thatcher becomes PM after Conservative election victory
USSR invades Afghanistan
Lord Mountbatten assassinated by the IRA
First referendum on devolution of powers from Westminster to Scotland fails

1980 Iran-Iraq War starts
Iranian Embassy siege in London

CND rally at Greenham Common airbase, England
IRA hunger strike at Belfast Maze Prison over political status for prisoners
Julian Barnes, *Metroland*

1981   Prince Charles and Lady Diana marry in St Paul's Cathedral with 750 million worldwide television audience
Widespread urban riots in UK including in Brixton, Holloway, Toxteth, Handsworth, Moss Side
AIDS identified
First IBM personal computer
Alasdair Gray, *Lanark*
Salman Rushdie, *Midnight's Children*, which wins Booker Prize for Fiction

1982   Mark Thatcher, PM's son, disappears for three days in Sahara during the Paris-Dakar rally
Falklands War with Argentina, costing the UK over £1.6 billion
Body of Roberto Calvi, chairman of Vatican-connected Banco Ambrosiano, found hanging beneath Blackfriars Bridge, London

1983   Klaus Barbie, Nazi war criminal, arrested in Bolivia
Beirut: US Embassy and barracks bombing, killing hundreds of members of multinational peacekeeping force, mostly US marines
US troops invade Grenada
Microsoft Word first released
Salman Rushdie, *Shame*, which wins Prix du Meilleur Livre Étranger (France)

1984   Miners' strike
HIV identified as cause of AIDS
IRA bomb at Conservative Party Conference in Brighton kills four British Telecom privatization shares sale

Thirty-eight deaths during clashes at Liverpool v. Juventus football match at Heysel Stadium, Brussels
Martin Amis, *Money: A Suicide Note*
Julian Barnes, *Flaubert's Parrot*
James Kelman, *Busconductor Hines*
Graham Swift, *Waterland*
Iain Banks, *The Wasp Factory*

1985   Famine in Ethiopia and Live Aid concert
Damage to ozone layer discovered
Mikhail Gorbachev becomes Soviet Premier and introduces *glasnost* (openness with the West) and *perestroika* (economic restructuring)
PC Blakelock murdered during riots on Broadwater Farm estate in Tottenham, London
My Beautiful Laundrette film released (dir. Stephen Frears, screenplay Hanif Kureishi)
Jeanette Winterson, *Oranges Are Not the Only Fruit*

1986   Abolition of Greater London Council and other metropolitan county councils in England
Violence between police and protestors at Wapping, East London after Rupert Murdoch sacks 5,000 print workers
Challenger shuttle explodes
Chernobyl nuclear accident
US bombs Libya
Peter Ackroyd, *Hawksmoor*

1987   Capsizing of RORO ferry, *Herald of Free Enterprise*, off Zeebrugge kills 193 people
London Stock Exchange and market collapse on 'Black Monday'
Remembrance Sunday: eleven killed by Provisional IRA bomb in Enniskillen
Ian McEwan, *The Child in Time*, which wins Whitbread Novel Award
Jeanette Winterson, *The Passion*

1988   US shoots down Iranian passenger flight
Pan Am flight 103 bombed over Lockerbie, 270 people killed
Soviet troop withdrawals from Afghanistan begin
Salman Rushdie, *The Satanic Verses*

1989   Fatwa issued against Rushdie by Iranian leadership
(Khomeini)
Fall of Berlin Wall
Exxon Valdez oil disaster
Student protestors massacred in Tiananmen Square,
Bejing
Hillsborough Stadium disaster in which 96 football fans
die
Kazuo Ishiguro, *The Remains of the Day*, which wins Booker
Prize for Fiction
Jeanette Winterson, *Sexing the Cherry*
Controversial poll tax introduced in Scotland (April)

1990   London poll tax riots
Fall of Thatcher; John Major becomes Conservative PM
Nelson Mandela freed from jail
Jeanette Winterson adapts *Oranges* for BBC television film
A. S. Byatt, *Possession*
A. L. Kennedy, *Night Geometry and the Garscadden Trains*
Glasgow is European City of Culture

1991   Soviet Union collapses
First Iraq War with 12-day Operation Desert Storm
Apartheid ended in South Africa
PM Major negotiates opt-out for Britain from European
Monetary Union and rejects Social Chapter of Maastricht
Treaty
Hypertext Markup Language (HTML) helps create the
World Wide Web
Hanif Kureishi, screenplays for *Sammy and Rosie Get
Laid* and *London Kills Me*
Pat Barker, *Regeneration*

1992   'Black Wednesday' stock market crisis when UK forced to
exit European Exchange Rate Mechanism
Adam Thorpe, *Ulverton*

1993   Black teenager Stephen Lawrence murdered in Well Hall Road, London

With Downing Street Declaration, PM John Major and Taoiseach Albert Reynolds commit Britain and Ireland to joint Northern Ireland resolution

Film of Ishiguro's *The Remains of the Day*, starring Anthony Hopkins and Emma Thompson

Irvine Welsh, *Trainspotting*

1994   Tony Blair elected leader of Labour Party following death of John Smith

Channel Tunnel opens

Nelson Mandela elected President of South Africa

Provisional IRA and loyalist paramilitary cease-fire

Homosexual age of consent for men in the UK lowered to 18

Mike Newell (dir.), *Four Weddings and a Funeral*

Jonathan Coe, *What a Carve Up!*

James Kelman, *How late it was, how late*, which wins Booker Prize for Fiction

Irvine Welsh, *The Acid House*

1995   Oklahoma City bombing

Srebrenica massacre during Bosnian War

Pat Barker, *The Ghost Road*

Hanif Kureishi, *The Black Album*

Leah Betts's Ecstasy-related death (November)

Braveheart (dir. Mel Gibson)

1996   Cases of Bovine Spongeiform Encephalitis (Mad Cow Disease) in the UK

Divorce of Charles and Diana

Breaching cease-fire, Provisional IRA bombs London's Canary Wharf and Central Manchester

Film of Irvine Welsh's *Trainspotting* (dir. Danny Boyle), starring Ewan McGregor and Robert Carlyle

Graham Swift, *Last Orders*, which wins Booker Prize

Sixteen children and one teacher shot to death at Dunblane School

1997   Tony Blair becomes Labour PM after landslide victory
Princess Diana dies in Paris car crash
Hong Kong returned to China by UK
Jim Crace, *Quarantine*
Jonathan Coe, *The House of Sleep*, which wins Prix Médicis Étranger (France)
Ian McEwan, *Enduring Love*
Iain Sinclair and Marc Atkins, *Lights Out for the Territory*
Devolution approved in referenda of Scottish and Welsh voters

1998   Good Friday Agreement on Northern Ireland and Northern Ireland Assembly established
Twenty-eight people killed by splinter group Real IRA bombing in Omagh
Sonny Bono Act extends copyright to lifetime plus 70 years
BFI/Channel 4 film *Stella Does Tricks*, released (screenplay A. L. Kennedy)
Julian Barnes, *England, England*

1999   Euro currency adopted
Macpherson Inquiry into Stephen Lawrence murder accuses London's Metropolitan Police of institutional racism
NATO bombs Serbia over Kosovo crisis
Welsh Assembly and Scottish Parliament both open
Thirty-one passengers killed in Ladbroke Grove train disaster

2000   Anti-globalization protest and riots in London
Hauliers and farmers blockade oil refineries in fuel price protest in the UK
Kazuo Ishiguro, *When We Were Orphans*
Will Self, *How the Dead Live*
Zadie Smith, *White Teeth*

2001   9/11 Al-Qaeda attacks on World Trade Center and Pentagon
Bombing and invasion of Afghanistan

Riots in Oldham, Leeds, Bradford, and Burnley, Northern England

Labour Party under Blair re-elected to government

Ian McEwan, *Atonement*

2002   Queen Mother dies aged 101

Rowan Williams named next Archbishop of Canterbury

Bali terrorist bomb kills 202 people and injures a further 209

Inquiry concludes English general practitioner Dr Harold Shipman killed around 215 patients

Zadie Smith's *White Teeth* adapted for Channel 4 television broadcast in autumn

2003   Invasion of Iraq and fall of Saddam Hussein

Death of UK government scientist Dr David Kelly, and Hutton Inquiry

Worldwide threat of Severe Acute Respiratory Syndrome (SARS)

2004   BBC Director General Greg Dyke steps down over Kelly affair

Bombings in Madrid kill 190 people and injure over 1,700

Expansion of NATO to include seven ex-Warsaw Pact countries

European Union expands to 25 countries as eight ex-communist states join

Jonathan Coe, *Like a Fiery Elephant: The Story of B. S. Johnson*

Alan Hollinghurst, *The Line of Beauty*, which wins Booker Prize for Fiction

Andrea Levy, *Small Island*, which wins Orange Prize for Fiction

The Queen opens the new Scottish Parliament building (9 October)

Edinburgh is UNESCO World City of Literature

2005   UK ban on foxhunting with dogs comes into force

7/7 London suicide bombings on transport system kill 52 and injure over 700 commuters in morning rush hour

Hurricane Katrina kills at least 1,836 people and floods devastate New Orleans

After four failed bombings are detected, Brazilian Jean
Charles de Menezes is shot and killed by Metropolitan
Police officers at Stockwell Underground Station
Ian McEwan, *Saturday*
Zadie Smith, *On Beauty*, which wins 2006 Orange Prize for
Fiction

2006   Jeanette Winterson awarded the OBE
Airline terror plot thwarted, causes major UK airline
delays
Israel–Hezbollah war in Lebanon
Five prostitutes killed in Ipswich in a six-week period
Saddam Hussein executed by hanging in controversial
circumstances

1

INTRODUCTION:
THE IRVINE WELSH
PHENOMENON

'The Power of Scotland', a lengthy article in the 14 April 2002
Scotland on Sunday, listing and briefly describing the one hundred
most powerful Scots, suggests a national confidence hardly imaginable just a decade earlier. Amidst all the bankers, business
people, government officials, newspaper editors, radio and television directors and other influential living Scots are four writers:
Alasdair Gray (#83), Liz Lochhead (#56), Irvine Welsh (#42) and J.
K. Rowling (#9). 'Once the enfant terrible of Scottish fiction, Welsh
exploded on the literary scene in 1993 with *Trainspotting*. He has
now returned to his native city after a period in exile, and has
arguably influenced Scottish literature – and the perception of it –
more than anyone else in the past decade'. To say that Welsh lived
'in exile' when in fact he had simply spent much of the previous
seven or so years elsewhere, including Amsterdam, London,
Chicago and Dublin, is understandable. However, this perhaps
unwitting attempt to mythify Welsh by linking him indirectly to
the greatest literary self-exiles of the twentieth century, the Irish
writers James Joyce and Samuel Beckett, is also unfortunate in that
it seems less a sign of Scotland's newfound power and self-confidence than a subtle reminder of lingering self-doubt. The linkage is
indeed doubly unfortunate because the more grandiose claim,
concerning Welsh's influence, is entirely true. Welsh and his work
constitute a cultural 'phenomenon' of considerable sociological as
well as literary interest, one in which the mythified Welsh plays an
important but nonetheless secondary role.

Welsh's immense influence is especially obvious in the potency of 'Irvine Welsh' as signifier and in the speed with which Welsh became literary benchmark and touchstone. New writers were greeted and graded according to the Welsh standard. They were as good as Welsh or not as good; in the tradition of Welsh or not in the tradition; half Welsh, the next Welsh, the female Welsh, the English Welsh, the Welsh Welsh, the Muslim Welsh. Edinburgh, the setting of most of his work, was remapped according to Welsh, and the BBC World Service, the *Daily Telegraph* and Britain itself were made over to appear more Welsh. 'Trainspotting', a term previously and pejoratively used in relation to the anorak crowd, suddenly became ubiquitous, in one form or another (trendspotting, bookspotting, etc.). Welsh's influence, or shadow, could be seen on the stage in the proliferation of in-your-face plays, in films (following the success of the 1996 adaptation of *Trainspotting*) and especially in British fiction, in what was published and how it was marketed and read. In 1997, one London bookshop, Prospero's, devoted an entire section to books endorsed by Welsh, so powerful was his cachet, even in the form of a jacket blurb. That same year, the new fiction section of Waterstone's, Britain's largest bookseller, was described as made in Welsh's ubiquitous image: 'a veritable King's Cross of urban angst, rough sex, graphic violence and rampant drug use. Ecstasy, heroin, handguns, trance music, deviant erotica and sexually transmitted diseases are the predominant currency: alienation, hedonism and nihilism the prevailing attitudes' (Amidon).

The present study examines Welsh's writings as part of the Irvine Welsh phenomenon and therefore as both aesthetic objects and as cultural products. Welsh's work and the Welsh phenomenon are best seen from the perspective of and as a contribution to British cultural studies which began in the 1950s concentrating almost exclusively on English culture (as fully representative of British culture) and which rapidly developed during the 1990s, when Welsh's influence became dominant. The Welsh phenomenon represents the most important but still contested shift from Matthew Arnold's theory of culture, as secular religion with its own set of values, to the more modern, or postmodern, theory of cultural materialism. Cultural materialism rejects the Arnoldian and later Leavisite faith in the beneficent, even saving effects of a necessary but embattled high culture and liberal humanism entrusted to the discerning few, and it rejects the crudely Marxist view that cultural products can only reflect the economic system that produced them. Neither merely reflections of the economic system nor completely independent of it, cultural products must be understood in terms of 'the continuing cultural practices in which they are presented' (Easthope 14). Accordingly, the emphasis in this study will be on Welsh's work and the Welsh phenomenon as the intersection of various forces, influences and consequences, foreground and aftermath.

One can trace the roots of both back several decades, not just to Leith, where he was born, and Muirhouse, where he was raised, but to the broader national contexts of Welsh's lifetime. (One must keep in mind that 'nation', as used here, is itself a complex as well as ambiguous signifier, referring to both the nation state of Britain and the stateless nation of Scotland.) This backward glance means taking into account the well-intentioned attempt to address inadequate housing that would lead to the construction of schemes such as Muirhouse which would soon become the breeding ground for many of the social problems that Welsh's fiction addresses. It also means noting how the further breakdown of the British Empire in the mid-1950s (the time when, as a result of the war effort and the postwar creation of the social welfare state, Scots' sense of their Britishness was at its height) resulted in the stirrings of Scottish nationalism in the 1960s which in turn fed the renewed interest in Scottish identity, politics, history and literature leading up to the failed referendum on devolution in 1979. The referendum failed to pass because a clause was inserted at the eleventh hour, requiring approval by at least 40 percent of all *eligible* voters. The failure came to be understood as further proof of both English treachery – of London's and therefore England's power over Scotland – and Scottish cowardice, thus provoking intense debates and feelings of self-loathing, national and personal.

Nineteen-seventy-nine was also the year Margaret Thatcher began her eleven-year reign as prime minister. This was a period in which Scots in general came to feel even more alienated from and oppressed by Britishness as the Tory-led, London-based government passed laws affecting a Scotland represented by fewer and fewer Tory MPs. Equally important, Thatcher's economic policies were at odds with Scottish interests and with Scotland's perception of itself as socialist, communitarian, and working-class. Thatcher's goals of denationalizing industry and easing the tax burden on the wealthy who formed the Tory base resulted in three historically significant and decidedly symbolic events. The first is the Falklands War, which Thatcher wildly oversold and then even more wildly claimed, against the backdrop of the nation's still declining international status and escalating violence in Northern Ireland, 'boosted Britain in the world colossally' (qtd. in Brantlinger 238). Ironically and understandably, the spike in Thatcher's popularity, as well as in British nationalism, occasioned by Britain's 'victory' led to the second historically and symbolically significant event, the miners' strike (1984–85), which replaced the war without (against Argentina) with the war within, which directly affected Scotland and Northern England the most. And the third is the imposition of 'the poll tax', which led to rioting (and eventual repeal) and which, for local scheduling reasons, was introduced in Scotland in 1989 (and in England and Wales one year later). Preceded by the inaugural meeting of the Scottish National Convention in 1989, the poll tax fiasco resulted in Thatcher's political demise and the introduction of her successor John Major's so-called 'classless society'. This was a time when inequality, disenfranchisement and disaffection were especially high in a winner-take-all 'society' symbolized by the gulf between the housing boom in the South East and the post-industrial economic hard times throughout much of the rest of Britain and symbolized for younger Britons by the Criminal Justice Act of 1994, part of which sought to control the rave movement and all it represented. The election of a New Labour government led by Tony Blair in 1997 proved a mixed blessing. It resulted in a second referendum on devolution, in September 1997, which voters approved by a three-to-one margin. Scotland now had its own parliament, its first in nearly three hundred years, but was and still is tied to Britain, its identity, independence and future still uncertain and still largely shaped by New Labour policies, Thatcher's legacy and a globalizing economy that made the unresolved question of national identity seem at once more pressing and less relevant.

There are, of course, few direct links between the events outlined above and Welsh's development. What matters is not direct linkage, however, but socio-political context. Two kinds of other changes were also in the air and therefore part of the times in which Welsh and his fiction developed. One involves youth culture in Britain. There is the combination of high unemployment, punk's aggressively anti-art, DIY aesthetic and anti-bourgeois ethic (a sneering, cynical distrust of authority and in-your-face rejection of middle-class values), the rise in the number of heroin addicts, especially among the underclass, and, throughout the 1980s, the number of AIDS- and heroin-related deaths which gave The Sex Pistols' famous phrase 'no future' from 'God Save the Queen' renewed relevance and darker meaning. This was followed by the different ethic and aesthetic of rave and club culture, with the cross-class use of Ecstasy and attendant media panic now that drugs were (once again) no longer just an underclass phenomenon. In one way, rave and club culture followed the same trajectory as punk, as rebellion became increasingly commercialized. The other kind of change is more general and institutional. It includes the devolution of the BBC in the early 1970s, the founding of Radio Scotland in 1978, the impact of Channel Four on programming at BBC Scotland, the revival of Scottish filmmaking (starting with Bill Forsyth's *That Sinking Feeling* in 1979), and the revival of Scottish theatre within the larger revival of theatre throughout Britain. Edinburgh's Traverse Theatre was founded in 1963 to promote new Scottish plays, theatre censorship was abolished in 1968, John McGrath's 7:84 Scotland began staging decidedly working-class plays for a largely working-class audience in the 1970s, and Mayfest, founded in 1983 and backed by trade unions, celebrated political and working-class plays. There were new plays for new audiences, often in new and unconventional theatrical spaces such as Glasgow's Arches and Tramway.

More generally throughout Britain and less conventionally 'cultural' are those changes that contributed to the making of the new cultural atmosphere which mainly derived from a very different (far more Thatcherite) ideology. These include changes in the British advertising industry following Saatchi & Saatchi's highly successful 'Labour isn't working' campaign for Thatcher, whose emphasis on private ownership and entrepreneurship were tailor-made for advertisers. The advertising industry in turn developed the kind of strategies used not only to market Welsh's books but to create a general as well as highly commercialized atmosphere of cultural transgression: from the Benetton ads of the early 90s to the French Connection's FCUK campaign in 1997 and the media hype and fury surrounding Young British Artists such as Saatchi-backed Damien Hirst and the Turner Prize. Something similar happened in British publishing as far-reaching in its way as the creation and the innovative marketing of Penguin Books in 1935. The change includes both the reorganization of British publishing from family-run businesses to the merger-and-acquisition mentality of multinationals, the proliferation of subgenres for carefully targeted markets, and the marketing of books via large book chains. This development was greatly enhanced by the collapse of the Net Book Agreement in 1995 that contributed to the emphasis on bestsellers and fastsellers and to the proliferation and hyping of literary awards (with their potential for increasing sales of individual book titles and of books generally). Under New Labour, these practices coalesced in the rebranding of Britain as Cool Britannia (the 1990s equivalent of Swinging London) and of Scotland as Cool Caledonia. In this way the two cultures – not C. P. Snow's earlier science and art, but corporate and 'cultural' – merge into that characteristically postmodern (and New Labour) phenomenon, the culture industries.

In the making of Cool Britannia and Cool Caledonia, the venerable and seemingly outdated form of the novel played a large role – surprisingly so because the novel is not only old but conservative and seemingly outmoded, which is to say superseded by newer media: television, film, digital. By 1993, the year *Midnight's Children* was selected as the Booker of Bookers to celebrate the prize's twenty-fifth anniversary, the British novel was once again in need of rejuvenation, this time by Welsh's hyper-Scottish novel *Trainspotting*. The controversial awarding of the 1994 Booker to James Kelman for *How late it was, how late* raised the contemporary Scottish novel's profile even higher. The sudden interest in Scottish fiction on the part of non-Scots, especially the English, was related to the slightly earlier interest in Commonwealth writers such as Rushdie and was, Welsh felt, partly the result of colonial guilt and partly the desire for something fresh. By 'fresh', Welsh meant something different from the 'Oxbridge' fiction that dominated the English novel then as now. 'Oxbridge' is Welsh's shorthand both for novels produced by writers educated at Oxford and Cambridge and for writers who subscribe to a vaguely similar set of aesthetic and cultural values: high art, *Granta*-ish, Arnoldian/Leavisite: the 'serious', 'literary' novels of Martin Amis especially. 'I think that a lot of people are sick of the kind of representations of the world that we live in as a kind of bland *Four Weddings and a*

Funeral sort of place', Welsh said; 'they want something that says a wee bit more about the different cultures within that society that tend to get ignored' (Macdonald).

As the work of Janice Galloway, A. L. Kennedy, Candia McWilliam and Ali Smith attests, 'fine writing' of the Oxbridge/ *Granta* kind exists in Scotland (or in the case of McWilliam and Smith, in Scots transplanted to Oxbridge), but even in these writers and more particularly in writers such as Alasdair Gray, Kelman, Duncan McLean, Alan Warner and Laura Hird, there is an important difference. There is the sense that Scots, as Angus Calder points out, by and large define themselves not by what they are but by what they are not and by what they have been made to feel they should feel/speak/write. I will address the question of language later. Here I want to emphasize another aspect of contemporary Scottish writing to which postcolonial theory has sensitized us and that makes up part of the context of the Welsh phenomenon – this despite the fact that the relationship between Scotland and colonialism is both peculiar and problematic. This difference is further complicated by Scots having been subjected to English narratives (Craig, *Modern* 13) which, in 'the development of the subject of "English Literature"', has constantly involved and reinforced an oppressive homage to centralism' (Crawford, *Devolving* 7). This 'oppressive homage to centralism' generally manifests itself indirectly through a subtle but nonetheless effective exclusivity, as in the 54-page chapter '1979 to the Present' in Malcolm Bradbury's *The Modern British Novel*, where contemporary Scottish writers receive, *in toto*, ten lines and Ian McEwan receives five pages. The regionalism, including regional writing, that characterizes Scottish literature simultaneously impedes Scotland's disappearance into English- and Anglo-centric Britishness (Ryan 88) and preserves a Derridean *différance* which the heightened regionalism of much contemporary Scottish fiction exploits with special effectiveness. This fiction inverts the perceived inferiority of Scotland as inscribed in the regional novel as an inferior subgenre and further suggests, as Liam McIlvanney notes, that 'the incompatibility of Scotland and the novel' may have more to do with the novel, or the English novel, as narrowly defined, than with Scotland (207–8).

The Scottish novel may, in fact, be better positioned than its English counterpart to exploit the dialogical, cannibalizing

qualities that for Bakhtin define the novel as an anti-genre, as
Robert Crawford was among the first to point out. Indeed, the
contemporary Scottish novel is in a particularly good position to
take advantage of the recent 'disarray' of an English literature 'that
has grown increasingly un-English': a literature of 'broken English'
(as Colin MacCabe calls it) in which the word 'broken' connotes
something positive (Brantlinger 236, 245, 247). This involves breaking down the unitary language needed for nation-building and
'subvert[ing] and refashion[ing] standard English into various new
forms of "english"' (McLeod 26). A literature of broken English
takes advantage of border lives and involves the combination of
conflicting forces and styles (realism and fantasy, for example) that
is so characteristic of many individual Scottish literary works (and
Scottish culture generally and even Scotland itself, Edinburgh
especially) as to have its own name. Caledonian antisyzygy is most
apparent in works such as James Hogg's *The Private Memoirs and
Confessions of a Justified Sinner* and Robert Louis Stevenson's *Dr Jekyll
and Mr Hyde*, and, as Crawford wittily notes, in Scotland's having
produced Britain's brains during the Enlightenment and, as early
as Roman times, the enduring image of the noble Caledonian
savage. Caledonian antisyzygy applies equally well to the dialogical interplay of Scottish and English languages and socio-cultural
elements. As Dietmar Boehnke points out, contemporary Scottish
fiction such as Gray's often involves 'a double refraction'; these
works intertextually exploit, integrate, and rewrite not only previous Scottish texts, but English ones as well. Furthermore, the
'break-down in the concept of literature, and in cultural authority
generally' which Alan Sinfield describes and which is so evident in
much contemporary Scottish writing, Welsh's above all, is conso-
nant with the carnivalesque tendency noted by Bakhtin, which
involves the temporary cessation, overturning or inversion of the
world of monological authority and orthodoxy and the eruption
of the liberating forces of lawless proliferation and renewal.

As Benedict Anderson and others have explained, 'the development of the novel is profoundly linked to the development of the
modern nation' (Craig, *Modern* 9). But what is true of nations in
general and Britain in particular is an even more pressing matter,
and arguably a more characteristic one, in stateless nations (or
now, semi-stateless nations) such as Scotland. This is the case not
simply because nations are narratives – the narratives which bind

the nation together imaginatively – but because, as Christopher Whyte has explained of Scotland after the Act of Union and before the convening of the new Scottish Parliament in 1999, 'In the absence of an elected political authority, the task of representing the nation has repeatedly devolved to its writers' (284). While true of Scotland generally over the past three hundred years, Whyte's view is especially so at particular moments in Scottish history: the Scottish renaissance of the 1920s and 1930s, when the poets carried the burden, and the more recent explosion of Scottish writing in the 1980s and 1990s, when the task of representing the nation devolved mainly to its fiction writers. Although begun two decades earlier, Gray's seminal *Lanark* appeared at a particularly propitious moment, two years after the failed 1979 referendum, just in time for an entire generation or two of Scottish writers to take advantage of and respond to his example. It is at moments such as this, when the sense, or awareness, of powerlessness is most acute that Scottish writing has flourished: times when, as Colm Toibin wistfully remarks, 'books are written, as in Ireland in the old days, to replace a country'.

The most noteworthy of the remarkably varied group of Scottish writers of the 1980s and 1990s have, Ian A. Bell explains, 'responded to the challenge thrown down by *Lanark*, revising the imaginary of Scotland through the form of the novel to such an extent that both the subject and the vehicle of expression have by now virtually been reinvented ... . These writers have sought to reclaim the right to represent Scottish culture on their own terms ... envisaging it from within and from below in ways far removed from the prevailing sentimental, romantic or 'realistic' paradigms ... [and] refusing to collaborate with a transcendental, totalizing and finally determining sense of national identity, be it supportive or critical' (Bell 219–20, 226). One of the strengths of Bell's analysis is his ability to translate literary concerns into political language and more especially to account for individual differences within the larger issue of these writers' shared 'commitment to an honest evaluation of contemporary Scotland' (233) – or contemporary Scotlands.

There is no direct line of descent from Gray to Welsh, as there is for several other contemporary Scottish writers, notably Kelman and Galloway. There is however a direct line in the minds of readers and critics linking Welsh to Kelman that needs to be closely examined in terms of important similarities between the two writers and even more important differences. However indirect it may be, Welsh's debt to Kelman's fiction and example is considerable in terms of use of the vernacular, depiction of underclass life, and urban setting. Within those similarities lie even more significant differences. One is political: the 'commitment and integrity' of the one, the 'anarchy and disintegration' of the other (Maley, 'Subversion' 194). Another difference is geographical. It is not an exaggeration to say that Welsh's fiction created an Edinburgh alternative to a Glasgow which was perceived as the centre of Scottish population, football, poverty and twentieth-century fiction, especially working- or underclass fiction. Glasgow's monopoly increased following its being designated 1990 European City of Culture, replete with smiley face logo and 'Glasgow's miles better' slogan. In reclaiming Edinburgh for literature, Welsh's fiction contributed to what David Punter terms the remapping of Britain over the past few decades, in terms both of Edinburgh's relation to Glasgow and Scotland's to England. The difference between Welsh and Kelman is more than geographical; it is also aesthetic: Kelman's grittiness is offset by a decidedly heightened literary style, a philosophical pedigree, and, Welsh rightly claims, a tendency to 'airbrush' his existential working-class characters in a way that makes them less sexist and/or racist than their real-life equivalents would be (Casper Llewellyn Smith, 'Credible').

The most important difference is generational. It is a difference obscured when the two writers are subsumed under the headings 'Scottish' and 'working-class', especially in the *anni mirabili* 1993–94 when *Trainspotting* burst on the scene, *How late it was, how late* won the Booker Prize and the profile of the contemporary Scottish novel and of Scotland generally increased dramatically. Kelman's winning bucked two trends: until 1994 no Scot had won the Booker and until then recent winners had seen sales of their books increase. The fact that there was no sharp increase in sales of *How late it was, how late* is made all the more significant in the context of how phenomenally well Welsh's books were doing. By 1995 his first three books were all on the bestsellers list simultaneously, in large part because they appealed to younger readers and to a much broader range of readers than did Kelman's fiction. Of course, it is unlikely that Welsh's fiction would ever have reached that audience had it not been for the development in Edinburgh of a support group modelled on Glasgow's a decade earlier and the creation of outlets such as Duncan McLean's Clocktower Press and Kevin Williamson's Rebel Inc which not only supplemented established showcases such as *New Writing Scotland* but were able to make the newest writing available in the shortest possible time. (All three, incidentally, published parts of *Trainspotting* in the early 1990s.) As McLean explained, 'Ezra Pound said that literature is news that stays news. Commentators tend to focus on the notion of permanence in that statement, but it seems to me that the 'news' part is at least as important' (x).

One aspect of the generational difference is also a consequence of the multiplying, or regionalizing, of Scottish literature during the 1990s, alluded to by Bell. This is the eroding sense of a singular (essentialist) Scottish identity and the growing acceptance, even assertion, of multiple identities: a *mise en abyme* of devolved identities, intra-, supra-, post- and extra-national, socio-economic, cultural and subcultural. These include the sense of Scottish identity as something performed, as in the case of the comedian Billy Connolly, the television character Rab C. Nesbitt and the television series *Hamish Macbeth*, in which the image of Scots and Scotland is produced, received and disambiguated in different ways for different audiences (markets): in the case of *Hamish Macbeth* as a stereotype recognized as such by the local (Scottish) audience, as a representation of Scotland for the English market and finally as a bit of Highland exotica for export to international audiences, including in the US and Canada (see Sillars). The Scottish identity which emerges from this context is multiple and contingent rather than essentialist, transcendental and totalizing, or existential in the Kelman sense. Although some worry that Rab C. Nesbitt and Welsh's characters perpetuate stereotypes or, worse, present Scots the way the English prefer to see them, representations such as these imply confidence. They suggest less an abject submission to the stereotypes than a postmodern and postcolonial willingness to invert and play with them in carnivalesque fashion, with 'the cultural fragmentation which earlier writers deplored ... recast throughout the 1990s as vital, invigorating diversity' (McIlvanney, 'Divided').

The risk of over-investing in national icons is real and made especially clear in the nineteenth-century exposure of the Ossian poems as modern fabrications, in *Empire* magazine's naming

Braveheart the worst film ever to win the Oscar for best picture and in the revelation that the painting *The Reverend Robert Walker Skating on Duddingston Loch*, its image now part of the design of the new Scottish Parliament building, may not be the work of Sir Henry Raeburn but instead of a little known French artist. Welsh's generation runs its own risks. One is dispensing with the past altogether in an effort to embrace the present more fully in order to escape the traditional which has often exerted so destructive and stultifying an influence on Scottish fiction. Another is being domesticated: 'the volatile brat of contemporary Scottish fiction' (Whyte and Galloway) becoming yet another Scottish icon along with heather, haggis, kilts, shortbread, Robert Burns and William Wallace. The painting of the new writers commissioned by the National Portrait Gallery seems likely to accomplish this goal. This enshrining is clearly related to the half-civic, half-corporate boosting of Welsh and others as part of Cool Caledonia, which is itself indicative of the transformation of Scotland and Northern England from industrial production to cultural production (from steel and coal and docks to *Trainspotting*, *The Full Monty*, *Brassed Off*, and *Billy Eliot*) described by Julia Hallam and trumpeted by former Minister for Culture, Media and Sport Chris Smith.

Concerns over *Trainspotting* and *Morvern Callar* creating a Scottish cliché just 'as dangerously delimiting as historical "tartanry" or the "kailyard" ever were' (Boddy, 'Scotland' 361) were first raised by conservative critics, as well as politicians such as Donald Dewar, who objected to the new dominant view of 'Scotland as Thug Central'. More recently critics such as Boddy present this concern in a less judgmental and more nuanced way which accounts for how the new images are circulated, received, deployed, perpetuated, and exploited. As Peter J. Smith notes, 'in the redefining of Scottish identity, 'Trainspotting' helped. Or hindered. It certainly did something'. It certainly did something politically. As did *Braveheart*, but where Gibson's 1995 film was embraced by the Scottish National Party, 'which appropriated the film as a whole into its party rhetoric and images from the film into its party literature' (McArthur, 'Braveheart' 177), *Trainspotting* was adopted by the SNP's youth wing, the Young Scottish Nationalists, for their leaflet *Toryspotting*, which the SNP quickly moved to have withdrawn (Deerin). *Trainspotting* also did something socially, focusing a great deal of positive attention on drug use – especially heroin addiction – in Edinburgh. *Trainspotting* also had an effect on Scottish education. As P. H. Scott notes in *Scotland: A Concise Cultural History*, published the same year as *Trainspotting*, 'It is possible to go through a Scottish education at all levels and emerge in almost complete ignorance of Scotland's contribution to civilization' (qtd. in Crawford, 'Defining' 91). Welsh soon became one of the top four writers studied in Scottish schools (William McIlvanney, Iain Banks and Muriel Sparks being the others), and *Trainspotting* became an approved book for the Higher English paper. Objections to both quickly surfaced, as well as to using public money to put copies of *Trainspotting* in school libraries. However, as one journalist wittily noted: '*Trainspotting* has replaced *Treasure Island* as a must for juvenile readers. To the consternation of traditionalists, Irvine Welsh's notorious best-seller is a favourite for personal reading amongst Higher pupils. What is the world coming to when a novel about drug abuse gains ground over a novel about theft and treachery, drunkenness and murder?' (Home).

The Scottish renaissance of the 1990s took place at a time and in a context that greatly complicates both its meaning and its appropriateness. As Ray Ryan sums up particularly well, 'Scottish writing in the nineties is part of a larger cultural effort to assert a national distinctiveness despite the levelling impact of globalization' (132). David McCrone takes issue with anyone who fails to show sufficient enthusiasm for the opportunities globalism affords. Scotland, he believes, is too mired in the past; its future lies with globalization, not with maintaining its distinctiveness as Cairns Craig, Tom Nairn and others believe. Scotland's future lies, one might say, with Renton's fleeing to Amsterdam at the end of *Trainspotting*, not with Craig's critique of that escape, because 'the search [for a distinctive Scottish identity] is increasingly becoming invalid' (McCrone 145). Where McCrone advises breaking with the past, Craig counsels a fuller understanding of the present and the future in terms of the ways that the Scottish myths impinge on and shape (or misshape) the Scottish present. If there is a shortcoming to Craig's analysis, it is not his critique of globalization; it is that his privileging of the novel precludes his taking into account the ways in which media, industries and technologies contribute to the making of the modern Scottish nation.

The possibilities as well as the limitations and liabilities of the local (variously defined) on one hand and the global on the other and the need to read Welsh's fiction within the context of an internal, ongoing debate about both are especially relevant to several areas not yet addressed. The most obvious of these is language. In Welsh's work, language is intimately and intricately tied to place and to what Gill Jamieson calls 'the architecture of despair'. (Audience plays its part here as well, in that the sense of place expands or contracts based on different audiences' finding Welsh's language either entirely familiar or exotic or impenetrable or vulgar.) Welsh's language is also tied to identity, from the most personal and local (mainly underclass, youth and Leith) through the national (specifically Scottish) to the broad question of 'how an un-English identity may be preserved or developed within "English Literature"' (Crawford, *Devolving* 6). Significantly, Welsh has spoken most often about the limitations of conventional language for fiction such as his own just as he became a more frequent user of it (from 2001 on). 'It would have been pretentious to have written *Trainspotting* in standard English', Welsh said in many interviews from this period. It is too unrealistic, too 'imperialist', too 'controlling' and not 'funky' enough to bring the characters to life (Novick). Welsh implicitly rejects Edwin Muir's call for a single language (English) for overcoming 'the ineradicable psychological damage of a divided linguistic inheritance' that results from Scots 'feel[ing] in one language and think[ing] in another' (qtd. in Craig, *Modern* 15). In this as in so many matters, Welsh normalizes what a previous generation either marginalized, questioned, excluded or felt compelled to assert. Welsh uses the vernacular urban Scottish dialect in a far more 'natural' and less self-consciously literary way than Kelman and with a greater ease and confidence than Tom Leonard in linguistically politicized poems such as '6 O'Clock News', where for reasons as much generational as political, Leonard must assert what Welsh all but takes for granted.

Trainspotting greatly expanded the linguistic resources available to Scottish writers. Welsh drew, directly or indirectly, on the example of West Coast writers such as Kelman, Leonard and McIlvanney, but he was motivated by a much more local imperative within the larger post-1979 national context. The Celtic oral tradition, lower-class Edinburgh slang, including rhyming slang and gypsy influences, and an intertextuality drawn from popular culture combine to form what the *Scotsman on Sunday* called 'a vernacular spectacular' and the *Sunday Times* 'the voice of punk, grown up, grown wiser, grown eloquent' (Andrew Smith, 'How'). This distinctive voice, quite apart from the political uses to which it would be put, provided a subversive alternative to the voice found in much Oxbridge fiction, which Welsh criticized less for its high tone and literariness than for 'its tendency to see itself as universal, rather than [as] just another subculture' (Berman 60). Welsh's narrative language also exposes the class-bias of works such as Martin Amis's *London Fields*. Stripped of the literariness of Kelman and the literary condescension of Amis, Welsh's language strikes a much more authentic note which in turn clearly struck a chord with readers. It is a language in whose rhythm can be heard the sneer of punk and the rhythms of rave and hip-hop, in whose design can be seen the influence of visual culture and whose intense physicality provided an alternative to the increasing abstraction of modern literature and life. Nowhere is this more evident than in the contrast between Welsh's language and the Orwellian rhetoric that characterizes 'the touchy-feely Blair era of superficial smarm' (Welsh, 'Hurting'), including the mind-numbing generalizations of Chris Smith's book on the culture industries in Britain. 'Fuck that', Welsh might have said, although he would have said it in a context which included not only *Trainspotting* but the British edition of American novelist Dale Peck's *Martin and John* published in the UK five months earlier under the title *Fucking Martin*. He would have said it, that is, in a literary and consumer context already primed for distributing and receiving 'shocking' language.

A second way that the conflict between the local and the global manifests itself in Welsh's work is in his treatment of masculinity in general and the iconic figure of the Scottish hard man in particular. Here too one must guard against reading Welsh too narrowly by recognizing the multiple contexts on which his fiction draws and to which it contributes. One is the hardened sense of Scottish masculinity which will be discussed later, in the *Marabou Stork Nightmares* chapter. Another is the unabashed reassertion of traditional masculinity in the spate of men's beer-and-babes magazines in Britain in the 1990s. *Loaded* (founded in 1994), *FHM* and *Maxim* are about more than 'men behaving badly'. Such magazines address in their own crude ways the crisis of masculinity, assuaging the crisis as well as exploiting it. Ladlit does the same in its fashion as it ranges over the full spectrum of male types, from hard men to new men, and at a time of increasing stratification of the literary marketplace with the advent of chicklit and the number of new magazines directed at girls and young women. Readers come to the ladlit in part to vicariously indulge themselves but also in part to escape the hardened masculinity that these writers variously critique. They come 'at a time when', as Stefan Herbrechter explains, 'masculinity has been forced out of its hegemonic silence, [when] feminism, gay, lesbian and transsexual movements and postcolonial and postmodern theories have been attacking the hegemonic model of the white heterosexual patriarch as masculinity's natural norm' (119). Growing up in a society in which 'the myth of the macho male' was alive and well, experiencing firsthand 1970s gender-bending (punk and glam rock), and writing his MBA thesis on the bias against women in the Scottish workplace made Welsh aware of the practical consequences of the abstract changes Herbrechter mentions. Although some feel that Welsh does not go far enough in his handling of these changes (Christopher Whyte), others (Herbrechter, Schoene and especially Zoe Strachan) feel differently. What is important is not Welsh's taking a position in his fiction, but his unprogrammatic inclusion of a broad range of gender identities as a natural part of his fictional world.

Welsh's handling of gender issues is just one example of how his fiction has moved on in ways that some readers have not. Another is his treatment of the working class. 'A lot of contemporary [Scottish] fiction is rooted in all that seventies nonsense about working-class solidarity and trade unions and stuff. There's that west-coast tradition of industrial socialism, with obligatory references to shipyards. I'm more interested in moving in and out of different cultures, getting away from those massive, mythical institutions' (Welsh, qtd. in 'It's Generational'). The working-class aesthetic and ethos form one of several contexts that Welsh's fiction rejects without escaping altogether. Just as his language looks to the present rather than to the past, Welsh turns away from 'revolutionary' Scottish working-class socialism because, he said, 'the old routes of radical change were destroyed by the 80s' (Berman 57). And he turns toward alternative, apolitical or post-political youth culture and, more recently, assimilation, in *Glue* and in his own pilgrim's progress 'from working-class to international leisure class' (Bearn). But as the treatment of Spud at the end of *Trainspotting* and throughout *Porno* suggests, mixed with Welsh's, Renton's and other characters' individual successes is a sense of guilt that may be read as the trace of the working-class ethos, with its sense of community and solidarity which individual success cannot entirely erase. In this context punk provided an important link between the working-class ideals at which punk could only cynically sneer and Thatcherite hyper-individualism which rave culture could only temporarily delay.

The style and subject matter of *Trainspotting* led to the early assumption that the novel was not only drawn from life but more particularly from the author's life. Welsh was born in Leith in 1958 and grew up in Muirhouse, where his family moved when he was four; he left school at sixteen, worked briefly as an television repairman before going to London, where he joined punk bands, lived in a squat, used heroin, ran afoul of the law. He then bought and sold London properties during the 1980s real estate boom before returning to Edinburgh, where he was employed in the local council's Housing Department. Subsequently, *Trainspotting* appeared, and Welsh, Scottish fiction, and Scotland have never been the same since. He was, in the words of John Walsh, writing in 1995, 'a pure writer, an *enfant sauvage*, a literary Kasper Hauser, raised in darkness, schooled in depravity, unread, unlettered and unlearned but capable, given pen and paper, of producing staggering feats of storytelling'. Soon dubbed 'the poet laureate of the chemical generation' by *Face* magazine, Welsh would by 1995 have three books on the bestseller lists at the same time (and four in 1996). Welsh's rapid rise to literary superstardom had consequences for both his writing and his reputation. Having been welcomed into the literary club on the basis of his dazzling prose, his shocking subjects, and his authentic voice, Welsh was suddenly finding his street cred questioned: whether he had ever been a heroin addict and whether he was indeed quite as young as he claimed to be (or as others claimed him to be), which is to say as young as many of his characters and especially readers. As early as 1995 Andy Beckett wondered whether Welsh had perhaps 'colluded' with journalists in the making of his image. In 1998, Welsh himself complained about the high cost of celebrity and the need to scale back his public life – to stay away from the Groucho

Club in London and perhaps even move to the United States – all this just as *Filth*, his first new book in two years, and the film *The Acid House* were about to appear and the *Scotsman* ran a five-article spread on him. The Edinburgh establishment's nightmare was looking like the dream creation of the Scottish culture industries. In Edinburgh, Welsh was included in an exhibit of the city's literary greats and, as previously noted, Prospero's Books devoted an entire section to books endorsed by Welsh, the former literary Caliban. What Beckett observed in mid-1998 – '*Trainspotting* has been appropriated so much it's like a Richard Branson product. A zone of identity that's used to sell products' – seemed equally true of Welsh. And yet, just a few months later James G. Ballard named Welsh as one of only two British writers (the other was Will Self) providing an alternative to the bourgeois novel, seeing not pound signs in his eyes but 'something sharp and glittering in [his] teeth' (Ellis).

Over the next four years, Welsh, who had said he would only write as long as he had something to say, was starting to find it necessary to write every day, was a regular at the Edinburgh Book Festival, a judge for literary prizes, a columnist for the *Daily Telegraph* and writer-in-residence at Columbia College in the United States. Earlier the papers had gleefully reported every instance of boorish behaviour and every arrest along with evidence of his newly acquired wealth, as if the flats he purchased in Amsterdam, London and Edinburgh were proof of his having betrayed his *Trainspotting* roots. Now, they reported his divorce and upcoming marriage plans, the renovation of his Dublin flat, his taking advantage of a tax shelter and *The Shorter Oxford Dictionary*'s use of quotations from Welsh's writings. Earlier he had contributed a story, introduction, interview or blurb to just about anyone who asked; now he contributed his time, work and name to various social, legal and charitable causes, and relocated to Dublin with his wife, Beth Quinn, in July 2005. Despite all this, the rude boy image persists, as in an 8 January 2004 article in the *Independent* reporting the literary tempest occasioned by a remark by the (then) latest Edinburgh literary sensation, Alexander McCall Smith: 'In one corner is the bow-tied, genial writer of detective stories which have become the surprise literary hit of recent years. In the other, the foul-mouthed, bullet-headed hardman of cutting-edge contemporary fiction' (Kirby). One year later, the lion lay down with the lamb in a contemporary rendering of *The Peaceable Kingdom*. At the literary hard man's suggestion, Welsh, McCall Smith and Ian Rankin joined forces to write a collection of interlinked stories to raise money for OneCity Trust, which promotes cultural inclusion in Edinburgh. If the picture of Welsh which emerges is complicated, even contradictory, the reason has less to do with confession and collusion, truth and fiction, than with the complex phenomenon that Joe Moran discusses in *Star Authors*: 'the phenomenon of literary celebrity – how it is produced and disseminated, what kinds of meanings are attached to it, and how celebrity authors themselves have grappled with and added to these meanings in their work' (in Welsh's case, in *Glue*, *Porno* and especially *The Bedroom Secrets of the Master Chefs*).

Welsh's appeal to the broadsheet and quality magazine audience of serious readers in and out of the UK has been vital to the Welsh phenomenon but hardly definitive. (In the US it was the glossy *New Yorker* that took special delight in presenting Welsh as drunk and disorderly for the benefit of its mainly older, upscale readership.) Welsh's audience has to be considered more broadly, in terms of a continuum having readers of literary fiction at one end and postliterate youth at the other, or perhaps further still, the kind of reader for whom Welsh intended *Trainspotting*, the kind of people found in the novel, the kind who generally don't read books. One of the most far-reaching consequences of the Welsh phenomenon is the way it has altered the demographics of fiction-reading and play-going. As Nick Hornby pointed out, Welsh 'writes with style, imagination, wit and force, and in a voice which those alienated from much current fiction clearly want to hear'. This is an audience more inclined to buying music CDs than novels and more inclined to buying novels in Virgin and Tower superstores than in bookshops. In Welsh, one finds the convergence of the people Hornby describes, hungry for the kind of fiction Welsh writes, and publishers hungry for new groups of readers who can be reached through the forms of marketing and advertising developed over the past decade to sell popular music. This convergence made moot the distinction found in the UK between books, which are not subject to VAT, and other consumer goods, which are. Admittedly, in attempting to reach the broad audience described above, Welsh and his publishers ran the risk of catering to cultural voyeurs. However, it is equally likely that non-underclass readers, especially young readers, have found in Welsh's work either a parallel to their sense of disaffection or an alternative to their increasingly virtual world.

Robin Robertson, Welsh's editor, first at Secker & Warburg and later at Jonathan Cape, may have had 'an evangelical feeling about the kind of publishing [he is] engaged in', i.e., using Welsh's and John King's fiction to 'convert' young people to reading and, in Welsh's case, to bring contemporary Scottish fiction to the wider audience (Cowley). Evangelism such as this is also good for business. In 'The Cult Now Arriving', Guy Russell explains that although *Trainspotting*'s 'success has a lot to do with its sheer brilliance ... the big-time crossover has also shown up the potential size of the audience for types of fiction in which the subject, politics or style don't fit the literary norm': the punk novels published by smaller firms which began appearing in the mid-80s. Once the audience for these books was established, firms like Secker, 'part of the media-poor Reed group', and W. W. Norton in the US, became interested. In the first six months of 1996, when Welsh was 'the undisputed leader of the new wave of contemporary British fiction', Waterstone's reported having sold more novels than in any other six-month period in its history (Arlidge, 'Return'). Clearly, one person's commodity is another person's cult fiction, with the emphasis on the important role that cult fictions, films and authors play in a post-religious, late-capitalist age. And just as one person's evangelism is another person's profit, it can also be someone else's pandering, as in Tom Morton's scathing dismissal of Welsh as 'a purveyor of pulp: cynical, calculated fiction making a commercial value of an underclass, broadly drawn for the benefit of the bourgeois readership ... . All you get in Welsh is a laddish grovelling in the lurid'.

In 1999, Elizabeth Young, who had written one of the earliest and most enthusiastic reviews of *Trainspotting*, wrote an end-of-the-decade assessment for the *New Statesman* in which she declared the British novel moribund. In 'The Long Slow Demise of Our Literary Culture', she lamented the abysmally low critical standards, the abundance of sentimental books, and the dearth of writers worth reading. Welsh isn't one of them; he isn't even mentioned. Three years later, Kate Mikhail looked back over the previous decade and found 'plenty to applaud'. Of the ten areas she identifies, seven are pertinent to Welsh and one, 'nihilist literature', focuses exclusively on him. As the leader for the article points out, 'Lottery money, extra funding for millennium projects, a new government with a professed commitment to the arts – the past years should have been a golden period for the established cultural institutions. So why did all the interesting movement happen on the margins?'. Therein lies the problem: Welsh isn't on the margins anymore. He is both out of the picture (Young) and in the mainstream. In 1993, the *Scotsman*'s literary editor Catherine Lockerbie said of the then unknown Welsh's reading from *Trainspotting* at that year's Edinburgh Book Festival, that this is 'just what the Book Festival should be doing: providing a platform for the cutting edge of the new amid the comfort of the established'. A dozen years later, Andrew Crumey, the paper's new literary editor, congratulated Lockerbie, the festival's director, for assembling an impressive list that featured high-profile writers such as Rushdie and Margaret Atwood but added a note of caution concerning 'the potential downside of the Book Festival's' blockbuster approach. You are less likely to see cutting-edge up-and-comers here; more likely to see how book marketing these days puts festivals high on the list of potential sales outlets'.

The city Welsh remapped – its recesses now extending well beyond the Old Town's closes and wynds that figure so prominently in the Edinburgh gothic imagination – has itself been made over. Britain's heroin- and HIV-capital has become host of the MTV Europe awards, International Man Booker award, G8 economic summit, UNESCO City of Literature and site of a booming literary tourism industry for which Welsh is no less responsible than *Braveheart*, *Harry Potter* and *The Da Vinci Code*. Like its new, abstract logo, Edinburgh's new slogan, 'Inspiring Capital', raises doubts that the 'progress' of the Edinburgh Book Festival over the dozen years since *Trainspotting* appeared clearly confirms and that Pierre Bourdieu's analysis of cultural and subcultural capital helps explain. One can hardly begrudge the urban renaissance which the Welsh phenomenon helped set in motion. On the other hand, one can certainly question whom this renaissance will benefit and whom it will not and what its short and long term effects on Scottish fiction and on Scotland will be. Among the 124 recommendations of the June 2005 report of Scotland's Cultural Commission are the spread of Tartan Days and Tartan Weeks (presently held in the United States), the transformation of the

Edinburgh Festivals into national companies having 'performance indicators' (i.e., targets), the formation of a quango (quasi-non-governmental organization) entitled Culture Scotland, and 'a culture bill' giving all Scots 'four cultural rights': to fulfil creative potential, to partake in cultural life, to lead an 'enriching communal life', and to help shape cultural policy. While it is certainly possible to say that the Cultural Commission's report is what *Trainspotting* in a sense wrought, it is no less certain that it is hard to see how *Trainspotting* could ever come out of the kind of cultural environment that the report envisions. In 1991, Whyte and Galloway wrote: ' "Scottish Literature" as a cosy study of the past is not enough, we must support the vital and volatile brat that is literature in the making'. It is hard to see the brat having a place in the report's cosy picture of Scotland's cultural future, unless the brat looks like thirteen-year-old Emma Maree Urquhart, whose fantasy novel *Dragon Tales* was the Scottish publishing sensation of 2005. At the end of *Fictions of State: Culture and Credit in Britain, 1694–1994*, published the year before New Labour came to power and Scots voted for devolution, Patrick Brantlinger quotes from The Sex Pistols' 'God Save the Queen': 'no future for you … no future for me'. 'In regard to postmodern culture', Brantlinger goes on to say, 'until there are clear, progressive alternatives to "Sado-mone-tarism" and to a Ukanian nation-state grown increasingly decrepit, ruinous and fetishistic (both incredible and uncreditworthy), Johnny Rotten's injunction "Believe in the ruins" may be as hopeful as anyone can reasonably get'. In the increasingly prosperous Edinburgh of 'inspiring capital' and in the Cultural Commission's report (and the trends from which they grow), the problem is not that there is 'no future'; it is the kind of future that has developed from the confluence of forces (not simple, linear causality) that the Irvine Welsh phenomenon highlights, draws on and contributes to.

PART II
Major Works

2

TRAINSPOTTING:
THE FIRST DAY OF THE
IRVINE WELSH FESTIVAL

'Critics, prize-giving juries, and readers alike are hereby served notice: *Trainspotting* marks the arrival of a major new talent', wrote Alan Chadwick in a brief but important review which appeared in the *Herald* on 31 July 1993. That was two weeks before the novel's release date and a month before Welsh's first appearance at the Edinburgh Book Festival. More than hype, Chadwick's announcement of *Trainspotting*'s and Welsh's arrival sought to create a space for both novel and author within the more or less closed ranks of the literary establishment of gatekeepers (reviewers and prize juries) and in the literary marketplace as part of the category that has come to be known as 'literary fiction'. Chadwick's announcement also opened up a space for the kind of readers *Trainspotting* would attract, whose readings of the novel would be outside mainstream considerations and standards and whose response would help create the space within which Welsh's reputation would develop and against which it would be measured. That audience was as specific as the young underclass Leithers who formed Welsh's ideal audience and, as A. L. Kennedy later noted, the broader audience of her and Welsh's generation of Scots (literary Scots, like Kennedy, the unread like many of Welsh's characters, and the postliterate). Matters of class and generation are further complicated by region, nation (both within Britain and without), language and time, with readings of *Trainspotting* affected by the subsequent but for many readers intermediary forms of highly successful stage and screen versions.

By then readers in Britain could read the novel in quite different and distinctive editions, with each of the four paperback covers orienting the reader in its own way. They could read the novel differently as well, as gritty realism, as black humour, as Scottish or as British, as postmodern or as postcolonial, as political or as post-punkishly post-political, as proof of Scottish confidence or as further evidence of the Scottish cringe in its presentation of 'Scots as the English like to see them: drunken or drugged, aggressive, illiterate, socially inept, boorish' (Gordon). The broad, but by no means universal, acclaim it received in Britain was due in part to the novel's 'brilliance' and in part to the British literary class's 'yearning for something fresh' (Innes). *Trainspotting*'s appeal was broader still (and more diverse). 'Market research found that half the people who had bought *Trainspotting* had never purchased a book before'. Whatever the actual percentage, and the figure Euan Kerr cites sounds more like hype than fact, the overall point is valid, as Richard Downes discovered while researching his 1995 documentary *In Yer Face* (Molloy). *Trainspotting*'s success is the stuff of which authors' and publishers' dreams are made. From a humble initial print run of 3,000 copies, sales mushroomed: 150,000 copies prior to the film's release, more than double that (according to Lesley Downer) soon after. By that time both the original Minerva paperback and the movie tie-in edition (also Minerva) were bestsellers in the UK (numbers 10 and 3 respectively) and *Trainspotting* was being billed as 'the fastest selling and most shoplifted novel in British publishing history' (Arlidge, 'Return'). (There were six printings of *Trainspotting* in 1994, nine in 1995, and at least twelve in 1996.) The 'most shoplifted' tag undoubtedly contributed to the book's allure and therefore sales, as copies left bookshelves with the speed new recordings left record shops (increasingly in venues where both were sold), with so many copies carried across the Atlantic by clubbers that publisher W. W. Norton moved up the novel's US release. As translations appeared in more than thirty countries, copies of the original Secker & Warburg clothbound edition were suddenly worth anywhere from £300 to £1,000 each. More important than the actual price is the general perception as Welsh's schemie novel entered auction house culture and began appearing on lists of The Nation's 100 Favourite Books, *The Times* of London's Top Ten Modern Classics, Favourite Books of the 90s (also *The Times*), Waterstone's Top 100 Books of the Twentieth Century, and *Melody Maker*'s Essential Brit-Lit novels.

Trainspotting's success in so many forms and on so many fronts eventually led Welsh to compare it to 'a bad curry after a few lagers. It keeps coming back' (L. C. Smith). The novel's success is especially startling in that it was written by someone who did not think of himself as a writer and for people who did not read books. (Only much later would he claim, inconsistently, that he had always believed *Trainspotting* would be successful [McMenanin].) At the outset of his career Welsh was no less dismissive of himself as a writer and the writing process than he was of *Trainspotting*'s chances of success. 'All you need is a 35p notepad out of Woolie's and a bookie's pencil and get on with it' (Farquarson). His attitude towards writing and especially Oxbridge writers is underscored by his accounts of how he wrote *Trainspotting*: the diaries he had kept, to counter the boredom, while riding from New York to Los Angeles on a Greyhound bus in the early 1980s; his seeing, upon his return to Edinburgh (from London) in the late 1980s, so many of his friends either addicted to heroin, HIV-positive, or dead or dying of AIDS or drug overdose. Then, while employed by the Edinburgh council Housing Department, he was sent to study for an MBA at Heriot-Watt University where he began writing again, once again to counter the boredom but also to help with the comedown from weekend clubbing, which he used to counter the boredom of the straight, middle-class life he had adopted, or adapted to, at the time and whose energy and 'urgency' he drew on in his writing. *Trainspotting* became the space where he could simultaneously relieve the boredom, try to understand why 'people I grew up with and went to school with were dying' (McKay) and 'express my anger over their deaths' in a city that was 'the HIV capital of Europe', not the Athens of the North (Welsh, 'Drugs' 7). 'What was hard for me was the way people seemed to just accept it, like it was something else on top of the poverty, like it was natural' (Black). Begun in the summer of 1988, *Trainspotting* 'came together in a rapid but intermittent burst, over a two year period' (Grant) and was completed in 1991, when Welsh sent it, at Duncan McLean's suggestion, to McLean's editor at Secker & Warburg, the Scottish poet Robin Robertson. (Having learned of Welsh from the *Trainspotting* excerpts published in *New Writing Scotland* and *West Coast Magazine*, McLean sought out Welsh, subsequently published other parts of *Trainspotting* as well as of *The Acid House* in three Clocktower Press publications, and recommended him to Rebel Inc editor Kevin Williamson.) With the publication of *Trainspotting* on 6 August 1993, Alan Chadwick's prophecy came to pass.

How it came to pass neatly sums up the way *Trainspotting* exists as the point of intersection of forces which the novel and its reception both release and contain. Immediately upon the novel's publication, the *Scotsman*'s literary editor, Catherine Lockerbie, hailed Welsh as 'a young writer of wild talent' who at times 'makes James Kelman sound like Anita Brookner'. Efforts to tame, exploit or in some cases subvert that 'wild talent' began quite early and continued through the release of the film version two and a half years later when Welsh acknowledged that in becoming a cultural phenomenon, the novel was no longer really his anymore; it was 'everybody's' (Thompson). Around the same time, reports began circulating that *Trainspotting* had failed to make the Booker shortlist three years earlier because the three male judges had been 'too gentlemanly' to override the two female judges whose 'feminist sensibilities' the novel had offended (Casper Llewellyn Smith, 'Club'; Porlock). While some critics, the conservative Scottish novelist Allan Massie, for example, and the Marxist cultural critic Alan Sinfield, took pains to say that *Trainspotting* was not nearly as unprecedented as its most ardent admirers (such as Lockerbie) claimed, English novelist Jonathan Coe wondered whether 'the rush to confer respectability on [Welsh and Kelman] stems largely from a desire to make dangerous writing safe by finding it a comfortable niche in the literary canon'. The fact that *Trainspotting* was chosen by the Softback Press book club and Quality Paperbacks Direct seems to support Coe's view, as did reviewers' efforts to boost the novel's stature by comparing it with other formerly controversial but now established and therefore eminently safe works such as James Joyce's *Dubliners* (story cycle) and J. D. Salinger's *Catcher in the Rye* (adolescent coming-of-age novel). The trend started early: Chadwick called *Trainspotting* 'a Last Exit to Lothian' and titled his review 'Fear and Lothian'.

The need to explain the new in terms of the familiar is understandable, but the gain in comprehension must be weighed against the loss to the novel and to the already marginalized segments of its audience. Efforts to make *Trainspotting* more accessible and therefore less strange are especially worrisome given its pervasive and, for some, pernicious influence: its spawning a host of imitators and 'warping' contemporary Scottish fiction. On the other hand, *Trainspotting* liberated the voices, talents and careers of writers such as Laura Hird, John King, Niall Griffiths and Alan Warner – by doing for this generation of Scottish, English and Welsh writers what Gray had done for Galloway and others in the 1980s and by making these writers more accessible and commercially viable. The ripple effect continues to be felt in works such as Stephen Smith's bestselling novel *Addict* (set in Aberdeen) and in 'one of the most startling novels to come out of Britain since Irvine Welsh's *Trainspotting*', Helen Walsh's novel *Brass*, a story of drug- and sex-filled angst set in Liverpool. In retrospect it is easy to compare *Trainspotting* with Britart, which Brett Jeffries has dismissed for being 'institutionalized and incapable of being subversive' – its shock tactics (like Welsh's wildness) just a sign of Britart's self-absorption. But, in making this connection, which depends much more (in relation to Welsh's early career) on the general cultural context than it does on direct contact and influence, it is easy to forget, as Duncan McLean has pointed out (responding to Welsh's supposed pernicious influence), that 'In those days, to write about heroin addicts on a run-down Edinburgh estate was far from the easy commercialism cynical critics often accuse Irvine of having adopted' (xiv).

Whatever the novel became in the eyes of critics who lamented or in some cases applauded not just *Trainspotting* but the *Trainspotting* effect, both novel's and author's power and appeal derive in large measure from the variously motivated energy and urgency with which Welsh wrote *Trainspotting*. This includes Welsh's writing it without quite knowing what he was doing and where the novel was heading. (This is true in two senses: within the covers and as a phenomenon; someone like Helen Walsh had, thanks to Welsh, different expectations and greater prospects.) As a result, *Trainspotting* is something of 'a Pandora's box' (as Xan Brooks said of the film, 103) and latterday *Frankenstein*.

The novel's 'broader network' (as Welsh called it) begins with his handling of place, space and time. *Trainspotting* is set in the space of the industrial and postindustrial city, but this is a city defamiliarized for most readers in multiple ways. The city is not only Scottish; it is not the familiar Scottish urban setting of Glasgow but the smaller, less frequently novelized capital Edinburgh. Equally important, the parts of the city that are featured are not those in the Old and New Towns that would make Edinburgh a UNESCO World Heritage site in 1995; rather they are the unpicturesque marginalized areas, including Leith. Nor is the urban space represented in the novel the abstract postmodern space produced by capitalism, as described by Henri Lefebvre in *The Production of Space* (1974). Instead, the city of *Trainspotting* is one described in all its particulars (real places and streets), traversed on foot and by bus and taxi rather than (as in Ian Rankin's Rebus novels) private car. It is a city divided in various ways: by economics, by drugs (or drug dealers), by familiarity. Just as the novel marginalizes touristy Edinburgh, it marginalizes, as well, the 1990 European City of Culture whose underclass appeared to have a monopoly on suffering. London figures more prominently and positively if only, as Mark says, because it is not Edinburgh (a spin not extended to Glasgow). It is a place of refuge ('we're all slags on holiday') and a place to make money (the site of two of Renton's five giro schemes, of his one foray into legal employment and of the £16,000 drug deal). It is also a place where Scots are invariably Jocks unless they disguise their voices (as Mark does) and where abstract postmodern space is more visible, as in the Rule Britannia pub, 'now a frighteningly sanitized hole' (not unlike the places taking over Leith a decade later in *Porno*).

Against the contrast of Old and New Towns peddled to tourists, Welsh divides Edinburgh socio-economically and linguistically rather than 'historically': 'the last thing I want is all these fuckers up in Charlotte Square putting on all the vernacular as a stage managed thing. It's nothing to do with them' (Farquarson). Begbie attests the difference between tourist image and lived reality when he tells the story of Monny's aunt who, having arrived in Edinburgh from the Western isles of Ireland, was immediately smitten and asked for a flat, thinking she would have a fine view of the Castle, not of the gasworks in Granton where the 'hot-line joab' in a rundown housing scheme leaves her. Although it appears in the novel only once, Leith Central Station, located at the foot of Leith Walk and closed since the 1950s (and demolished in 1989), is representative of the distressed state of the parts of the city in which the novel is mainly set. Like the novel itself, the station is a gathering place for drunks and addicts as well as the homeless. The disused station not only suggests Leith's dependency on (and socio-economic and cultural distance from) Edinburgh; Leith Central Station anticipates the financially troubled Waterworld that opened on the site the year before *Trainspotting* was published. It also anticipates, however distantly and indirectly, the colossal failure of the Millennium Dome a decade later and those more successful colossi dedicated to seeing and being seen, Tate Modern in a disused power plant and London Eye.

But what can be said about the differently colossal success of *Trainspotting* itself, starting with Chadwick's review and Welsh's appearance at the 1993 Edinburgh Book Festival? Angus Calder claims that 'Hypers of Scottish Culture should have problems with the *Trainspotting* phenomenon' (238). Calder makes the common-sensical mistake of underestimating the consumer culture's and the culture industry's ability to profit from transgression by incorporating it, not only in Welsh's appearance at the 1993 Edinburgh Book Festival but in *Trainspotting*'s and Welsh's becoming catalysts for the Athens of the North's transformation into UNESCO World City of Culture (Tim Bell's guided *Trainspotting* tour included and Auld Reekie's resurrection as Inspiring Capital, as Edinburgh's new London-designed, punningly apt slogan has it). The novel's setting can also be read in terms of the larger political situation. As Welsh has noted, 'Leith and Edinburgh are quite analogous to Scotland and England' (Beckett, 'Irvine'). Although certainly valid, this analogy is useful only insofar as it is not allowed to displace the physicality of the actual city as depicted in the novel. Leith does not so much stand in for anything (Edinburgh, Scotland, etc.) as stand against them as proof that Whyte and Galloway were right. '"Scottish literature", as a cosy study of the past, is not enough'.

As Gérard Genette explains in *Narrative Discourse*, narrative time is spatial in its duration, and in *Trainspotting* this spatializing of time is especially (albeit unselfconsciously) complex. The novel marks (and masks) time in several ways. There are the temporal markers, relatively infrequent, to help orient the reader in time. Begbie takes off for London on page 119 and has already returned by 120. Renton shoots up on page 86, is 'still clean' on 112 and clean for weeks on 131. June is pregnant but not yet showing on page 119 and in hospital giving birth twelve pages later. Billy reenlists in the army (page 132, mentioned again 172) and is killed in action on 210. Spud is sentenced to ten months in Saughton Prison on page 168 and just released (in time for Billy's funeral) on 211. Renton is in London on page 122 and back in Edinburgh for his 'first shag in ages' on 130 and back in London three months later on 228. There are also temporal markers tied to annual public events, including the Edinburgh Festival (August), New Year's Day, the Orange Day parade (12 July), the London Fleadh (June). There are other markers tied to one-off public events such as the introduction of the infamous poll tax (first in Scotland, 1989, and in the rest of Britain the following year). 'If you're being pedantic about it, you could say it [*Trainspotting*] was set in Edinburgh between 1982 and 1988', Welsh claimed (Macdonald). Textual evidence from within the novel and elsewhere indicates that *Trainspotting* is actually set between 1988 and 1991. In *Ecstasy*, Mark is 16 years old in 1979; he is 25 early in *Trainspotting*, making the year of 'the first shag in ages' 1988. Internal evidence supports this dating: references to 'back in 1985' and 'the mid-eighties', 1970 and '20 years later', the release of the film *The Accused* and The Proclaimers' 'Sunshine on Leith' (both 1988), the Simple Minds' going political (1989), Mandela's release and the fall of the Sandinistas (both after February 1990), and the Pogues' appearance at the London Fleadh at the end of the novel (June 1991). This chronology, which is established by dating undated events mentioned in the novel, indicates that the Iggy Pop event Tommy attends early in the novel must have been the one on 15 December 1988 (not the one two years later). However, Welsh has Iggy Pop sing 'Neon Forest', a song not recorded until 1990. There are other chronological errors, both of dating and duration: Nina's mother could not have watched *Bruce Forsyth's Generation Game* in 1988 as Forsyth did not resume hosting the show until 1990; by the time Mark and Franco stand inside, Leith Central Station would already have been demolished, and the 'several months' that have elapsed between Tommy's first having tried heroin (91) and 'Winter in West Granton' (316) are far too few.

On the one hand, such mistakes matter because they indicate the kind of slippage that has occurred in postmodern times identified by Fredric Jameson, involving an attenuated sense of history. At the same time, these mistakes (and others like them) do not matter because the specificity of political and pop cultural references creates a sense of the times as lived by Renton and others. The passage of time is registered in personal terms, as in Davie Mitchell's recollection of his family's flat in Oxgangs, which anticipates Welsh's much fuller treatment of this subject in *Glue*: 'The place had always seemed so modern to me when I was a kid. Now it looked like a shantyhouse relic of a bygone era' (250). The historical and more numerous musical references create a clear *sense* of when the novel takes place while at the same time contributing to the very different sense created by the vague internal markers and more especially the frequent slippage of verb tense, as past and present lose their distinctness and create an almost claustrophobic sense of immediacy, a present from which there is no relief and no escape. The markers, along with this slippage, create both a familiar world and the temporal equivalent of the characters' spatial confinement. It is a world that is relentlessly now, and yet, as the film version's Diane (not the novel's Dianne) says to (and of) Mark and as the frequent references to pubs rather than clubs suggests, it is also a world that is strangely and subtly dated (1982–88). The combination of immediacy and the 'weakening of historicity, both in our relationship to public History and in the new forms of our private temporality' (Jameson 6), contributes to the novel's appeal as much as characters and overt content do. The very few exceptions – patriotic songs, Spud's family history – do not really provide relief from this intense and claustrophobic immediacy. Rather they underscore the general absence of connection to any larger context. Thus, the novel's 'debunking of the Western Enlightenment tradition' centred in eighteenth-century Edinburgh and the characters' lack of interest in the ideals of liberty, equality or fraternity ... or in self-improvement, rationality and citizenship – all those codes and dead narratives' (Haywood 158). Both in style and effect *Trainspotting* also creates a counter-history of pre- and post-acid house. Combining punk's rebelliousness and rave's hedonism, the novel rejects the temporal distance and (presumed) cultural proximity of heritage fiction and film that were so popular in the 1980s and 1990s in favour of intense temporal closeness and (for many readers) cultural distance. Once again, one must not be too dogmatic about what something in this Pandora's box of a novel 'means'. The slippage in verb tense found in *Trainspotting* is also characteristic of oral storytelling, where switching from past to present signals a change in importance and a sign of what Ronald K. S. Macaulay calls oral storytelling's 'extremely common eloquence' (42).

The novel's tenuous connection to this oral tradition notwithstanding, the horror of *Trainspotting* is the apparent absence of connection to anyone or anything. There is no connection to Britishness, which Renton dismisses as 'ugly and artificial' (228), and certainly none to the role Scotland has played in constructing and preserving Britishness: whether Billy's role as a British soldier in Northern Ireland or, in the chapter titled 'A Scottish Soldier', Johnny Swan's pretending to be a disabled veteran of the Falklands War in order to raise drug money. 'A Scottish Soldier' alludes to the maudlin song of the same name and to 'one of the abiding icons of Scottishness ... which confirmed that being Scottish and British were not at all at odds' (McCrone 15). Just as none of the characters feels connected either to the nation-state of Britain or to the stateless nation of Scotland, neither do they feel connected to culture, as commonly defined, meaning high culture, but also much of mass culture, especially television. Nor do they feel vitally connected to nation writ small, the *natio-*, or local community, especially Edinburgh and not even Leith, which was unwillingly incorporated into Edinburgh in 1920. Nor, except in the most attenuated form, are the characters connected to youth culture. If, as Mick Brown notes, 'Youth Culture is all about belonging' and British youth culture is 'traditionally tribal', then Welsh's characters appear deprived even of this sense of cohesive community, except for the music. The films are American; Hibs football works only slightly better as a binding agent and families not at all. Nina would rather go clubbing than stay with her mother, watching *Bruce Forsyth's Generation Game,* the night of her uncle's death. Death abounds in *Trainspotting* but does not serve to bind together the living. At Matty's funeral, characters retreat into their private memories, and following Dawn's, they retreat into separate states of heroin-induced oblivion. Phil Grant's death, from a heart attack at age 27 or so, leads to a vicious kicking, and Tommy's imminent death promises to be lonely. Having grown up in an era of Thatcher-induced mass unemployment, the characters are also cut off from their parents' working-class roots. Scottish manhood and industry appear only in perverted forms, approved by his parents but understood all too well by Mark: Billy as soldier, Begbie as husband and father, Simon as go-getter. Drug culture proves no less inimical to community: 'Nae friends in this business, only associates', Johnny Swan says in a line that Mark finds so impressive he repeats it and which nicely updates for the children of Thatcher's revolution the sentiment expressed by Alexander Trocchi in *Cain's Book*: ' "Capacity for love?" George asked. "I don't know anything about that. I have noticed that Jody has a capacity for horse" ' (227).

In *Trainspotting*, positive is negative (as in HIV-positive); so is sharing (as in sharing needles). The needier one is, the more vulnerable and alone he or she becomes: Julie Mathieson (78) and Tommy (after becoming HIV-positive). The trace of friendship and communal feeling appears fleetingly the last time Mark sees Tommy: their eyes meet 'and something flashes between us. It's something ah cannae define, but it's something really good. It's thair jist fir a second; then it's gone' (317). It is apparently scenes such as this that led Dominic Head to find in the novel 'a disguised lament for a simpler and more human world – the stereotypical home and hearth values of the pre-war working classes, perhaps' (44–5). However, *Trainspotting* is observant rather than nostalgic, often mordantly so. Like the 'something' that momentarily flashes between Mark and Tommy, the 'shockingly close' engagement of reader and characters (Turner, 'Sick Boys') is offset by the failure of the characters to actually communicate with one another. Their fear of intimacy is underscored by outbreaks of desperate camaraderie especially evident in 'New Year's Day' (in listening to and singing along with political songs such as 'James Connolly' and 'The Boys of the Old Brigade') and in 'There Is a Light That Never Goes Out' where Spud's yearning to 'jist huv somebody' is made even more intense in the midst of so much social pathology played out against the grim lyrics of the Smiths' song to which the chapter title alludes, and in a novel where addiction plays itself out against the backdrop of abuse of all kinds (spousal, child, physical, sexual, mental).

It is hardly surprising that fearing intimacy, needing someone and the presence of so much social pathology should lead Mark and others to 'ma beautiful heroine's tender caresses' in this first of Welsh's chemical romances. Heroin becomes a potent floating signifier of social pathology, political dependence, and consumer capitalism. The novel offers a host of explanations for why the characters use heroin. Each is compelling but none is definitive: to counter the boredom, to induce oblivion, to escape consumer capitalism's endless choices, to participate in the consumer culture as both consumer and entrepreneur; as 'psychic defence', as reasonable response on the part of Thatcher's Army of the Unemployed (see Mount, 240), as a purely arbitrary but nonetheless effective way of organizing one's life, as the epitome of consumer capitalism's 'algebra of need' and of 'the Thatcher government's politics of competitive individualism', and as the logical consequence of classical liberalism which illogically and hypocritically proscribes certain drugs (heroin, for example) but not others (from alcohol to credit cards). Although clearly marginalized, socially, economically, politically and culturally, *Trainspotting*'s addicts reflect the ethos of mainstream society in the age of late capitalism: 'Consuming, not working, becomes the "hub around which the life-world rotates". Pleasure, once seen as the enemy of capitalist industriousness, now performs an indispensable role' (Lyon 66).

Unlike Christoph Lindner, who compares Welsh's novel unfavourably with Mrs Gaskell's nineteenth-century 'condition of England' novels (*Trainspotting* never gets beyond the diagnosis of a symptom [heroin]' [41]), Carol Gow couches her approval of the novel and its appropriateness to young British readers in language that suggests just how inescapable consumer capitalism is. Contrasting *Trainspotting* with the government's ineffectual 'just say no' anti-drug programmes, Gow praises Welsh's novel because it allows young readers to make an 'informed choice'. While it is certainly true that 'drug addiction has become the demonic and demonized reflection of a commodified, fetishized and irresponsible capitalist system' (Haywood 158), it is no less true that, as Claire Squires argues, *Trainspotting* is in effect, if not necessarily in authorial design/intention, part of that system ('Trainspotting'). Taking the wider view, Squires correctly understands the parallel between selling smack and selling *Trainspotting* (and Scottishness more generally) to a new market of eager young readers who are asked to 'Choose *Trainspotting*', a novel in which Mark punkishly dismisses the 'Choose Life' ad-speak mantra of contemporary consumerism. As Terry Eagleton explains, 'Postmodern culture may be anti-patrician, but its demotic disdain for elitism can sit easily enough with an endorsement of conservative values .... The market is the best mechanism for ensuring that society is both highly liberated and deeply reactionary' (71).

It is of course *Trainspotting*'s liberating possibilities that were first noticed, especially the 'dazzlingly self-assured' prose and seemingly unselfconscious stylistic virtuosity. Welsh effectively, perhaps intuitively combines the oral/aural and the cinematically visual, 'wild talent' and 'pitch-black wit', gritty realism, grotesque realism, and 'social surrealism' in a wildly divergent yet strangely coherent whole which remains steadily grounded in the characters' actual lives and in the author's intensely physical writing. The proliferation and intersection of so many styles transform the novel into a carnivalesque space, where languages and styles jostle one another in 'joyful relativity'. The carnivalesque is always implicitly political; at the very least it disrupts the basis of the modern nation in 'the standardisation of *one unitary language* that all its members can understand' (McLeod 72). More constructively (for Bakhtin, carnival is always far more creative than destructive), *Trainspotting* evidences the ways 'dominated social groups can reappropriate language, allowing it once again to become a medium for expressing the needs of individuals and groups' (Jochen Schulte-Sasse, qtd. in Nehring 132).

The reappropriation of language in *Trainspotting* is most apparent in Welsh's use of dialect which both 'add[s] up to something greater than the sum of the individual parts' (Paget 133) and 'gestures to the lost community which dialect had represented in the Scottish tradition and which has now been corrupted into fearful individualism' (Craig, *Modern* 97). The sign of fearful individualism and of collective defiance, dialect in *Trainspotting* is heard against a linguistic background which includes not only English, but the more familiar Glaswegian. As John Skinner points out, 'Welsh's metropolitan Scots is actually far more impressive than the more homogeneous Glaswegian demotic forged by Kelman' (220). Certainly more impressive than the language of the European Union techno-state, the novel's vernacular stands in solidarity with readers in other fearful nations facing gradual extinction in United Europe. One also hears in the dialect what Henry Nash Smith, writing about *The Adventures of Huckleberry Finn*, called 'the vernacular perspective': the value system which a vernacular implies. In Welsh this system includes his interest in 'physical' as opposed to 'cerebral' writing (Romero) and his interest in 'the body as the locus of meaning' (Jamieson 221–2). It is also writing clearly linked to the Scottish oral story-telling tradition that the Scottish Storytelling Festival, begun in 1989, has helped revive (see Donald Smith 167). But this linkage is complicated by the emphasis on page design and typography (admittedly less extensively here than in *Marabou Stork Nightmares* and *Filth*), which underscores the material existence of both the literary text and the reality it seeks to represent.

Dialect in *Trainspotting* is not quite as natural and artless as it seems and at times differs considerably from the language found in the previously published excerpts. The fact that the language of the first of the nine, 'The First Day of the Edinburgh Festival', published in *New Writing Scotland 9*, is more conventional than that of the novel is more likely the result of Welsh having begun writing *Trainspotting* in Standard English, which he abandoned because he found it 'pretentious' ('On Language'), than of editorial interference on the part of Whyte and Galloway. Thus, these representative differences between excerpt and novel: of/ay, anyway/anywey, I've/ah've, was/wis, parting/partin, I am/ah'm, thaire/thair (the former being the usual spelling in most of the excerpts and therefore clearly attributable to Welsh) and this longer passage: 'I have distinctive ginger hair and Forrester can obviously see my reflection through the window … ' (excerpt), 'Forrester can obviously see the reflection of my ginger hair through the dimpled window' (novel). The dialect used in seven of the eight other excerpts on the other hand is more pronounced than in the novel. (The eighth excerpt, 'Traditional Sunday Breakfast', published in *DOG* magazine [December 1991] and narrated in the first person and in Standard English in the novel, was not located.) 'It Goes without Saying' (*West Coast Magazine*, 1992), 'Trainspotting at Leith Central Station' (*A Parcel of Rogues*, 1992), 'Grieving and Mourning in Port Sunshine' (*Rebel Inc* #2), 'Her Man', 'The Elusive Mr. Hunt', 'Winter in West Granton', and 'After the Burning', the second part of 'Memories of Matty' (all four in *Past Tense*, 1992) do not just include several grammatical peculiarities clearly attributable to Welsh (e.g., no apostrophe for the possessive), 'wifes' for 'wives', 'the gather' for 'thegither' (i.e., together). The dialect of the excerpts also places greater demands on the general reader than either the novel or 'The First Day of the Edinburgh Festival' published in *New Writing Scotland*, whether this general reader is in Edinburgh's Charlotte Square, Glasgow's George's Square, London's Russell Square, or New York's Washington Square: ehs (excerpt)/us (novel), it wis/it's, o'/ay, out o'/ootay, shi/she, wis/was, ehs o'/us ay, eh/he, wid/would, like eh/likesay, ahywis/eywis, nuebodies/naebody's, hudin/haudin, mibye ehs/mibbe he's, bit/but, ur/her, coz/cause, hur/her, lits/lets, ursell it/hersel at, ehsel/hissel, zat/s'at (is that). There are also several instances where the dialect in the previously published excerpt is less demanding than in the novel: could/kin, know/ken, from/fae. As this brief summary indicates, the role that language plays in creating *Trainspotting*'s air of authenticity proves more complex and crafted than readers of the published novel can possibly suspect.

That the novel is, as a genre (as Bakhtin defined it), a point of intersection of various dialogized voices, each with its loophole and sideward glance, is a now familiar concept. However, it is also clear that certain novels are more dialogical than others, and that the way Welsh structures *Trainspotting* contributes to its intense dialogism. Attempts to define that structure and thereby understand and contain the novel and limit its contextual possibilities are instructive: 'anecdotal collage', 'set of loosely linked improvisations', etc. Where Will Self compared the narrative to 'a torch of awareness, passed from one character's internal monologue to the next', Welsh likened it to 'a bunch of voices shouting to be heard' (McGavin), to a puzzle and to a DJ's mix where the intention is 'to keep the pages turning, to keep the action moving, just like a dj' (Reynolds, 'Angel') in a way akin to the way postmodern, postliterate youth engage the world (Berman 59). Clubbers who came to *Trainspotting* via *The Acid House* would have intuited this connection, one largely lost on mainstream readers and reviewers. Rather than trying to understand *Trainspotting*'s structure in either/or terms (pub or club, torch of awareness or bunch of voices), one should think in terms of both/and. That way one can appreciate the way the novel evokes the engagement of dance culture while at the same time appreciating the way the structure makes

Trainspotting 'feel like an exercise in futility' (Ian Bell) which effectively locks the characters into 'the hell of a narrative without end, without purpose' (Craig, *Modern* 131). It is the latter which prevents each of them from 'becom[ing] an independent "I", a fully formed stable self with the power of agency … to act in history', and which condemns them to 'suffer[ing] the stasis of existence outside of social progression' (Freeman 256).

Trainspotting accommodates, indeed invites, complementary readings of its structure and therefore its meaning, which, like the novel's ending, is penultimate and incomplete, and for which Berthold Schoene's description of the fourth part of *Glue*, 'tumultuous kaleidoscope', seems particularly apt ('Nervous'). On one hand, the novel's characters exist not only in a kaleidoscopic relation to one another, but 'in an eternal present' (Hagemann) that subjects Apollonian order to 'Dionysian rendering' (Lasdun). One result of this Dionysian rendering is the atomized individual of late capitalism. Another is the exhilarating novel and its effect on Scottish and British fiction that it engendered out of junk, shit and death, transforming punk's buses to boredom and to nowhere (from the posters advertising The Sex Pistols' 'Pretty Vacant') into the Welsh phenomenon. To understand the novel's structure requires understanding its complexity, and that means comprehending that some of this complexity is by design, some not. The table of contents creates an expectation of order and progression at odds with the way the reader actually engages with the novel. The publisher's summary, printed on the front inside cover of the original Secker & Warburg paperback, narrows the focus even more by declaring Renton the novel's protagonist and then going on to raise many of the points repeated by reviewers. *Rebel Inc*'s endorsement, 'The best book ever written by man or woman … deserves to sell more copies than the Bible', appears on the front cover of all British paperback editions but is relegated to the back cover of the US edition. Jeff Torrington's lengthy and enthusiastic endorsement appears in the first edition of the British edition and in abbreviated form on subsequent British paperbacks but is not included at all in the US edition. Torrington, a Scot, came to writing late but achieved fame quickly, in the UK, with his first novel *Swing Hammer Swing* (1992). Instead of Torrington and blurbs from the *Herald*, the *Independent on Sunday*, *Sunday Times* and *Scotland on Sunday* featured on the Minerva editions (the *Independent on Sunday* blurb was dropped from the 2003 Vintage edition), Norton substituted blurbs more likely to resonate with American book buyers: *Time Out*, *TLS*, David Foster Wallace (riding high following the publication of *Infinite Jest* the same year) and Nick Hornby (by then author of two ladlit books, *Fever Pitch* and *High Fidelity*, addressed to a youthful, not young, middle-class audience). The covers themselves help create reader expectations. The mainly black and silver of the first British paperback, with traces of red and white and its figures in skull masks, is at once stylish and macabre, more Goth than punk, and well suited to the way characters are presented in the novel, with little attention to physical details. The US edition, released at the same time as the film, substitutes publicity shots of five of the principal actors from the film. The first British movie tie-in edition features Ewan McGregor / Renton on the front cover, the other four relegated to the back, with the back inside cover given over to an ad for the film soundtrack (a spot used in the 2003 paperback edition to advertise the new 'definitive' edition DVD).

It is not only the film (in all its various forms) which makes Mark Renton appear to be *Trainspotting*'s central figure. To the extent that *Trainspotting* is read as a novel about drugs, Renton is clearly the focus. The novel is shaped by his drug use and the reader vicariously experiences heroin use and withdrawal through him. Renton represents the junkie's social withdrawal in its purest form, stripped of Begbie's pathological violence, Sick Boy's predatory 'numero uno'-ism, Spud's terminal passivity, and Tommy's sense of loss. In the novel's first chapter, the only reason he tears himself away from the Jean-Claude Van Damme video to accompany a shivering Sick Boy to the dealer Johnny Swan's is that he knows his own withdrawal pains are 'in the post'. Mission accomplished, he chooses to return to his flat and the video rather than visit Kelly who, as Alison says, 'really needs [him]' following her abortion. Renton's self-centredness is even more glaringly and dismayingly apparent following the death of baby Dawn. Asked by Lesley, the baby's distraught mother, to cook up a shot, Mark obliges as the others gather round. 'Lesley comes first', Mark says, 'eftir me. That goes without saying' (56). Renton's pursuit of 'ma heroine's beautiful caresses' and 'the cause ay oblivion' (11, 222) is nonetheless offset by a sympathetic understanding of others that sets him apart from the rest of the novel's male characters. He frequently recalls the way Johnny Swan and others were when they were children:

innocent, hopeful, full of promise. And he is mindful of those less fortunate than himself: Julie Mathieson, for example (78), 'perr Lesley', 'perr Mally' and 'poor Matty'. Although he takes sexual advantage of Sharon, his dead brother's pregnant girlfriend ('Bang to Rites'), Mark's preying upon the vulnerable, grieving as well as desperate Sharon is more complicated than it may at first seem. Their sex in the locked bathroom transforms the family's 'festival of grief' into something close to, even if hardly identical to, the carnivalesque defeat of death which Bakhtin discerns in Rabelais (discussed below). Equally important, Mark takes the time to listen to Sharon, and therefore to understand her, before relapsing, as it were, into social withdrawal. He does something similar with Giovanni a few pages later, in 'London Crawling', a chapter in which Mark shows his openness not only to others' stories but to a much more flexible sense of sexual identity than do any of the other male characters.

Renton is also more self-aware, more self-critical and more self-deprecating than the others, and much less self-deluded. He is intellectually aware of his self-loathing and of the seeming inescapability of his world; he is also ultimately less willing to be content with temporary escapes, both geographical and pharmacological. In London ('Straight Dilemmas No. 1'), Renton realizes that he has given up one kind of boredom and desperation (Edinburgh junkie) for another ('the nine-to-five arsehole' [300]). Returning to Leith a few pages later, he realizes what 'home' means as he walks from the city centre towards Leith: 'the further ye go doon the Walk at this time ay night, the mair likely ye are tae git a burst mooth. Perversely, ah feel safer the further doon ah git. It's Leith. Ah suppose that means hame' (306). Going home and travelling down the Walk means running into Begbie, whom Renton has been trying to get away from since their school days (prompting Renton to work harder at his studies than he otherwise would have, even going to university in Aberdeen, where he spends his grant on drugs and prostitutes). After a brief stop at the derelict Leith Central Station, the chapter, like the first chapter and like Mark's brief university experience, comes full circle, with the likelihood of a 'burst mooth' mentioned at the beginning becoming a reality at the end. As Begbie takes out his rage on a nameless youth, Renton looks on: 'Ah didnae even feel like tryin tae intervene, even in a token away' (309).

What chiefly characterizes this passage is neither Renton's fatalism nor his indifference. Rather, it is his awareness of both. This awareness puts Renton's social withdrawal in a different light, as signifying both the junkie's habitual self-centredness and Renton's no less habitual ambivalence about 'home' and all it implies. For Renton to go see Kelly because 'she really needs ye', as Alison says, would be to commit himself to home. Not to see Kelly, however, results in Mark feeling guilty. This guilt evidences itself not in anything Renton says about his failure to act (a very Catholic sin of omission); rather it evidences itself in (and derives from) his awareness of his privileged position as one who is aware, ironically so. This self-awareness is connected to Renton's being the most verbally adept, varied and resourceful of all the novel's characters. His articulateness evidences itself in numerous scenes and forms: at the job interview, at his court appearance, and in his dealings with his doctor, his psychologist and his counsellor. It also manifests itself in his vivid, grotesquely realistic descriptions of others and of the drug experience ('each bone in ma body wis simultaneously being crushed in a vice n set aboot wi a blunt hacksaw' [8]). Renton also has the novel's best lines (his 'Choose Life' and 'I don't hate the English' raps), and he is the character who verbally and artistically resembles Welsh the most as he turns the bluebottle fly which has been tormenting him into 'art' by spelling out the word Hibs on the toilet wall. Asked what he does by Dianne's parents, he imagines a job that curiously parallels *Trainspotting*: 'Ah work wi the social history collection, based mainly at the People's Story in the High Street … . Ah rake around in people's rubbish for things that've been discarded, and present them as authentic historical artefacts ay working people's everyday lives. The ah make sure that they dinnae fall apart when they're oan exhibition' (146–7). Renton's tale serves as the glue which holds together the unofficial People's Story – 'the bunch of voices shouting to be heard' – that is the novel *Trainspotting*, which succeeds so well *because* it risks falling apart.

If, as Douglas Gifford claims, Renton emerges as the novel's 'complex centre' ('Lonely'), he does so in a novel in which 'no single narrative voice is allowed to dominate' (Boddy, 'Scotland' 371). In much the same way, *Trainspotting* exists within and against the traditions of the Scottish and 'English' novels, as something marginal that quickly came to occupy the centre. Just as

'*Trainspotting* is not reducible to simple drugs novel unless 'you discount its social panopticon' (Linklater, 'Irvine'), neither is it reducible to its ostensible main character. Renton is prominent but not dominant; he exists as part of the 'broader network', as Welsh called it (Young, 'Blood'). *Trainspotting*'s seven sections ('Kicking', 'Relapsing', 'Kicking Again', 'Blowing It', 'Exile', 'Home', and 'Exit') comprise forty-three sections (344 pages); thirty-three are narrated in the first person (approximately 250 pages), twenty-one (160 pages) by Renton and fourteen (96 pages) by seven other first-person narrators (two in Standard English). One section, 'Speedy Recruitment' (Renton and Spud), is narrated in both first and third persons. Nine sections (100 pages) are narrated in the third person (and in Standard English): one by Renton, three by Renton and others, and five by others only. In other words, not only is much of the novel narrated in the third person and in Standard English; much of it is narrated by and is about others.

Instead of linear progression and the emergence of a main character which the contents pages suggest, *Trainspotting* offers a variety of structuring devices to create a sense of a localized world at once coherent and under threat. These devices include the recurring references to popular culture (especially music), parallel scenes and situations, 'inter-echoing vignettes' (Lockerbie), novelistic equivalents of hyperlink and quick cuts, 'sudden swerves between wit, rage, cynicism, and unexpected tenderness' (Lasdun), minor characters (at times just names) that weave their way through the novel to create a sense of local community (however dysfunctional), the tropes of return and futility and the desire for, as well as failure or fear of, intimacy. Perhaps more important in creating a sense of coherence despite the apparent narrative discontinuity is the network of decrowning doubles that give *Trainspotting* its distinctive air of punkish cynicism and festive carnival. As Bakhtin explains, 'The primary carnivalistic act is *the mock crowning and subsequent decrowning of the carnival king*', a parodic act ('parodying is the creation of a *decrowning double*' – of a 'world turned inside out') which undermines monologic authority and underscores 'the *joyful relativity* of all structure and order, of all authority and all (hierarchical) position' (*Problems*, 124–7). Some of Welsh's decrownings are quite general: the novel itself is the decrowning double of the Oxbridge British novel; *Trainspotting*'s Edinburgh and London turn the touristy cities on their heads; Renton chooses not to choose life; the Falklands War is part of a con to secure drug money; brother Billy is not 'the brave young man' who died for his country but 'a spare prick in a uniform' and 'exactly the kind of cunt they'd have branded a cowardly thug if he wis in civvy street rather than on her Majesty's Service' (211). The night before her essay on 'whether morality is absolute or relative' is due, Kelly exacts her revenge on the three middle- to upper-middle-class English white settler types who make her feel inferior by adding her menstrual blood, infected urine and excrement to their food. In taking this Rabelaisian form, Kelly's comic revenge forms part of the novel's larger privileging of the intensely physical over the transcendentally abstract. Kelly's waitressing, Mark's giro schemes, Johnny Swan's and Mikey Forrester's drug-dealing, Begbie's and Spud's thieving are the decrowning doubles of the Edinburgh virtues of hard work, respectability and godliness. Political rhetoric is similarly debunked on two notable occasions by being relegated to the realm of the purely personal; thus Lizzie turns Tommy's going to the Iggy Pop concert into 'a pure referendum on [their] relationship' (72) and in 'House Arrest' Mark, after allowing his mother to decide whether he will have coffee, quotes Enoch Powell's famous line, 'Power devolved is power retained' (202). Sentimentalism is seen as either dangerous (the singing of patriotic songs such as 'James Connolly' being the Catholic equivalent of Mark's father's and brother's Orange bigotry) or ridiculous (Mark's mother) and is attacked with particular venom in Welsh's transformation of lines from Chris de Burgh's top-of-the-pops 'Lady in Red', 'I have never had a feeling / Such a feeling of complete and utter love / As I do tonight', into Mark Renton's 'Ah've never known such ay sense ay complete and utter hopelessness, punctuated only by bouts ay raw anxiety' (201). Significantly, on occasions when Mark does feel emotion, he either expresses it in plain but highly affecting language, as in his memory of Julie Murchison (78), or by lapsing into silence (the several unfinished sentences in 'Bang to Rites').

Billy's is just one of the many deaths in this novel of 'bleary waste and menacing mortality' (Spencer). Although Welsh would later be unfavourably compared with Don DeLillo upon the UK release of the latter's *Underworld*, which features a waste management executive, *Trainspotting* is all about waste. Junk, wasters, the waste produced by consumer capitalism (and the government policies, such as Thatcher's, which promote it) all contribute to what Jamieson calls the novel's 'excremental motif'. The number of deaths in *Trainspotting* is astonishing: both of Renton's brothers, his Uncle Alex and Billy's friend Phil Grant (heart attacks), two infants (cot death), David Ross (injecting whisky directly into a vein), Julie Murchison (AIDS complications), Matty (toxoplasmosis), Ventners (murdered before he can die as a result of AIDS), at least one of NaNa's many husbands and partners, Goagsie and Tommy (AIDS) and Lesley attempting suicide (but surviving, as the reader is surprised to learn in *Porno*, a far more upbeat work than *Trainspotting*). Death here, despite all the Rabelaisian humour, is not 'cheerful' because productive, as it is in Bakhtin's reading of *Gargantua* and *Pantagruel*. Death is not defeated, does not bring forth life, at least for the characters, who lose limbs and lives and who find their community wasting and whittled away. Waste is productive only for Welsh and for others who have profited in various ways from his example and success: writers such as Niall Griffiths, Laura Hird, and John King; Scottish and British fiction; their publishers; Cool Britannia and Cool Caledonia by following Renton's example in transforming the vile bluebottle fly that has been tormenting him in the bookie's toilet into a primitive but ultimately profitable early example of Brit Art.

Another way Welsh achieves coherency in *Trainspotting* even as he downplays or undermines linear progression is by creating an ensemble novel. Admittedly, some characters are more important than others and all either allegorical types – hard man, soft touch, scheming schemie, drug dealer, lad o' pairts, etc. – or R. Crumb-like cartoons, but more than most novels, *Trainspotting* depends upon them all. Also, although Welsh focuses here (as in his other fiction) on male characters, leading some to read *Trainspotting* as an egregious example of ladlit of the 'men behaving badly' kind, female characters are surprisingly numerous and play a greater role late in the novel (but not, as in *Glue* and *Porno*, because Welsh is having them do so by design).

To read *Trainspotting* as a carnivalesque ensemble novel in which everyone and everything exist in close proximity and as part of a 'broader network' of narrative and of material culture requires a more complex and comprehensive approach to the novel (especially the final section) than it has thus far received. The ending ('Exit', the only one comprising a single chapter, 'Station to

Station') has been read as proof of Renton's triumph (and therefore proof of Renton's role as protagonist), of Renton's 'capacity to survive … based on his ability to adapt' (Freeman 260), and of his 'fight[ing] back from the brink through a combination of life-affirming intelligence and wit' (Petrie, *Contemporary* 91). Such upbeat readings, while by no means unwarranted, must nonetheless be carefully qualified. They must be read in the context of the rest of the novel, where change is generally associated with the very young (Dianne), the desperately hopeful (Sharon, Davie Mitchell, Kelly) and the completely deluded (Johnny Swan's dream of going to Thailand). And it should be read in the context of Welsh's later novels as well, where the endings seem either melo-dramatic (*Filth*) or unconvincingly optimistic (*Glue* and the ever upbeat *Porno*). *Trainspotting*'s ending is certainly consistent with 'the desire to leave it all behind' that is so 'prevalent in contemporary Scottish fiction' (Boddy 366) – perhaps nowhere more so than in Sammy's long goodbye at the end of *How late it was, how late* – which plays off, and with, the long history of Scottish emigration dealt with more extensively in *Marabou Stork Nightmares*.

The ending can also be read as autobiographical revelation: Welsh's own desire to escape from what Sick Boy says spells 'limited', including 'the nine-to-five arsehole' that Renton fears becoming in London and that led Welsh to turn away from his own nine-to-fine job and MBA studies, and towards clubbing on weekends and of course writing. *Trainspotting*'s ending has been read even more broadly by Angus Calder, looking ahead to the 1997 referendum, by Grant Farred (recklessly so), and Robin Spittal who reads Renton's leaving for Amsterdam in the context of David McCrone's enthusiastic embrace of a post-national Scotland free of 'the regressive Scotch myths', rejecting the tartanry, kailyard, and red Clyde which he feels have hampered Scottish nationalists no less than nostalgic Scots and positively regarding the nation as part of the European Union and the global economy. Taking the opposite and more nuanced view, Cairns Craig reads *Trainspotting*'s ending as a prime instance of 'the persis-tence of the self-mutilating ethic' of the fearful and fearless that he finds central 'to some of the most innovative writing of the 1980s and 1990s' (*Modern* 154). Craig reads Renton's freedom at novel's end as irresponsible, insofar as it leaves the dialectic of the fearful and the fearless in place, his freedom founded on fear, his own and that of others. While some critics are far too eager to endorse Renton's escape, Craig is too reluctant and in his reluctance fails to give its due to a second dialectic, one more pronounced in the film, between the local and the global.

Even as the novel appears to endorse Renton's Kierkegaardian leap of faith, or self-interest, it qualifies that endorsement in several ways. First, it begins with a sentence which includes the Scots word, *dreich*, which, unlike much of the Scots vernacular used elsewhere in the novel, strikes a decidedly old-fashioned and therefore discordant note. Second, except for dialogue, the chapter is narrated in Standard English as well as in the third person and, except for the last page and a half, the past tense. In addition, the narrative focus moves back and forth between characters, except for Secks (unlike in 'Memories of Matty' where the focus moves from one character to the next) before finally settling on Renton. Third, the carnivalesque, Dionysian style which characterizes most of the novel is absent here as the novel grows increasingly less dialogic. Overall, the ending returns *Trainspotting* to its genesis, to the Standard English in which Welsh began writing it but then abandoned because it sounded pretentious and affected and a world away from the published novel's opening, 'The sweat wis lashing oafay Sick Boy'. Thus, even as the novel ends by looking ahead to Amsterdam (and all it implies), it looks back and in so doing creates yet another of the closed circles which *Trainspotting*'s vernacular perspective drew on in 'celebrat[ing] the wit of self-loathing' (Milne 163). As Jamieson correctly notes, 'although Welsh is critical of Scottish society, he appears reluctant to relinquish the distinctive Scottish voices that populate his fiction or indeed to distance himself from the place they inhabit' (226). In the novel's final sentences – 'Now, free from them all, for good, he could be what he wanted to be. He'd stand or fall alone. This thought both terrified and excited him as he contemplated life in Amsterdam' – with their echoes of Margaret Thatcher and James Joyce (*Portrait of the Artist as A Young Man*, or perhaps resonating Trocchi's allusion to *Portrait* in *Cain's Book*), one also hears *la nostalgie de la boue*. The faraway gaze of the ending's transcendental signified only throws into higher relief the carnivalesque nature of all that precedes it, the joyful relativity, the grotesque realism, the Nietzschean *ressentiment*, the heteroglossia, the decrowning doubles, the intertextuality, the intense physicality. By ironizing the ending (perhaps intentionally, perhaps not), they render any reading (especially of the ending) incomplete, as befits a work which exists in so many forms. One must similarly resist reading the return to Standard English too narrowly, as a sign either of Mark's betrayal or of his confidence. It is just as likely that it underscores Mark's (as well as the others') sense of discomfort and inferiority as Jocks among non-Scots, whether in London or in Amsterdam, as in the story 'Eurotrash', or of Scots tending to be 'less broad' in their speech generally when dealing with non-Scots (Macaulay 64).

Coincidentally, about the time Renton trawls through the foul waters of the bookie's toilet in search of his 'two nuggets of gold', the opium suppositories he unwittingly shat out, consumers of 'literary fiction' were reading a passage in another novel, *The Remains of the Day*, about waste that makes much the same point, albeit much more delicately. In it an elderly servant 'walk[s] back and forth in front of the summerhouse, looking down at the ground as though he hoped to find some precious jewel he had dropped there' (Ishiguro 50). The juxtaposition of these two passages nicely underscores the loss felt at *Trainspotting*'s end. This is a loss that has less to do with Mark's leaving Scotland behind than with the carnivalesque energy that one mistakenly assumed would go on forever: an energy arbitrarily and with no apparent irony curtailed, only to be resumed, in different form, in the 1996 film version.

3

TRAINSPOTTING:
THE FILM

Concerning differences between novel and film, Welsh noted that 'The novel is a bunch of voices shouting to be heard … you're inside [the characters'] heads rather than just watching them on the screen' (McGavin). Rather than comparing book and film, this chapter examines some of the cultural and critical voices shouting to be heard and therefore contributing to the cultural significance of arguably the most influential film of the 1990s and one of the most free-floating signifiers of the past decade. To do so requires one's viewing the film the way the film views London: as a montage, or more specifically as a montage of cultural signifiers within the larger cultural consumerscape. *Trainspotting*'s success in so many forms over so short a time makes comprehending its enormous cultural impact especially challenging; it also makes it difficult to measure the extent to which the film version may be said to re-present or repackage Welsh's novel: whether the one supplements, supersedes or supplants the other and suppresses or releases the novel's multiple voices.

Welsh's attitude towards and comments about the film offer an appropriate starting point. After signing over the film rights (twice in fact, first to Nick Gay), Welsh took a hands-off approach, appearing in a cameo role but never interfering in the film's production in any way. He not only denied that any film adaptation could or should be 'true to the book'; he welcomed the creative aspect of adaptation, comparing it to a DJ's remix (Welsh, 'She's'). 'The more transformation the better. I know what is in my head; far more interesting to see what's in someone else's. Often aspects of the material are brought out that I was previously disinclined to engage with' (Macdonald 118). Welsh has also noted that filmmakers are in general much more constrained than writers, especially an author who had not expected his novel would ever be published.

Hailed as 'the best Scottish film since *Gregory's Girl*' (Arlidge, 'Dynamic'), *Trainspotting* arrived at a time when Scottish films were much in the news, though the term 'Scottish film' was something of a moveable feast, referring to everything from *Small Faces* and *Shallow Grave* to *Braveheart* and *Breaking the Waves*. The film that the *Economist* claimed in 1997 had 'smashed confidently through all national borders' ('Will') also managed to raise the hopes of other small national cinemas, both within Britain and without. John Arlidge may have been waxing a bit hyperbolic in claiming that movie culture was moving north of the border ('Dynamic'), but there is no doubt that film played an important part in the revived nationalism leading up to the successful referendum on devolution. Differences aside, the Hollywood kilt epics and *Trainspotting* offer different versions of the same type, the outlaw hero (or antihero), and of Scottish identity. This is an identity fragmented and dispersed in the novel but much less so in the film and in the publicity surrounding it which tended to emphasize the undifferentiated Scottishness of its cast and crew and even a link to the past in the form of Macdonald being the grandson and biographer of Emeric Pressburger. *Braveheart* was made by an American-Australian actor-director-star, largely with American money; it was largely shot in Ireland and, in creating a rousing but hardly realistic Passion of the Wallace, looked to a mythified and mystifying Scottish past. *Trainspotting* was more home-grown and, more importantly, attempted to represent Scotland by contesting the dominant iconography and conventional wisdom in ways that *Braveheart* did not. In turning tartanry and the Scottish cringe on their heads, *Trainspotting* also created a few problems. Its demystifying deconstruction of mythified Scotland – Scotland the theme park – was so successful as to risk becoming yet another Scottish icon along with William Wallace, Harry Lauder, Sean Connery, the Highlands, kilts, kailyard, haggis and whisky.

Trainspotting was also read as a British, rather than a Scottish film, and thus as a sign of the resurgence of national cinema in

Britain. One of the reasons for the 35 per cent rise in film attendance in Britain during the first quarter of 1996, 'the most successful British-funded film of 1996' was situated in a context that included *Four Weddings and a Funeral* and *The Full Monty* rather than *Gregory's Girl* and *Small Faces* (Jury; Brooks 95). *Trainspotting* soon became the poster-child for contemporary British cinema, at least for academics and journalists if not for the government's guardians of the culture industries, who adopted a much more cautious approach. One important if indirect consequence of *Trainspotting*'s success was its impact on funding. With few exceptions, British films had been low-budget and poorly distributed outside the UK; concerns over poor funding, distribution and exhibition crested about the time of *Trainspotting*'s release. Its success provided the impetus for change, including in 1999 the earmarking of lottery revenues for British films. (Two years earlier, *Four Weddings and a Funeral* had been an even bigger success, but that was an American-financed film which became a hit in the UK only after becoming a hit in the US.) *Trainspotting*'s influence on funding has turned out to be something of a double-edged sword, however. On one hand, it led to improved funding, to increased visibility and confidence, and to the making of films that in style and/or subject bear *Trainspotting*'s imprint. On the other hand, *Trainspotting* seems to have been the catalyst for a very different change, as hopes raised by the film's success turned into charges of wasted opportunities and misdirection. As David Aukin and Geoffrey MacNab point out, the expansiveness that *Trainspotting* engendered may have been a misstep from the start and the recent downsizing of the British film industry, including the folding of FilmFour back into Channel Four, may, in Aukin's words, create an 'environment where once again films that have no obvious commercial value can be commissioned and surprise us all'. (Ironically, it had been *Trainspotting*'s success which led to FilmFour's creation [Murray Smith, 'Transnational' 226].) Scottish actor Kevin McKidd, *Trainspotting*'s Tommy, makes the same point about the Scottish film industry; *Trainspotting*'s success led to an emphasis on big-budget films 'instead of using the money to help new actors and filmmakers get on their feet' (Qureshi and Smith).

As part of British national cinema, *Trainspotting* played its part in redefining British identity at a time when this identity was perceived as under threat from within and without. Although interpreted by some as a sign that the breakup of Britain was imminent, others saw it as 'an assertion of a healthy cultural diversity' (Kelly 72). The fact that *Trainspotting* and *Sense and Sensibility* were released the same week led to much discussion of the differences, not between Scotland and England but instead between Trainspotters and Janespotters, bulging veins and stiff upper lips, young and old, as urban kailyard was made to play its part in the making of Cool or Ghoul Britannia. *Trainspotting* became the leading exhibit in the late 1990s rebranding which included Brit Pop, Young British Artists such as Damien Hirst and of course the rejuvenated and confident British film industry *Trainspotting* helped create. *Trainspotting* thumbed its nose at two British film traditions simultaneously while effectively creating one of its own. One was the heritage film – Jane Austen remakes and all things David Lean and Merchant-Ivory – whether set in the past (as most were) or in a tarted-up present, such as *Four Weddings and a Funeral*. The other tradition is the Kitchen Sink realism most closely associated with 1960s film adaptations of the 1950s Angry Young Men novels and more recently with Mike Leigh and Ken Loach.

'Disaffection is all the rage' (LaSalle), but this 'rage' had as much to do with the discovery of the buying power of the youth market as it did with a 'mainly youthful constituency [that] has been misread, overlooked and downgraded, while an older generation in Britain allowed itself to be heritaged to death' (Paget 139–40). The connection with the youth audience/market affected the selection of Stylo Rouge, best known for its work in popular music, to handle the design of the poster and other aspects of the film's advertising. Although the campaign's and the film's visual style, often likened to MTV, became hugely influential – for many annoyingly so – it was, like so many aspects of the film's edge, hardly unprecedented. Indeed, the film's deliberately postmodern intertextual recycling and recombining of elements contributes to its allure, as in the supposedly cutting-edge posters, which in fact imitated ads for Quentin Tarantino's *Reservoir Dogs* (1992). As the prospect of commercial success increased, the early emphasis on publicizing the film via 'exclusive' behind-the-scenes features in magazines such as *Face*, *Sky* and *Time Out* was expanded to include mainstream publications such as *The Times* of London, where the emphasis was (as in Miramax's US marketing) on hipness, not drugs and HIV. (For more on the film's marketing, see Westbrook; Rawsthorn.)

Much of the film's appeal to the youth audience derives from the style and substance of what appears on the screen, but another part derives from what this audience hears and how it is heard. As with its handling of drugs and the changing drug scene (see below), the film's use of pop music creates a sonic bridge between the time of the novel (the late 1980s to 1991) and the release of the film, between the music the main characters grew up with in the late 1970s and 1980s to the dance music of the 1990s. To the value of the music aesthetically and narratively, one must add the value of the music in cementing the connection between the film and a target audience quite unlike Welsh's intended audience, comprising people like the characters in the novel, who (except for Renton) didn't read books. The film's target audience is quite different, more like those same characters as they appear in the film: this is 'the youthful, liberal, "cool" audience whose approval the film seeks' (Murray Smith 50), only more well-to-do, more in tune with the mainstream economy.

The relationship between the film and its target audience needs to be parsed still more closely, for this audience is not just young and generally middle-class; it is, as Claire Monk has noted, largely male. In this *Trainspotting* is in the vanguard of British films of the 1990s which 'address the anxieties of young male viewers in terms of an appealing subculture of dissent from the demands of adulthood, women and work' ('Men' 160). Films such as *Four Weddings and Funeral* and *Brassed Off* present the anxious male in his most benign form, as the 'new man'. Films such as *Naked* and *Nil by Mouth* present the anxious male in a more malevolent, pathological way. *Trainspotting* is different in that it mediates between the two extremes as it draws on the new-lad phenomenon associated with the magazine *Loaded* yet critiques the new lad as well. It plays Renton's new man (and Diane's treatment of him) against Begbie's hard man, the new lad at his most menacing, ridiculous, outdated and unadaptable. In expanding Diane's role (especially in the advertising), the film is even able to connect with the young female audience by offering a female version of the new lad, the ladette, who anticipates *Glue*'s Charlene and *Porno*'s Dianne.

Trainspotting's appeal to disaffected youth is undeniable but not easily separable from its appeal to the youth market. Recognizing the film's potential for attracting a wider audience, PolyGram decided to market *Trainspotting* at 50 percent of the production cost, rather than its more usual 10 percent: £850,000 for a £1.7 million film. The film's marketability involved more than riding the novel's and Welsh's coattails. (Even here, however, one needs to proceed cautiously: recall that the novel that caught on with clubbers had already received favourable to rave reviews in the mainstream press written and read by people no longer young.) It also involved the complicitous relationship between the autonomous aesthetic object and late-capitalist, postmodern consumer product in which PolyGram's international distribution network was as much a player as Ewan McGregor. The book's US publisher, the generally staid W. W. Norton, best known for its mammoth and generally canon-conserving anthologies of American (i.e., US), World (i.e., almost exclusively European), and 'English' literature, entered into cross-promotional arrangements with Capitol Records and Urban Outfitters, 'a 50-store apparel chain catering to the young and disaffected' (Bing). It is worth recalling that in the UK the film appeared as the (then) climax of Welsh's meteoric rise from the 1993 publication of *Trainspotting* through *The Acid House*, *Trainspotting* the play, and *Marabou Stork Nightmares*. In the US the film (released five months later than in the UK) in effect introduced Welsh to an audience for whom the publication of *Trainspotting*, *Marabou Stork Nightmares* and *Ecstasy* more or less coincided with the film's release. (*The Acid House* was first published in the US in 1995.) Although *Trainspotting* went on to become the most successful independent release of 1996 in the US, its very status and cachet as an 'independent release' is complicated by the fact of its US distributor Miramax's own status as an 'independent subsidiary' of the Disney Corporation with a reputation for successfully handling films that could 'be marketed on controversy alone' (Lawson). *Trainspotting* was so successful that it became a prime example of a contemporary phenomenon associated with Hollywood studios: the film as brand name, 'a locomotive dragging behind it many other sectors of the economy' (Watson 86),

Although shot in Scotland with a largely Scottish cast and crew, *Trainspotting* is in many ways a very American film, far less indebted to Forsyth and Loach than to Tarantino and Scorsese. And although American reviewers praised the film for having 'a verve and vitality' lacking in Hollywood films (Street 208), it is the film's linkage to American cinema that makes it seem at once so familiar and so distinctive. The expanded importance of Iggy Pop and Lou Reed in the film and the addition of little touches such as the Warhol-style poster in Diane's bedroom and Mark's copy of a biography of Montgomery Clift contribute to 'the lure of the American' (Murray Smith, 'Transnational') in a film that, as noted earlier, has been variously enlisted to represent and speak for Scotland, Britain, youth and of course Welsh's novel. One can read this intertextuality in postmodern terms and therefore as a sign of the film's appeal to young viewers in the global village, whether those viewers are in Edinburgh, Scotland or Scotland, Ontario. One can also read it in economic terms, as part of American cultural hegemony. Or one can read it in post-national terms: the lure of things American as a rejection of both Britishness/Scottishness and the narrow as well as outdated sense of national identity they imply. However, as Murray Smith has cautioned, 'Even in a film as emphatically specific as *Trainspotting*, the local and the global cannot easily be disentangled' ('Transnational' 226); 'it is the call and response between the regional and "Hollywood International" that is so seductive' (*Trainspotting* 20). On one hand this dialectic of the local and a global rendered in decidedly American, Hollywood-international terms implies that the cultural and subcultural specificity that is central to the novel becomes subservient to the demands of the larger culture of the global marketplace. On the other hand this dialectic unwittingly underscores the one aspect of Alexander Trocchi's writing and career that Welsh admires: the international perspective that freed him from a constricting sense of Scottish identity (Welsh, 'A Scottish'). In this sense, the film, far more than Welsh's novel, is something of a foundational text for understanding the interaction of two opposing forces. Prior to devolution, these forces were associated with independence and alignment with the European Union (with Renton's self-imposed exile to Amsterdam made to play a major symbolic role). More recently, these forces have been defined along slightly different lines by Allan Massie: 'the more powerful the forces pushing towards assimilation [in the global culture], the more strongly and self-consciously Scottish culture has reasserted itself'. Read subcultur-ally, this conflict evidences the essential ambivalence that Karen Lury finds in Scottish youth films of the 1990s that 'articulate the tension between staying and going', 'growing up and leaving home'. This subcultural reading cannot easily be disentangled from the political context which has novel and film poised between Edinburgh and Amsterdam, Scotland and Britain, UK and US, UK and EU, local and global, and the Scottish political activism which Welsh felt had been thoroughly discredited during the Thatcher years and an Ecstasy-fuelled rave culture that is either a viable alternative to the despised Choose Life ad-speak or a disguised form of the hyper-individualism that is the most enduring and corrosive legacy of Thatcher's economic policies.

The film's success, and with it the greater availability and success of Welsh's novel, derives in part from certain commercially driven aesthetic choices made in the process of adapting page to screen. As Hodge explains in his introduction to the published screenplay, 'My intention was to produce a screenplay which would seem to have, approximately, a beginning, a middle, and an end, would last ninety minutes, and would convey at least some of the spirit and content of the book. This involved amalgamating various characters, transferring incident and dialogue from one character to another, building some scenes around minor details from the book and making up a few things altogether' (x). If the narrowing of the narrative range to Renton represents the film's chief concession to the mainstream film market, the oft-criticized lightening of the tone and far greater use of fantasy in the film than in the novel suggest something more: the filmmakers' need to make the film their own. Doing so cinematically was made difficult both by the novel's having so recently achieved critical and commercial success and by its having already been successfully adapted for the British stage. In adapting Welsh's novel, Gibson and Hodge faced many of the same problems and handled most in much the same way. Gibson, however, adheres much more closely to Welsh's self-effacing monologue style and structure and range of incidents, themes, and voices. Gibson's self-effacement is so complete that it is Welsh's name, not Gibson's that appears on the published script. Gibson does leave his mark on the play in one especially notable way. Instead of ending with Mark's theft of the money from the drug sale and his leaving Scotland, and England, for Amsterdam, the play, which ends at Leith Central Station, emphasizes the futility of the characters' lives. The film ends as does the novel, with Mark's theft and flight, but with Mark repeating the Choose Life rap with which the film began (and which appears just once, midway through the novel). Where Gibson stressed futility and Welsh uncertainty and possibility, the film creates a very different effect: more gleefully ironic, or sardonic, thus underscoring an aspect of the novel from which Welsh's ending itself shies away. Or seems to: recall that the novel's final section is one of the very few rendered in Standard English. There are other ways in which the filmmakers make their presence known: substituting for Welsh's detachment their own 'visual flourishes' (McCormick) or introducing little bits like the Clift biography and Warhol-style poster already mentioned, and the English translation of the French Situationist International slogan that appears on Renton's wall: 'Never work ever'. The slogan is certainly appropriate to a film and a novel in which thievery and giro schemes are the chief sources of income. But the slogan also measures, if not the degree to which the filmmakers are willing to adopt Sick Boy's exploitive use of politics (Mandela and Sandinista T-shirts), then the distance separating the student activism of 1968 Paris and the post-political cynicism of Renton. The filmmakers chose to hedge their bets in a postmodern world in which commitment appears naïve and consumption is *de rigeur* if accompanied by the kind of self-awareness evident at the end of the film in which self-deprecation and self-indulgence combine in peculiarly postmodern fashion.

Change is also evident in the film's handling of drugs. This is obvious when one compares *Trainspotting* with more conventional drug films. Although the manner in which it depicts shooting up may allude to *Pulp Fiction* (which created considerable controversy upon its release in the UK sixteen months earlier), the jokiness is combined with and deepened by a grittiness that derives from both Welsh's novel (including the handling of the drug culture as a mirror of rather than an aberration from the hyper-capitalism of Thatcher and Reagan) and from the assistance provided by Calton Athletic, the Glasgow-based drug rehab service. Boyle is right: 'All the commotion wouldn't have occurred had the movie not crossed over into the mainstream' (Lawson). So is Macdonald in saying that the film tries to be 'honest' about drug use (Brooks 89). However, what was honesty to some was irresponsibility to others, especially now that the writer formerly known as a literary Kasper Hauser had become the poet laureate of the chemical generation. Charges of moral irresponsibility competed with the news that Calton Athletic would receive 5 percent of the film's profits and that police in Quebec took five hundred youths to see the film, believing that it discouraged drug use. Lost amidst the moral panic was the simple fact that events that occurred between the release of the novel in 1993 and the film in 1996 entailed a refunctioning of heroin from novel to film. The Criminal Justice Act of 1994 which was the focus of so many articles in youth-oriented publications and the Ecstasy-related death of Leah Betts in 1995 which attracted so much attention in the mainstream press suggest that whereas heroin is a specific drug in the novel, it is a synecdoche in the film for drugs in general and the broad-based youthful disaffection associated with their use, particularly at a time (the mid-1990s) when drug use came to be perceived as a middle-class, rather than an underclass problem. (In the US, where the film's July release coincided with the presidential campaign, as well as with the publication of Welsh's first three books, the film became the *sine qua non* of heroin chic.)

A trio of 1996 articles by three influential writers – one English, one American, one Scottish – highlight both the potency of *Trainspotting* as a cultural signifier and the need to situate it in a broad context. Will Self's 'Carry On Up the Hypodermic' appeared in the *Observer* at the time of the film's release in Britain. Self begins by carefully distinguishing between Welsh's novel (one he later admitted he had not finished reading) and a film he disparages as 'an extended pop video', 'a meretricious adaptation of an important book', and an example of 'recent drug pornography'. Self then proceeds to use the film (and Welsh's cameo appearance in it) to discredit Welsh both for giving his 'imprimatur' to the film and for claiming to be what Self, speaking from on high and playing the more-drugged-than-thou card, says Welsh clearly never was: an IV drug-user. Thus the doubly moralistic thrust of Self's critique: at the infidelity of the film and at the author of the novel on which that faithless film is based. The *New York Times* chief book reviewer Michiko Kakutani proves equally moralistic in a prominently placed essay in the *New York Times Magazine*, though her outrage is differently directed. 'Welsh's nasty first novel', the film adaptation, the popular musical *Rent*, and Larry Clark's film *Kids*, Kakutani claims, 'are just the latest offerings from a thriving brand of tourism that offers bourgeois audiences a voyeuristic peep at an alien subculture and lets them go home feeling smug and with it'. Although there is some merit to Kakutani's claim, much the same can be said about anyone who, as The Sex Pistols sang, goes slumming in other people's misfortune, including readers of Jacob Riis's *How the Other Half Lives* and the audience leaving a performance of *Oedipus* twenty-five hundred years ago. Although not presented as such, A. L. Kennedy's op-ed piece in the 20 July 1996 *New York Times* can be read as a reply to Kakutani which very effectively counters Kakutani's one-size-fits-all brand of cultural imperialism. Noting that the success of the *Trainspotting* film offers 'a chance to examine the current allure of contemporary Scottish literature and culture', Kennedy distinguishes between American and Scottish reactions. Americans, she speculates, may find Scottishness exotic, but Scots of Welsh's and Kennedy's generation find *Trainspotting* (novel and film) neither exotic nor chic. Instead, they find it all too familiar: the long repressed Scottish voice singing of 'death, brief joys, dark longings, hilarious despair'.

Finally, one needs to consider the film's status as both cultural critique and as commodity within the consumer culture, both for what the film signifies and for the way the film has influenced subsequent readings of Welsh's novel. For Sarah Street 'The assimilation of *Trainspotting* [into mainstream culture] indicates that "feel good" can be combined with social comment in perhaps a more radical manner than in films such as *The Full Monty*' (*Transatlantic* 221). For Murray Smith, *Trainspotting* strikes 'a chord with a large audience because it addresses big issues with a deceptively light touch' (*Trainspotting* 87). According to Karen Lury, '*Trainspotting* achieved both international and domestic success primarily because it was not about its apparent subject matter – British youth – but was made to appeal to the youth of a global, hybrid culture, where the ambivalent play, negotiation and celebration of the commodity was unavoidable in the making and understanding of identity' (107). Although he is initially more critical, claiming that 'The subculture depicted in the movie, as well as the movie itself (staged as a subcultural event) is not a form of radical resistance to, but to some extent an integral part of global consumer culture' (160), Jürgen Neubauer nonetheless finds 'kernels of hope ... in *Trainspotting*'s critique of consumerism' (162). Alan Sinfield makes no such concessions. Unlike the novel which Sinfield rightly argues 'is acutely attuned both to the local issues, antagonisms, and atavisms of modern Scottish culture, and to the international subculture of drugs', the film narrows its range to 'the problem most accessible to media consternation and liberal goodwill', drugs. As a result, the film 'diminishes or removes most of the challenging aspects of the book': the racism, sexism, domestic abuse, class conflict, sectarianism, and 'most disappointingly … the contrast' between Renton and the more Thatcherite Sick Boy. Overall, these changes signal not just the 'shift towards a more market-driven imperative' (Petrie, *Screening* 130) but something worse, 'the capacity of modern societies to contain dissidence' and profit from it.

Sinfield's analysis is important but not entirely persuasive. Analysing the film in light of Robert Stam's theory of adaptation, for example, might have led Sinfield to take a more nuanced approach and to understand that, even as the film blunted the novel's edge in certain respects (racism, sexism, sectarian conflict, for example), it sharpened others, however selectively. (This sharpening includes the recontextualizing of Renton's 'I don't hate the English' speech, adopted by the youth wing of the Scottish National Party.) Moreover, the distinction Sinfield makes between the film as part of and complicit with commodity culture and Welsh's novel as a critique of that culture creates the misleading impression that the novel is not itself a commodity. Equally important, Sinfield's critique of the film recalls Craig's critique of the novel's ending in which, according to Craig, Renton's ripping off his mates and self-exile to Amsterdam represents the triumph of Thatcherite hyper-individualism that Craig and Sinfield both rightly bemoan, albeit in rather different ways. Just as Craig's reading of the novel's ending is based upon a politics with which Welsh is in sympathy but which he also feels is no longer viable, Sinfield's reading ignores the possibility of the film being in any way satirical. If it is satirical, however, then one needs to understand, as Bert Cardullo does not, that the satire is postmodern rather than conventional and as such is consistent with other ways in which the film so often criticized for its reductive approach to Welsh's complex novel also translates it for another age, even if those two ages – or rather sensibilities – are only a few years apart. One is the way the film substitutes for the novel's gritty realism what John Orr calls 'the burning intensity of the copy' that is characteristic of the hyperreal. The other, clearly related to the first, is the way the film 'forges a new sophisticated urban aesthetic, the combination of young cast, edgy subject matter, vibrant colours, visual pyrotechnics and a pounding soundtrack a direct allusion to the pleasures of club culture' (Petrie, *Screening* 196). In creating this 'new sophisticated urban aesthetic', the film does more than translate the novel into a visual idiom. It also returns to and teases out both the implications of a novel Welsh wrote while heavily involved in the club scene and its reception by postliterate clubbers via *The Acid House*. However, in doing this so successfully *Trainspotting* came to have, as noted earlier, a negative effect on a British and Celtic film industry that Colin McArthur ('Cultural'), Steve McIntyre and others believe can be most culturally relevant when it is small and poor: when it is what *Trainspotting* (the novel) was, not what *Trainspotting* (the film and subsequently the novel) became.

4

THE ACID HOUSE,
ECSTASY AND *FILTH*

Welsh's second book, *The Acid House*, was well received upon publication, proving that *Trainspotting* was not a one-off and showing the author still 'pushing the limit of his versatility' (Birch), 'experimenting with form and voice' (Boddy), 'mapping a linguistic and geographical domain either disregarded or disenfranchised' (Maley, 'Subversion' 191). 'How shockingly different is the Edinburgh and debatable land of Irvine Welsh in *The Acid House*', Douglas Gifford noted in an omnibus review in which his enthusiastic comments on *The Acid House* immediately followed his remarks on Candia McWilliam's novel *Debatable Land* ('Lion'). The question raised in the Paul Reekie poem which serves as the collection's epigraph, 'Do you hope for more / than a better balance / Between fear and desire', forms a recurring theme in the stories, and all the fiction through *Filth*, which follow. Part of what makes *The Acid House* so impressive a follow-up to *Trainspotting* is not only Welsh's stylistic virtuosity and ventriloquism but his range of subjects and settings as he explores the balance between fear and desire. Clearly, as Hugh Barnes and Willy Maley point out, the *Acid House* stories concern 'people who have been trapped' (Barnes 31), 'fringe figures, migrant and vagrant ... [who] are not part of any mainstream movement' (Maley, 'Subversion' 193). Welsh is not only interested in detailing their powerless states; he is also interested in how these trapped and marginalized figures exercise whatever limited power they have.

Timing, which is crucial in telling a joke, is often so in the publication of a book. *The Acid House* was published in the UK in March

1994, just seven months after *Trainspotting*. Evidence that the collection may have been rushed into print to capitalize on the novel's success among broadsheet reviewers can be found in several printing errors (including an entire section that should have appeared in italics). Where *Trainspotting* initially took off with the literary set, *The Acid House* struck a nerve with the postliterate club crowd, in large part, as Welsh has acknowledged, because of the title and the packaging – two factors which played large roles in the making of the Irvine Welsh phenomenon. The cover was designed by Peter Dyer and Conor Brady of React, best known for music album covers. Although *The Acid House* was not the first paperback to create a point of sale at which book and album, literature and music intersect, it was nonetheless one of the most influential, both in the marketing of other books and in the cultivating of a relatively untapped, arguably insufficiently exploited market. That audience included Americans (and others) no less than British youth, and Gerald Howard, an editor at W. W. Norton, has provided a useful if partisan account of how 'a formerly conservative publishing house' became the US outlet for the 'scalding and controversial new literature' of Welsh, Kelman and McLean. Failing to mention Norton's Secker & Warburg-like need to establish its own 'street-cred', Howard emphasizes *The Acid House*'s literary merits as the basis of Welsh's 'daring' collection and by implication Norton's no less 'daring' decision to publish it. In Britain however, where *The Acid House* was the second book by Welsh to appear and where most reviews ranged from the approving to the enthusiastic, reviewers had already begun raising questions, as well as doubts, about Welsh's fiction and more importantly about both its critical reception and its publishers' motives. Recall Jonathan Coe's 'suspicion that the rush to confer respectability on [Welsh and Kelman] stems largely from intimidation, from a desire to make "dangerous" writing safe by finding it a comfortable niche in the literary canon'. Elizabeth Young, whose *Guardian* interview had helped introduce Welsh to the mainstream literary audience, now wondered whether Welsh's fiction possessed the 'genuinely existent thing', that, along with voice (which she felt Welsh did have), is necessary to the 'art' of fiction. This Oxbridge definition implies the literary establishment's ambivalence about not only Welsh's 'dangerous' writing but the increasingly naked exploitation of literary fiction, or if not the exploitation *per se*, then the brazen way *The Acid House* was being pushed: titled, designed, marketed.

Clearly, and Welsh's status as a cult writer, as opposed to 'major literary figure', confirms this, for many young readers *The Acid House*'s importance is to be measured in cultural, or subcultural terms, rather than in aesthetic ones, especially as determined by solitary readers. *The Acid House* underscores the existence of three at times overlapping communities, none of which is nearly as monolithic as the following terms suggest: youth, 'literary' and commercial (publishers and booksellers, increasingly large corporate chains pushing books, at times flouting the Net Book Agreement). *The Acid House* appeared in the UK at a particularly opportune moment: when rave, especially tartan techno, was at or near its height; when media panic over drugs (especially Ecstasy) was high; when government efforts to control youth culture resulted in the passage of the Criminal Justice Act of 1994 and when opposition to those efforts culminated in the mass occupation of Castlemorton, in Worcestershire, the same year. Like the rave experience, *The Acid House* is decidedly carnivalesque; it combines joyful relativity, decrowning doubles, playful intertextuality and intense physicality for an audience that feels cut off from past, present and future. As the narrator-protagonist of one story puts it: 'I started to think about the politics of European integration, whether it was a good or bad thing. I tried to marry up the politicians' vision with the paradox I saw in the miles of these ugly highways of Europe; absurd incompatibilities with an inexorable shared destiny. The politicians' vision seemed just another money-making scam or another crass power-trip' (27–8). Equally important, as Simon Reynolds points out in *Energy Flash*, the Ecstasy that fuelled club culture seemed 'a miracle cure for the English disease of emotional constipation, reserve, inhibition' (47). 'The acid-house revellers often compared the feeling in the summer of 1988 [the second summer of love] to punk rock – the same explosion of suppressed energies, the same overnight Year Zero transformation of tastes and values' (49) as well as a similarly iconoclastic, DIY aesthetic and slippage into a parallel universe which corresponds to Welsh's use of fantasy (including grotesque realism).

Disambiguating *The Acid House* is thus a complex task, in which many textual and especially contextual factors have a part to play. Measuring the collection's importance by comparing it to works securely placed within the literary canon has the effect of elevating Welsh's stature at the expense of the collection's disruptive energies. Welsh's attitude towards adaptations of his work – the more transformation the better – suggests the need to consider his work less in terms of simple pedigree and causality and more in terms of a complex contextualism and an *apparent* immunity to any anxiety of influence. *The Acid House* may be variously read as a miscellaneous collection, a *Trainspotting* follow-up, a commercial venture, a consumer object, a narrative equivalent of the acid-house experience, among others. Reading *The Acid House* in terms of acid-house culture accounts for the interplay of a basic four-four beat within and against which the various voices, settings, tones, styles and settings are played as parts of a DJ's mix. Just as the proliferation of voices, forms, etc. implies a typically postmodern disbelief in metanarrative, this same proliferation emphasizes the importance of voice that, as Duncan McLean points out, was of special importance to Edinburgh-based writers of his and Welsh's generation in the early 1990s. These writers were interested not only in being heard but in being heard immediately, as indeed they would be, first through publishers such as Clocktower Press and Rebel Inc, and subsequently via large London- and New York-based houses.

Significantly, although the majority of the stories are set in Edinburgh, none of the first four are. Moreover, although dialect plays a large role in the collection, it is used differently than in *Trainspotting*, with mimicry playing a much larger role, along with humour and more direct depictions of dysfunction (individual, social, cultural), guilt, identity, and, as noted earlier, power. The first three stories feature displaced Scots: two in London, one in Amsterdam. All three limit dialect to dialogue and are serious in tone, the first one menacingly so. A story of revenge among petty criminals (two English, one Scottish), 'The Shooter' very effectively builds up the narrator's fearfulness, switching at the very end from the relative safety of the past to the present tense. 'Eurotrash' is similarly sombre but much longer and more intricate. Euan is a version of Renton, recently arrived in Amsterdam, cynical, self-loathing and, like Sick Boy, exploitative. He chiefly exploits the story's most vulnerable character, Chrissie, the ultimate displaced person and Eurotrash whose various confused identities (sexual, national, class) reflect those of post-punk youth culture and of the collection as a whole. As Euan defines them, Eurotrash are people just trying to get by, and getting by is the most that the characters, including Euan, returned to London in 'Stoke Newington Blues', can manage, hoping for nothing more than a place to sleep and score. A police raid leads to Euan's arrest and the racist police exploiting his desperate need for heroin so they can fit up Duncan Prescott, who is black. Played against a background of sexual abuse (the gang rape of Ange some time before), police corruption and racism (in the context of the murder of Stephen Lawrence in 1993), 'Stoke Newington Blues' has Euan betray Duncan for heroin and then rationalize his betrayal as well as his failure to help expose police racism and brutality. 'Vat '96' switches from the present to the near future, from Eurotrash to yuppies, from grim realism to comic fantasy, while nonetheless expressing the same sensibility evident in the first three stories. In the 1959 sci-fi horror film *The Brain That Wouldn't Die*, a scientist keeps the brain of his girlfriend, who died in a car accident, in a state of suspended animation in his laboratory until he can find a replacement body. In Kelman's 'Acid' (a story in the form of a single short paragraph), after a young man falls into a vat of acid at work, his father uses a long pole to duck his son below the surface. 'Obviously the old fellow had to do this', Kelman grimly adds, 'because only the head and shoulders – in fact, that which had been seen above the acid was all that remained of the young man'. In 'Vat '96' Welsh has a young, well-off woman keep the head of her otherwise dead boyfriend (another car crash victim), but as a decorative item in her well-appointed flat where she has occasional sex with the insurance man who helped her secure the money for the machine that keeps Keith's ahead alive.

Helpless males appear in most of the stories, most obviously the ones which immediately follow 'Vat '96', playing variations on its theme. Told in dialect and in framed flashback, 'A Soft Touch' is the hapless Johnny's first-person account of his marriage to Katriona Doyle, whom he wedded in the hope of gaining prestige and protection from association with her thuggish family. The marriage only leads to a series of physical and emotional pratfalls – beatings, harsh words of advice, sexual betrayal. It is a Punch and Judy show in reverse which ends with the inexorable punchline of Johnny taking a pregnant Katriona back, thereby inaugurating another round of abuse. Katriona is not just a comic caricature; she is also, as Toni Davidson points out, a type 'all too familiar' to working-class Scots (Redhead 29). In 'The Last Resort on the Adriatic', the punchline is the suicide of Jim Banks, whose insufferable middle-class voice and values probably contributed to his wife's suicide ten years earlier, also from a cruise ship and at the very same spot in the Adriatic where he jumps overboard. From the comic send-up of British stuffiness and sexual reticence in 'Last Resort', Welsh drops to the underclass vernacular of three of the very short stories that make 'Sexual Disaster Quartet' so effective. The first of the four, 'A Good Son', begins 'He was a good son' and continues in this deadpan style until the final line, 'Aye, Oedipus, yir a complex fucker right enough'. The comedy is bleaker still in 'Snuff'. Narrated almost entirely in Standard English, it deals with another dysfunctional male who prefers films to life and sets himself a task even more asocial than heroin addiction, one that is the polar opposite of club culture: watching alone and on video every film listed in *Halliwell's Guide*. 'A Blockage in the System' presents dysfunction in 'more explicitly political' fashion (Maley, 'Subversion' 201). Reading the story in political as well as postcolonial terms, Maley concludes that 'the workers, who quibble on the nature of the blockage, are themselves the blockage'. Although he rightly calls attention to the workers' subaltern status, he neglects the story's larger implication. The workers' resistance to work means that the most vulnerable tenant, the 'old geezer' who lives on the first floor and who could not have thrown into the 'system' the nappies and sanitary pads which the workers claim have caused the problem, must bear the blockage's foul effects as the workers exact their revenge on the system in general and their supervisor in particular. Maley does not so much exclude this reading as sidestep it. He also sidesteps the way the workers' vernacular serves as the decrowning double of the heightened language of the several conflicting managerial styles successively endorsed by management and practised by the supervisor, much to the dismay and even more the amusement of the workers dedicated to blocking the system.

A different carnivalesque reversal forms the basis of 'Where the Debris Meets the Sea', a title borrowed from an Iggy Pop song about Los Angeles. In *Teaching Scottish Literature: Curriculum and Classroom Applications* (1997), a resource for secondary school teachers, educator and (more recently author) Anne Donovan explains that the story's humour depends on reversals of roles and languages. In a California beachfront house, four sexy celebrities – Madonna, Kylie Minogue, Victoria Principal, and Kim Basinger – ogle three Edinburgh removals workers – Dode Chalmers, Deek Prentice and Tam Mackenzie – in the glossy magazines *Wide-o*, *Scheme Scene* and *Bevvy Merchants*. While the women speak the way working-class Leithers such as Dode would – 'Phoah! Ah'd shag the erse oafay that anyway' – the men speak the way the real Madonna et al. do in celebrity magazines: 'In all honesty I don't have time for heavy relationships at the moment'. Reversals such as these are common throughout *The Acid House*. Sometimes the reversal is used for comic effect, as in 'Where the Debris Meets the Sea', 'Across the Hall', a story in double columns about sexual repression, and 'Wayne Foster', whose title alludes to the strug-gling Hearts striker whose winning goal against Hibs on 20 February 1994 redeemed his otherwise lacklustre performance that year (and previous ones too) and extended his team's streak to 21 successive derbies without a loss to Welsh's beloved but humili-ated Hibs. Sometimes Welsh uses reversal to more serious effect, as in 'The House of John Deaf' and 'Snuff'. (Just as 'Across the Hall' anticipates the cover of *Porno*, 'Snuff' anticipates the ending of *Filth*.) The range of targets is remarkably broad: lower-middle-class sycophancy ('Lisa's Mum Meets the Queen Mum'), a Glaswegian philosophy professor's feigning hard man status, sexual fantasies born of sexual repression. Just as impressive as Welsh's command of various dialects is his command of various narrative structures: alternating narratives – the equivalents of split screens and parallel editing – and the escalating series. 'The Granton Star Cause' is an especially effective example of the latter. In it Boab Coyle suffers a series of humiliating defeats: rejected by his team, his parents, his girlfriend and his employer. After meeting god, a drunken Scot, Boab, transformed into a fly, avenges himself on all but one of his abusers before being squashed ('as flies to wanton boys', or, in this case, a sexually wanton mother).

Perhaps the most intricate use of alternating narratives occurs in the enigmatically titled 'Snowman Building Parts for Rico the Squirrel'. The story is, like 'Where the Debris Meets the Sea', set in two countries, the US and Scotland, and offers diametrically opposed views of childhood and family life. The California story is the kind that can only exist on television (especially American tele-vision). Rico, a magical forest creature, helps a family through difficult times – excessively and therefore comically so as Mrs. Cartwright recites the litany of misfortunes in a voice faintly reminiscent of June Lockhart. (Lockhart played Timmy's mother in the American television version of *Lassie*.) Rico gives the Cartwrights the greatest gift of all, 'making us remember just how much we loved one another', before departing, much to little Bobby's dismay, on his 'mission to spread love all over the world'. The story of the Cartwrights (the name of one of American television's best-known and most cohesive – as well as all-male – families, from *Bonanza*) alternates with that of the dysfunctional Scottish household comprising Maggie Robertson, her two fearful children and her sexist lover Tony Anderson. Set off in italic type and within a rectangular frame, the Scottish story is the Cartwrights' decrowning double, possessing all the sex, abuse, and vulgarity studiously missing from the other. Its opening line, '*Switch that fuckin telly oaf!*', suggests that the fearful Robertson children have been watching *Rico the Squirrel*, but at story's end it is Mrs. Cartwright who tells Bobby to turn off *The Skatch Femilee Rabirtsin*, whose content and language seem a cross between Rab C. Nesbitt and Billy Connolly, with a dash of 'Where the Debris Meets the Sea' when Tony, while having sex with Maggie, fantasizes that he is Keanu Reeves and she is Madonna. The humour derives from juxtaposing the two parallel yet contrasting narratives and from using typography to emphasize the material aspect which the American story so cheerfully transcends and in which the Scottish story is mired. The humour also derives from the punchline, in which Rico is given the final (indeed his only) word, on his going to 'help the little Skatch boy n girl on the television', as Bobby hopes and his young sister believes. ' "Don't hold your fuckin breath on that one honey", Rico the squirrel muttered, but the family failed to hear him, as they were so consumed with joy' (144). The humour also derives from the collision and subversion of several popular culture icons: most obviously *Lassie* and *Swiss Family Robinson* and more importantly two works alluded to in the story's title. *Snowman* is the animated film based on the 1978 children's book by English author Raymond Briggs, which first aired in 1982, has been broadcast every Christmas since, and is now enshrined in the British Film Institute's list of 100 Greatest British Television Programmes. Rico is a character (a lawman gone bad) in the popular British comic-book series, *Judge Dredd*, by Scotland-based John Wagner and

Scottish-born Alan Grant. (In a particularly bizarre example of life following art, in 2005 the BBC announced a new television comedy for the mainstream middle-class audience: *Brit Family Robinson* – 'they put the FUN in dysfunction'.)

The contrast between the two narratives, the two cultures and the two traditions in 'Rico' becomes the conflict between two social classes in Edinburgh in the last two short stories, where Welsh again employs typography and page design to underscore verbal and thematic doublings. 'Sport for All' uses double columns as a Hibs supporter and football casual, member of the Capital City Services, carries on two conversations. One is with a young man named Alistair, an accountant and rugby fan ('a poof's game') from upscale Marchmont whom the cashie chooses to verbally intimidate; the other is with the Begbie-like character's friends, Skanko and Kirsty, who try to dissuade him as he intimidates Alastair into answering his questions, buying a round and singing 'Distant Drums'. In each conversation, only the hard man's part appears; the parts of the others can be inferred but their actual voices exist off the page. As in 'The Shooter', the menace grows, but this time the ending is comical in both senses of the word: Alastair is allowed to go on his way and the hard man seems strangely softened, or at least bemused, by the confrontation. Class looms much larger in the title story, as do typographical pyrotechnics, where, as in 'The Granton Star Cause', there is a magical and decidedly comical transformation which recalls fairy tales (toads turned into princes), *The Prince and the Pauper*, and *Dr Jekyll and Mr Hyde* done as comic-book pantomime. The story begins conventionally; then, after inserting a second, alternating narrative, Welsh uses the page to reflect Coco Bryce's acid trip (compounded by a lightning storm): different fonts, words all in upper-case, text that goes from right to left as well as left to right, up and down the page, boxed insets, pages made up almost entirely of one repeated word, 'LIGHT', blank sections, and strobe-like effects before returning to a more conventional dual narrative. The lightning strike results in Coco and a yuppie couple's newborn child, Tom, changing places and bodies to hilarious effect. Coco is misdiagnosed as suffering severe brain damage, while the baby is judged preternaturally intelligent. Welsh uses Coco, trapped in (but also liberated by) baby Tom's body, to expose the pretensions and assumptions of the young, upper-middle-class couple, Jenny and Rory, who 'were located in an eighties English-speaking strata where culture and accent are homogeneous and nationality is a largely irrelevant construct' (162). Coco enjoys the comforts they provide but on his own linguistic, cultural and sexual terms.

Although it resembles *Trainspotting* in many ways, 'A Smart Cunt' is much more narrowly focused on a single character, Brian, and takes place over a single year, ironically so for the end finds Brian back where he began. As such, this novella is far more critical than the novel in emphasizing the purposelessness of Brian's life and implicitly criticizing him for it. Indeed, Simon Reynolds reads 'A Smart Cunt' as Welsh's way of confronting the 'idea of Ecstasy as counter-revolutionary force', with 'the explosion of pent-up social energies that occurred in the late eighties … channelled and corralled into a highly controlled and controlling leisure system' (*Energy* 424). 'A Smart Cunt' is in effect a waster's diary, a diary of an underground man, simmering (rather than boiling) with resentment which he directs at others but which stems from knowledge of himself that he fears others share. Having so little life himself, Brian lives vicariously by reading biographies and eventually claiming to have played a much larger part in the death of the Blind Cunt than he (perhaps) actually did. (As in *Marabou Stork Nightmares* and *Glue*, questions of guilt and responsibility loom large but are handled ambiguously.) Brian is, as each of the chapters appears to be, connected to nothing and to no one, so that the novella seems at once far less substantial and grounded than *Trainspotting* and yet in its way more frightening even though it lacks the novel's blackly humorous fury and power. What makes 'A Smart Cunt' disturbing is how, within its tight, year-in-the-life structure, the reader experiences each of the fifteen chapters as a separate burst that creates a sense of immediacy and disconnection similar to *Trainspotting*'s, rather than the sense of progression and causality that one expects in a work focused on a single character. Brian manages nothing more than exercising the little power he has in pointless ways, as in 'A Blockage in the System', but without the decrowning quality that redeems the workers in the earlier story. Brian is not wrong to reject the political commitment that his friend Donny Armstrong embraces, but the alternative that he adopts is nothing more than 'stick[ing] to drugs to get me through the long dark night of late capitalism'. Rather than (or in addition to) the critique of Ecstasy-fuelled rave culture that Reynolds claims it to be, 'A Smart Cunt' seems to place the blame squarely on Brian whose greatest fear is being seen for what he is, a smart cunt. In this sense, 'A Smart Cunt' looks ahead to Ecstasy.

'Irvine Welsh has become something other than a writer and Ecstasy shows it', Candia McWilliam wrote of Welsh's fourth book in three years. Ecstasy sold 15,000 copies in the first week and topped the bestseller list in the UK despite receiving reviews that were decidedly mixed and at times remarkably hostile. Welsh's editor at Jonathan Cape, Robin Robertson, conceded that the writing was poor: 'Ecstasy was a rushed job. The film of Trainspotting was about to come out, so we wanted a book. We were victims of his momentum'. And Robertson says the same is true of the short stories Welsh wrote during this period: 'The magazines were besieging Irvine for new work. They wanted rave stuff and he obliged them … . I was worried at the time that Ecstasy came out. The bubble might burst' (Beckett, 'Irvine').

It was not only the supposedly poor writing that made Ecstasy such an easy target. Another was the seeming omnipresence of Welsh and the Welsh phenomenon; Ecstasy appeared a few months after the film Trainspotting's release and at a time when Welsh seemed everywhere: film, novel, four books on the bestseller lists, two stage adaptations, a song made with Primal Scream. A third factor was the mainstream culture's need to put the literary upstart back in his place now that his success had exposed the extent of the commercialization of culture. And a fourth was Welsh's flaunting his connection to drug culture at a time when media panic over the transformation of drug use into a middle-class youth phenomenon was at its height. Ecstasy's merrily in-your-face cover – a man's blue head (shaved) and neck, pink tongue and gums, yellow plastic 'e' between the white teeth, with the back of the head visible on the back cover, quite literally making the contents, the three novellas, into a headstate – flaunts Ecstasy's status as an illegal drug. The book's release – played against the backdrop of the Scotland Against Drugs campaign begun in January and based on grass-roots organizations such as Muirhouse Against Drugs mentioned in 'A Smart Cunt' – proved even more trend-setting than its cover (adapted for an ad for Jolly Rancher sweets) as staid publisher Jonathan Cape and equally staid book-chain Waterstone's combined to launch Ecstasy at clubs such as the Blue Note in London and the Hacienda in Manchester.

Just as *Ecstasy*'s bestseller status tells us more about Welsh's appeal and celebrity and the efficacy of new marketing techniques than it does about the book's literary merits, the hostility on the part of literary reviewers tells us less about *Ecstasy*'s literary short-comings than it does about the inappropriateness of the standards being used by mainstream reviewers to judge Welsh's fourth book and to find it wanting. For example, claiming that 'it was simply tonic to read stories unashamedly cynical about [almost] every-thing' and comparing *Ecstasy* favourably with Janice Galloway's *Where You Find It*, even as astute and sympathetic a reviewer of Scottish literature and of Welsh's fiction as Douglas Gifford complained that Welsh's 'Achilles heel lies in his unsure handling of psychology – of some women's, some classes, some types – which he reveals he just doesn't know well enough and which he disguises through violent melodrama' ('Clever'). As the collection's subtitle clearly indicates, these are 'three chemical romances', not works of psychological realism. *Ecstasy* not only parodies the kind of familiar Catherine Cookson romance novel that Welsh's mother liked to read, as *Marabou Stork Nightmares* parodies the children's adventure stories of Enid Blyton and others. It also updates the genre for a chemical age, doing for postliterate (and literate) clubbers what David Lodge did for academics in *Small World* (1984). But where Lodge, as a campus novelist writing in the age of the global campus, drew upon Patricia Parker's scholarly study of the romance tradi-tion, *Inescapable Romance*, Welsh draws upon pop culture sources. In doing so he unselfconsciously wrote works that measure up quite well to Northrup Frye's definition of romance in *Anatomy of Criticism*. This feat is not so surprising given how much rave and romance have in common. Both resemble wish-fulfilment dreams, involve a 'paradoxical' antagonism between the real and the ideal, follow a particular form of the adventure plot (the quest), have a threefold structure and have a hero associated 'with spring, dawn, … fertility, vigour and youth' (188; Frye adds order, which clearly does not apply to Welsh). The hero battles an 'enemy … associated with winter, darkness, confusion, sterility, moribund life and old age'; this enemy is the dragon of early romance, the 'boredom and indifference' noted in *Ecstasy*'s epigraph, taken from Iggy Pop. Characterization 'follows romance's general dialectic structure, which means that subtlety and complexity are not much favored. Characters tend to be either for or against the quest' (195).

In much the same way that raves created a new kind of social and psychological space (and new uses for old industrial and agricultural space), *Ecstasy* creates a new kind of narrative space by adapting romance to recreate the energy and excitement of raves and clubs. 'Lorraine Goes to Livingston', the first of the three, interweaves the intersecting narratives of four major characters and two secondary ones, rave and Regency romance-in-progress, a host of addictions (none of them to drugs) and Bakhtinian decrowning doubles, several magical transformations and humiliating exposures, all in 70 pages divided into 25 short chapters. Rebecca Navarro, a writer of a bestselling series of Regency romances, is big with her readers and big physically. Her husband Perky is addicted to the lifestyle which her writing makes possible, including the porn he voraciously consumes. Television celebrity Freddy Royle's success in raising funds for the hospital where Rebecca is taken following her stroke provides him with access to the corpses he likes to bugger in the hospital morgue. Lorraine, a nurse, inspires Rebecca to change her life (slim down, start clubbing, try Ecstasy) and becomes the inspiration for the central character in Rebecca's latest, and presumably last (because of its gleefully vengeful pornographic turn) Regency romance. Along the way, Welsh adds a number of blackly humorous touches. He titles one Freddy Royle chapter 'Lord of the Rings' and has Rebecca cleverly insert into her porn romance a Criminal Justice Act-inspired diatribe against the waltz 'as an underhand tactic of our foreign foes to import this decadent music to our shores ... to weaken the resolve of the British officer by facilitating the erosion of his moral fibre and lubricating his fall to debauchery' (37). Welsh also creates a comic version of poetic justice by having Freddy grieve over the corpse of his friend Perky in Freddy's usual way. Yet Welsh also adds a touch of class, as it were. He comically thwarts the efforts of the new pathologist to put a stop to Freddy's necrophilia for no other reasons than his being public-school-educated and a threat to the working-class registrar's financial well-being.

'Fortune's Always Hiding: A Corporate Drug Romance' is another revenge story in an altogether darker mode. If 'Lorraine Goes to Livingston' recalls R. Crumb-style comics, then 'Fortune's Always Hiding' is much closer to the noirish style of the graphic novel. Once again addiction plays a role, this time addiction to greed, violence and legal drugs such as the pharmaceutical Tenazadrim, a lightly fictionalized Thalidomide. Just as the tone and atmosphere are much darker than in the first novella, the narrative web is much more complex, covering seven main characters over 30 years in semi-linear fashion, with the two main narrative lines developed slowly, then coming together in a final rush as Welsh modulates the story's pace and tone in expert DJ fashion. Part of what makes this seemingly over-the-top story particularly interesting is the way Welsh plays the inevitability of the revenge plot against the backdrop of the global pharmaceutical industry (this novella's dragon) from 1961 to 1991 and 1970s–1980s Euro-terrorism. The ending is not so much melodramatic as deliberately ludicrous. Samantha, who has flippers rather than fully formed arms, exacts a certain poetic justice of her own by cutting off the arms of the irresponsible pharmaceutical executive who put profit over safety, holding the chainsaw in her feet as Dave, the sexist football hooligan who has fallen in love with her, uses his arm to bar the door so that Sam can complete her grisly work before the police break in. Interpreted according to the usual literary standards, 'Fortune's Always Hiding' fails badly – as badly as a Catherine Cookson or a Rebecca Navarro romance. Read as a kind of literary comic book, or graphic novel (John Wagner's *The History of Violence*, for example, published two years later), it is much more successful and interesting and much less objectionable, especially to any young readers who may find the prose of Ian McEwan or Salman Rushdie both irrelevant and pretentious.

The last of the three novellas, 'The Undefeated: An Acid House Romance', is structured so as to lead much more directly to its conclusion than are the previous two. Its title drawn from an Iggy Pop song, 'The Undefeated' is a tale of two cities, urban Leith and suburban Dunfermline, of two people, ne'er-do-well Lloyd Buist and middle-class Heather, told in alternating 'Heather'/'Lloyd' chapters and in two symmetrical parts, 'The Overwhelming Love of Ecstasy' and 'The Overwhelming Ecstasy of Love'. Although the two parts are equally long (54 pages each), the second (17 chapters and epilogue) moves along at a faster pace than the first (prologue and 12 chapters), as Welsh creates the narrative equivalent of 'the dance NR G the dance U4E ahhhh' mentioned in the prologue. As Thomas Jones notes, 'In *Ecstasy*, Welsh makes us feel what other writers of club culture only tell us'. Lloyd's story is, like 'A Smart

Cunt', the tale of a thirty-year-old waster. Heather is no more satisfied with her life and husband than Lloyd is with his life and friends (the Poisonous Cunt, the Victim, et al.): her boring job, useless English degree, bad marriage and worse sex. Lloyd's aimlessness is reflected in his narration; Heather's greater frustration is highlighted by her Nick Hornby-like lists, several in framed boxes. Lloyd lives for his highs, Heather for her 'giggles' with her friend Maria, which she prefers to the Prozac prescribed by her doctor. Appearances notwithstanding (the cover especially), neither Welsh nor the closing novella exactly prescribe Ecstasy other than as a temporary measure. What he does prescribe is what Ecstasy represents but can only temporarily induce. (Recall that Welsh wrote *Trainspotting* in part as a way to deal with the come-down effect following a weekend of clubbing that made his nine-to-five Monday-to-Friday life tolerable.) It is not Welsh, Lloyd or Heather but a minor character who sees Ecstasy as God's gift and who turns rave into religion (175). Just as Marie warns Heather of the dangers of a chemical romance, Lloyd's friend Nukes tells him 'Tread warily .... Ye ken how easy it can be tae feel great aboot somebody when yir eckied up' (260). The trick is to transfer the feeling when 'eckied up' at a rave or club 'tae the outside world'. It is this transfer that the novella counsels and that makes *Ecstasy* a strangely moralistic work which at once feeds the media panic over drugs, offers an alternative to what Welsh has called the negative use of drugs (to negate rather than enhance or facilitate), begins the Welsh backlash, and creates a bridge between the explosion of narrative and cultural forces in Welsh's first three books and the controlled and contrived as well as consumer-friendly narratives to follow, especially after *Filth*.

The main character of *Filth* understands club culture very differently. He sounds in fact like the character in Rebecca Navarro's pornographic Regency romance-in-progress who rails against the dance culture of that time: 'It's a threat to the great British way of life and it has to be stopped before it gets a toehold' (84). However, since *Filth* is set in late 1997, club culture had not only gained a toehold but was already past its prime, as Welsh knew, even if his narrator-protagonist, Detective Sergeant Bruce Robertson, does not. Equally dated is Robertson's taste in music (the improbable but in Robertson's case appropriate combination of heavy metal and Michael Bolton). That Robertson is based in part on Ian

Rankin's music-obsessed Edinburgh police-detective John Rebus is obvious. Rankin achieved fame when his novel *Black & Blue* won a Gold Dagger award in 1997, the year before *Filth* appeared and just when Rankin, Christopher Brookmyre, Val McDermid and others had made Edinburgh 'the crime-fiction capital of Britain ... fictionally speaking'. Far from taking offence at the somewhat parodic borrowing, Rankin wrote a characteristically generous review of Welsh's novel, perhaps understanding that *Filth* is as much homage to the Rebus series as parody. Curiously, for a writer so interested in his characters' musical tastes, Rankin did not realize that Robertson's musical preferences for both heavy metal and Michael Bolton offer an early clue to the divided nature that links him to the same Scottish tradition that Hogg and Stevenson drew on in *The Private Memoirs and Confessions of a Justified Sinner* and *Dr Jekyll and Mister Hyde*. The tradition of the divided personality is also hinted at in Welsh's naming his central character after the traitor-hero Robert the Bruce (as well as Welsh's editor, Robin Robertson). Although he seems a departure from Welsh's earlier characters, Robertson is a variation on the type represented earlier by Roy Strang's father, another reactionary, racist, Anglophile Scot. Robertson is dismayed that ravers will invest vast sums for a sound system but not own a television set, like the one on which Robertson watches *Jim Davidson's The Generation Game* and a special on Margaret Thatcher. And he is equally incredulous about 'what they call art now': 'some fuckin schemie writing aboot aw the fuckin drugs him n his wideo mates have taken. Of course, he's no fuckin well wi them now, he's livin in the south ay fuckin France or somewhere like that, connin aw these liberal fuckin poncy twats intae thinkin that ehs some kind ay fuckin artiste' (37).

The schemie turned artist's first new book in two years and first novel in three received a decidedly mixed response. (*The Irvine Welsh Omnibus*, which repackaged Welsh's first three books in one volume, was released in 1997.) On one hand there were enough enthusiastic reviews to support Robin Robertson's hardly disinterested claim that *Filth* restored Welsh's reputation after the bruising receptions of *Ecstasy* and *You'll Have Had You Hole*. On the other, there is ample evidence in *Filth*'s reception that the backlash was still strong. Hostile reviews which derided the novel as a 'shambolic scatological mess' and 'exercise in misanthropy and hatefulness' did not prevent *Filth* becoming Welsh's 'biggest seller outside

Trainspotting in the UK' (Monteith et al. 177) as well as an international bestseller, selling more than 250,000 copies in the first two years. *Filth*'s success derives at least as much from Welsh's earlier successes and cult status as from the new novel's literary merits. It certainly benefited from deft marketing. The cover and posters (done in four different colour schemes) featured an anthropomorphic pig's face, topped by a comically undersized constable's helmet, staring fiercely (but again comically) straight ahead. News that police in Southampton and elsewhere had seized the 'offensive' posters from bookshop display windows provided free publicity even as the police action raised an interesting question. How offensive could the novel or its cover possibly be given that the novel was featured in the November 1998 Quality Paperback Books and Book of the Month Club catalogues as a 'Holiday Best Bet', the top half of the page devoted to *Filth* ('offensive' cover and all) and the bottom to six other books that would 'turn up the heat' during the winter reading season?

Welsh began writing *Filth* no later than April 1995, while he was also writing his 'trio of drug-induced romances' (Beckett, 'Raving'), and frequently alludes to, and in its reception benefits from, recent events. These include Thomas Hamilton's slaughter of sixteen children and their teacher in Dunblane in 1996, the racially motivated murder of Stephen Lawrence in 1993 and subsequent inquiry into the police's flawed handling of the case in 1997 and the release of the commission's findings in early 1999, and New Labour's victory in the 1997 general election. The departmental reorganization of Robertson's Serious Crimes Unit, to which Robertson objects, reflects changes ushered in by New Labour policies and the inquiry into the Lawrence investigation. The rise of the Young British Artists, especially the 1997 Sensation Exhibit at the Royal Academy and the awarding of that year's Turner Prize, forms part of the context in which *Filth* was received. Welsh's own contribution to shock art, the play *You'll Have Had Your Hole*, immediately preceded *Filth*'s release, which came on the heels of the controversy surrounding the broadcast of the film version of 'The Granton Star Cause' over its depiction of God as a mean-spirited drunk.

Unlike Don DeLillo's massive novel, *Underworld*, published in the UK in 1998, and which might be regarded as historically expansive, intellectually daunting, and narratively challenging, *Filth* could be regarded as nasty, brutish and short. However, such a reductive comparison would miss an important point. *Filth* offers its own voyeuristic glimpse into a sordid underworld of its own in the wake of devolution. *Filth* also connects with, and to a degree deconstructs, the tradition of the Scottish detective novel, from William McIlvanney's Glaswegian Laidlaw books to Ian Rankin's Rebus series. Welsh's examination of masculinist canteen culture also connects with the popular 'quality' British *Prime Suspect* television series, starring Helen Mirren, which aired between 1991 and 1997 and in which 'the strict duality' of the detective genre (detective's mind, victim's body) is greatly complicated (as in *Filth*) by gender. The emphasis on *Filth*'s scabrousness – all the more glaring in light of the highly stylized as well as stylish delicacy of John Lanchester's highly acclaimed 'foodie thriller' *The Debt to Pleasure* two years earlier – obscures its evocativeness, the way *Filth* draws on or connects with the cultural phenomenon mentioned above, as well as with 'the tabloid nightmare' crime fiction of James Ellroy and the Harvey Keitel film *The Bad Lieutenant*.

The relationship between the protagonist and the larger masculinist Scottish culture at a time of national change and crisis is the focus of important essays by Stefan Herbrechter and especially Berthold Schoene. In what follows, I want to take up a different aspect of the novel's depiction of Bruce's psychic disorientation, one embedded as it were in Schoene's description of Bruce as 'embody[ing] a grotesquely caricatured example of contemporary Scottish masculinity' (128). More specifically, I want to consider how this grotesque caricature has been misread in a way that illuminates a further contrast between differing sets of cultural and aesthetic assumptions and values. Neither problem nor flaw, excess, in all its forms, is, along with the novel's melodramatic revelation of Bruce's childhood, part of the appeal of a work which reads like the curious offspring of a Billy Connolly comedy routine and a graphic novel.

What the literary culture (or subculture) sees as a limitation – for example, Robertson as a caricature rather than a character, 'almost nothing but a monster' (Beckett, 'Irvine') – strikes those steeped in the visual culture quite differently, as it would have struck Bakhtin with his eye for and keen appreciation of the grotesque realism of Rabelais's monstrous creations, *Gargantua* and *Pantagruel*. Robertson has at least as much in common with Scottish caricatures Rab C. Nesbitt and Billy Connolly as with

Rebus and Laidlaw. Furthermore, as Schoene points out, Bruce
Robertson alludes to the iconic Robert the Bruce. Where the one
fought the enemy without, the English, the other fights the
enemies within: both within Scotland (gays, miners, rivals for
promotion) and within himself. Welsh's readers would of course
have primarily thought of Robert the Bruce as depicted in Mel
Gibson's *Braveheart* in which outlandish caricatures and historical
inaccuracies are rendered as if real by means of cinematic
verisimilitude coupled with postmodernism's attenuated historical sensibility. In effect, *Filth* answers *Braveheart*'s comic-book-
style super-heroism and 'empowering fantasies of the
dispossessed' (151), with a very different kind of cartoonishness,
closer to sci-fi, porn and video games, covers for albums such as
Iggy Pop's *Brick by Brick*, graphic novels and dark comics such as
Judge Dredd, about a futuristic fascist lawman. Bruce is not merely
sexist, abusive, resentful, and vicious; he is monstrously so. He is
monstrous because the outsize is the *lingua franca* of a postliterate
generation, for whom 'fine writing' and psychological realism are
passé.

'Nobody tells me what to do', Robertson says at the beginning of
a novel in which he experiences a series of rejections and reversals.
His comment strangely echoes *Marabou Stork Nightmares*' Roy
Strang and the refrain in Frank Norris's novel *McTeague* (1899). 'You
can't make small of me', the miner turned outsize dentist repeatedly says in a novel in which everyone, including his diminutive
wife Trina, does just that. As his name suggests, McTeague is the
eponymous Irishman (or Irish immigrant) and therefore the counterpart of Bruce Robertson's eponymous Scot. He is the very type
– or, reversion to type in Norris's Max Nordau-Caesar Lombroso
inspired novel – to an earlier form of masculinity now marginalized and resentful, fated to meet his melodramatic end. The same is
true of Robertson. As Amanda Drummond, who replaces him as
leader of the murder investigation while Bruce is in Amsterdam for
sex and drugs, says, ' "Bruce, you're an ugly and silly old man.
You're very possibly an alcoholic and God knows what else. You're
the type of sad case who preys on vulnerable, weak and stupid
women in order to boost his shattered ego. You're a mess. You've
gone wrong somewhere pal", she taps her head dismissively' (338).
Bruce is the abject 'hero': the self-hating figure, seething with
resentment and self-loathing and associated with 'those waste

products of the body that, by their nature, evoke both excess and the threat of death' (Julia Kristeva, qtd. in Gilbert 82).

Especially striking is Welsh's largely (but not entirely) comic handling of the abject figure in a novel which 'turns into an excruciatingly reticent talking cure' (Schoene 430). The logorrheic nature of what is essentially a nearly 400-page monologue cries out, as it were, for Freudian analysis, particularly in light of Freud's *The Joke and Its Relation to the Unconscious*. As the novel slowly and copiously reveals, *Filth* is, in the vulgarity of language and situation, an example of unbridled *id* and a study in repression, guilt and shame. The novel takes pathological yet strangely childlike delight in all forms of play, starting with Welsh's beginning the novel with a murder which occurs on Edinburgh's quite real but the novel's nonetheless jokingly symbolic Playfair Steps, leading down from the cramped dreamscape of the Old Town to the New Town, centre of Enlightenment reason, wealth and repression. 'Caricature, parody, travesty, just like their counterpart in real life, unmasking, are aimed at persons and things with a claim on authority' (Freud, *Joke* 193), including, for Welsh, the literary novel. The humour in *Filth* is not, as some claim (e.g., Oliver 120), a version of Shakespearian comic relief. There is Bruce's verbal play (puns, such as murder victim Efan Wurie being an 'Effen worry tae me', and rhyming slang, especially of the abusive kind: 'Judi Dench' for 'stench'), and there are his vicious practical jokes, aimed at enemies, rivals, colleagues, friends, Masonic brothers and sex partners alike, and his sex games. These please not only Bruce. Many of them also please the reader, the young Scottish reader in particular: Judi Dench won a BAFTA Scotland award for her role as Queen Victoria to Billy Connolly's loyal Scottish retainer in *Mrs. Brown* (1997) and an Academy Award the following year for playing Queen Elizabeth in *Shakespeare in Love*. These forms of play are a sign of Bruce's operating in 'zones of relative freedom' and power which, even as they grow ever smaller, do not disappear entirely.

They are also a sign of the resentment that is the inverse of carnival's joyous relativity and that results when carnival turns bitter, as Michael Andre Bernstein argues in his Nietzschean reading of Bakhtin. It is this bitterness born of resentment that John Carey sees as crucial in Freud's treatise on the joke, particularly the Jewish jokes Freud collected. In this context, the games Bruce plays with Bladesey, a 'wee [English] joker wi specs' whom Bruce befriends because Bladesey is friendless, are especially interesting. Bruce plays these games not because Bladesey, a fellow Mason, is a rival but because he is weak and therefore like Bruce's women and like Bruce himself. Nominally trickster to Bladesey's fallguy, Bruce also resembles the most vulnerable character in a novel loaded with vulnerable characters. This is the murder victim, 'an outsider, alone in a strange city, which seemed to have excluded him' as Bruce's superior, Robert Toal, describes him in the highly derivative television script he is writing on the side. Like Toal, Bruce is carefully closeted, in Toal's case on disk and hard drive. And like Toal's version of Efan Wurie, Bruce is 'excluded' socially (by class), geographically (from the mining district where he grew up and to which he can never return), and culturally. Indeed, Diane's words to Renton in the film *Trainspotting* seem even more appropriate to Bruce: 'You're not getting any younger, Mark. The world is changing, music is changing, and drugs are changing. You can't stay in here all day dreaming about heroin and Ziggy Pop' (Hodge 76). It is not surprising that Bruce should be drawn to *Jim Davidson's Generation Game* and approves of the host's habit of humiliating contestants – 'keeps the trash in their place' – and of all kinds of zero tolerance campaigns (Blair's keeping 'the jakeys off the street'). 'The same rules apply', as Bruce likes to say, as long as they do not apply to his own paranoid schizophrenic self. The chaos of his own life and literally disintegrating body contrast with his paranoid compulsion to control others that is one of the many 'compensatory fantasies of the dispossessed' which Welsh explores in his fiction.

Of the novel's several related tropes – mining, policing, investigating, consuming, fucking – filth is the most punningly playful and powerfully, as well as ambivalently, deployed. Most obviously, filth signifies the police, or more specifically any politically or economically or culturally marginalized group's view of the police (a reverse, that is, of the police's view or valuation of the marginalized group). Implicit in the latter is filth as the synecdochic representation of modern society's obsessive desire to rid itself, or at least manage, filth, which is to say its own waste products. Filth also connects Welsh's novel to his punk roots and to one of punk's formative moments, The Sex Pistols' 1 December 1976 expletive-rich appearance on Bill Grundy's television talk show which resulted in the famous *Daily Mirror* front page headline, 'The Filth and the Fury'. The cover art connects *Filth* to pig, the more

American slang for police as well as for a male chauvinist like Bruce, and to Damien Hirst's *This little Piggy went to market, this little piggy stayed home* at the 1997 Sensation exhibit. Less obviously but no less powerfully, pig connects Welsh's novel with religious prohibitions against unclean foods. This play of connotations combines with Bruce's deeply repressed, anal retentive, paranoid-schizophrenic personality and deteriorating physical and mental states to produce a scathingly funny, scatological as well as inter-minable monologue. Welsh's shaggy dog, or tapeworm, story demonstrates Alasdair Gray's point about creation as excretion and Georges Bataille's understanding of 'the double nature of filth', that it is both dangerously polluting and bounteously providing' (Cohen and Johnson xvii).

Offering a different kind of *Waste Land*, *Filth* revels in the immense variety of its inserted forms and voices, many of which reflect Bruce's schizophrenic, anal retentive, omni-consuming self. The inserted forms include lists, letters, crossword puzzles, the 'Carole' sections which punctuate Bruce's narrative and the many tapeworm passages which visually consume it or obliterate it, leaving only a trace in the margins of its vermicular form. The tapeworm's narrative not only literally exceeds Bruce's (which paradoxically contains it, being just one of Bruce's own voices). The tapeworm also exceeds Welsh's curiously flat explanation of it. To call the tapeworm 'a voice of reason kicking against the psychopath' (Cavenett) underscores one aspect of the tapeworm's hilariously stilted voice while obscuring, if not quite obliterating, others, some of which carry their own intertextual echoes. These include Hanif Kureishi's 'The Tale of the Turd', from *Love in a Blue Time* (1997), and less obviously but perhaps more relevantly Trocchi's 'Tapeworm', reprinted in *A Life in Pieces* (Campbell 27–34), also published in 1997 and including an interview with Welsh on Trocchi. Trocchi's tapeworm is the need for heroin which compels him to write to earn the money to support his habit; as long as Trocchi writes, the worm sleeps. (Trocchi uses the same trope in *Cain's Book*: 'The notes are not consecutive; they go on and on like a tapeworm' [238].) There is also the consciously comical disconnect between the worm's existing amidst the filth inside Bruce's intesti-nal tract and the worm's stilted style, especially as existential exploration and detective story turn into love song or when the worm, telling Bruce that he has potential, sounds suspiciously like

Laura in Nick Hornby's *High Fidelity*. The problem with failing to appreciate the novel's humour is particularly evident in Herbrechter's reading of the role Carole, or the 'Carole' sections, play in the novel. 'Bruce's scornful male chauvinism is in a sense "sanctioned" by its inverted other: traditional femininity. Carole's interspersed comments … represent woman conspiring in her own oppression, thus illustrating Simone de Beauvoir's idea of women as men's other' (120).

Herbrechter acknowledges 'that Welsh's text leaves open the possibility of Carole's interventions actually being projections or discursive appropriations by Bruce's imaginary'. He fails to understand, however (1) that these 'interventions' are very clearly projections on the part of a Bruce who is both transvestite and ventriloquist and (2) that, whatever she may have been before, Carole eventually became strong enough to leave Bruce, rescuing their daughter from an abusive situation and taking a black lover in a racist society. The Carole of the 'interventions' is the carica-ture of a 'real woman' who stands by her man as created by that man in ideal form when he literally stands in for her when the actual Carole leaves. (Her departure leaves Bruce at a disadvan-tage in defining himself as a man in the hothouse of patriarchal society that is canteen culture.) 'Carole' is as much a male fantasy as the *Sun*'s page three girls that Bruce ogles and uses to mastur-bate. Indeed, together they form the opposing views of women that the neurotic male, in this case Bruce, cannot reconcile. (The same virgin-whore duality recurs in Bruce's relationships with Carole and her sister Shirley.) It is important to understand that what Freud diagnosed as neurosis, the youthful segment of Welsh's audience see very differently, in the punk and post-punk parodying of this stunted male view of women in, for example, Siouxsie Sioux and Madonna as well as Anita Drummond, but not in Shirley, who is not only sex partner and handy outlet for Bruce's scorn, but also the muse of his transvestite fantasy: 'Everything's fake about her, but with her skill at applying the make-up she can approximate how she used to look … . After we've blown our muck, all we can see is her as a caricature of a former self' (234).

The novel's ending is marked by a similarly ambivalent serio-comic quality, with the emphasis on the serious appearing to work against Welsh this time. Read conventionally, the ending is, as many reviewers complained, both sentimental and melodramatically contrived. Read differently, in the context of the postmodern era of music videos, video games, graphic novels and the like, the sentimentalism and melodrama seem less like aesthetic flaws than acceptable, even effective narrative choices that are quite consistent with the novel's roots in visual culture: Stevie's burial in a coal pile, for example, or Rhona, her leg in a calliper, struck by lightning on a golf course. Even as Bruce's suicide, at Christmas time, serves the reader's desire for poetic justice and Bruce's need to inflict an additional measure of guilt and pain on others, there is something blackly humorous about his demise, which recalls 'Snuff' from *The Acid House*. It is not just the tapeworm finally being expelled, dripping out of its host like shit down the page, but the grimly funny and satisfying thought that even in committing suicide Bruce may fail, as the novel makes a point of saying about Bruce's fellow officer, Andy Clell, whose suicide attempt leaves him broken and further humiliated. Instead of a culmination, Bruce's suicide attempt may be just one more in the long line of indignities he has suffered in the novel's final pages, nightmarish for Bruce, nightmarishly funny for the reader. A vengeful and guilt-ridden Bruce, crossdressed as Carole, is picked up and tortured by his worst enemies, rescued by his supervisor Toal, seen while still in drag ('undercover') by the mother and son whose husband he had tried (unsuccessfully) to save earlier, and seen finally by the daughter who will find her abject father hanging from a rope, a chip off the paternal block: the rapist-father known as 'the Beast' seen for the weak 'pathetic thing' he is.

5

MARABOU STORK NIGHTMARES

Do not make me remember more. I do not deserve mercy but I need it.
Alasdair Gray, *1982 Janine*

This chapter examines the way in which a particular myth, that of the 'hard man', is depicted and deployed in Irvine Welsh's 1995 novel, *Marabou Stork Nightmares*. The hard man is not, of course, an exclusively Scottish myth or social type. Ben Kingsley's East London gangster Don Logan in *Sexy Beast* exudes just as much hard-man menace as Robert Carlyle's Begbie in the film version of *Trainspotting*. Nonetheless, the hard man is such a characteristically Scottish figure as to constitute a myth in the sense that Ascherson uses the term in *Stone Voices*: 'a historical narrative [or type] which is used to support wider assumptions about moral worth or national identity' (185). Myth in this sense 'refers to a set of self-evident truths which are not amenable to proof' (McCrone 90) and constitutes 'a psychic resource which can energize us for better or worse' (Mantel 104). Its two strands – memory and imagination – intertwine to form the 'tissue of fictions' 'by which individuals relate the personal shape of their lives, both retrospective and prospective, to the larger trajectory of the life of the community from which they draw their significance' (Craig, *Modern* 10). To conceive of national imagination, or 'national psyche' (Kennedy), in this way helps explain why Ascherson's distinctive weaving together of history, memoir, myth and reportage proves so effective even though so different from Tom Devine's similarly revisionist effort in *The Scottish Nation* 'to represent a coherent account of the last 300 years of Scotland's past with the hope of developing a better understanding of the Scottish present' (ix). As Ascherson notes, 'Some countries are tidy with their past … . But there are also countries which have left the past in its original condition: a huge, reeking tip of unsorted rubbish across which scavengers wander, pulling up interesting fragments … ' (v). Such scavenging and weaving prove especially effective in addressing what Colin McArthur terms the Scottish Discursive Unconscious, 'the bricolage of myths, images, and narratives' which includes everything from the Highland mists and mystifications of *Brigadoon* to the fascistic idealizing of hyper-masculinity in the quasi-historical *Braveheart* (*Brigadoon* 6). In doing so, *Marabou Stork Nightmares* in effect updates and furthers the work *Lanark* began: 'not the much demanded escape from the past, but a much more complex understanding of past Scottish culture and its imaginative products' (Craig, *Modern* 35).

Marabou Stork Nightmares is best approached and appreciated as both an example of and a critique of the hard man as an integral part of the Scottish Discursive Unconscious. This may seem a rather large claim to make about a work that Welsh admits he wrote in just five weeks, but it is also a work that Welsh has been unusually protective of, refusing to sell the film rights because he believes the novel is too complex for a ninety-minute film (Bresnark). One should also realize that the novel's origin in a complex of intersecting influences is particularly well suited to a trawl through the depths of the Scottish Discursive Unconscious, to wandering and scavenging through 'the huge, reeking tip of unsorted rubbish' that is Scottish history. 'The genesis of this book happened when I was tripping on acid one lunch-time in this pub. These guys next to me were discussing what kind of casual violence they were planning for the football. On the telly was this David Attenborough wildlife documentary. In the corner an old man was blowing off about how crap life was. Everything just became a strange soup of different things. I just started reconstructing these characters in my mind and let them take off' (Christopher). It is precisely the speed with which Welsh wrote the novel, coupled with its multifarious conception and diverse yet self-imposed structure, that gives *Marabou Stork Nightmares* the raw power that makes Welsh's portrayal of the hard man an important contribution to the reexamination of Scottish identity in terms of its 'four great formative experiences': Reformation, Union, Enlightenment and Empire (Fry 498).

The hard man has long been a familiar type in Scottish fiction, at least since Alexander McArthur and Kingsley Long's *No Mean City* (1935). Tom McGrath's 1977 play *The Hard Man* presents its main character, Johnnie Byrne, based on Jimmy Boyle, in a gritty but largely sympathetic way; Byrne is a vicious thug who is both a product of his society and its mirror image. (Boyle's allure lives on in the recent French film, *La rage et le rêve des condamnés* [2003].) Welsh's portrayal of the hard man is different in *Marabou Stork Nightmares* as well as in his earlier works; it is less overtly political, more critical, much more contemporary in its post-working-class sensibility, and much wider in range. 'Ah hate cunts like that', Mark Renton says in *Trainspotting*. 'Cunts like Begbie. Cunts that are intae baseball-batting every fucker that's different; pakis, poofs n what huv ye. Fuckin failures in a country ay failures' (78). And as Brian says in 'A Smart Cunt', 'One thing about hard cunts that I've never understood: why do they all have to be such big sensitive blouses? The Scottish Hardman ladders his tights so he rips open the face of a passerby. The Scottish Hardman chips a nail, so he head-butts some poor fucker. Some other guy is wearing the same patterned dress as the Scottish Hardman, and gets a glass in his face for his troubles' (275–6). Wary of the hard man's propensity for violence, Renton is also aware of the myths that sustain him. In this sense, the hard man represents not just a Scottish social type, but the Scottish male writ large and Scotland in general. He is the urban equivalent of the mythologized Highlands whose significance Tom Devine describes so well: 'it was in the Highlands, the poorest and most undeveloped of all [Scotland], that produced the main elements of cultural identity for the rest of the country. An urban society had developed a rural face' (231). It is a face re-urbanized by the hard man, as clans give way to gangs and crews, claymores to baseball bats and Stanley knives. (See also Plain; Sillars 250–1).The hard man's allure manifests itself not only in the recurrence of this figure in Scottish fiction and film but more subtly and perhaps more insidiously, as Liam McIlvanney suggests, in its having become a highly prized stylistic feature of much contemporary Scottish fiction, James Kelman's in particular ('Politics').

Welsh's depiction of *Marabou Stork Nightmares*' hard man, Roy

Strang, teases out what Bert Hardy's well-known 1948 photograph *Gorbals Boys* suggests. Welsh's Edinburgh novel works back to origins and ahead to consequences while simultaneously treating individual psychology, or psychopathology, in broad socio-cultural terms. Roy's condition is at once genetic, environmental (socially determined), individual and oedipal. There is the literal wound inflicted by his staunchly Unionist / hard man father's beloved dog Winston which leaves Roy badly scarred and with a permanent limp. And there are the figurative wounds inflicted by his father's genes, his father's frequent absences (in prison) and the boxing lessons during which Roy is bullied into pummelling his effeminate half-brother Bernard. Roy's future as a hard man is both pre- and over-determined, and the constellation of factors associated with the hard man is especially evident in the scene in which a barely pubescent Roy consciously embraces his future. Ordered by his father to pick up food at the chip shop, a reluctant because fearful Roy is accosted by a group of slightly older youths, including two girls, who witness the spectacle of Roy's debasement. Sex, fear, violence, humiliation, shame, resentment and revenge play their parts in this key scene in the making of a hard man, each intricately and inextricably linked to the others. Roy's refrains – 'Nae cunt laughs at Roy Strang' and 'Nae cunt tells me what to do' – echo the self-doubt masked as mistrust and self-assertion that Ascherson associates with 'the Scottish trauma' (85), also evident in Roy's presenting himself in first and third person, as subject and object. Fear of humiliation combined with the sense of inferiority results in fantasies of power, revenge and respect, both at the national and individual levels, so that Roy's psychological profile conforms to the curious mix of nationalist pride and inferiority complex that Richard Todd believes characterizes contemporary Scottish fiction in general.

In *Marabou Stork Nightmares*, nationalist pride devolves to the individual hard man and to the football casuals Roy joins. This pride never translates into real power and real confidence because Roy can never quite eradicate his sense of inferiority and otherness. As a result, he can only retreat further into himself, hardening himself in various ways: increasing his tolerance for pain and 'not giving a fuck about anything' (153). Significantly, the hard man derives from the same source as the Scottish work ethic, which prizes hard work, or overwork, which 'many psychiatrists and health professionals believe ... may well be the result of a deep cultural pressure to prove your worth' (Carol Craig 267). Proving himself is something Roy chooses to do largely outside the accepted middle-class routes of employment and higher educa- tion. He disparages the one (despite the money that enables him to be seen as someone other than his father's 'silly wee laddie') and eventually rejects the other out of hand despite having demon- strated academic ability. His reason? 'No cunt told me what to do'. As Ian Spring explains, 'The hard man mythology is ... a particu- larly potent form of inferiorist discourse in which the characteris- tics of the peripheral culture are not exactly the opposite of the core culture, but instead a carefully delineated perversion of them' (211). The symbiotic relationship between Roy's two sides is embodied in the line 'Remembering hurts'. As noun, 'remember- ing' is what makes Roy vulnerable; and as verb, 'remembering' is the source of his resentment, the recalling of past hurts that in turn fuels his rage.

Roy feels the need to armour himself against real and imagined enemies and more especially against real and imagined wrongs. What better defence than the ready-made image and posturings of the hard man who reduces the world to a series of binary opposi- tions: hard/soft, male/female, masculine/feminine, self/other, straight/gay? The Scottish hard man is pathological masculinity writ large. He is the other side as it were of Kafka's Gregor Samsa metamorphosed into a gigantic vermin, in which one witnesses 'patriarchal man's ... pathetic wrangle with his own inadequacies and insecurities' (Schoene-Harwood 130–1). Roy's hatred and abuse of gays, soft touches and especially women evidence the self- doubts that gnaw at him from within and that part of himself that he strives to compartmentalize and deny as a form of 'psychic defence'. This defence should be seen in national rather than in narrowly personal terms and compounded by class, as proof of both the 'the emotional poverty of being Scottish' (Ewan Baird in Devine and Logue 12) and, how 'in a context such as Scotland's where national self-determination continues to be a burning issue, gender antagonisms may be aggravated rather than resolved' (Whyte 284). That the hard man needs gays and other soft touches in order to define himself is fairly obvious. 'Whair's the fucking Glesgay hard men now, eh?' Roy's fellow casual (and role model), Lexo, crows triumphantly. 'Fuckin queers!' (172). Less obvious, as

Christopher Whyte points out and as *Braveheart* makes dismayingly clear, being gay and being Scottish 'are still mutually exclusive conditions'. *Marabou Stork Nightmares* thus dramatizes in more extreme, urgent and updated fashion the problem treated in *Lanark*, in which the tale of 'a man dying because he is bad at loving' is enclosed within a second story 'which shows a civilization collapsing for the same reason' (484).

Marabou Stork Nightmares is a study in and critique of 'fantasies of total male control' (Gray, 1982 *Janine* 58), from the comic books and television cartoons into which Roy retreats as a child to the old well in which he finds refuge from his paedophile uncle, from his pyromania, sexual abuse of women and running with the casuals to his suicide attempt and African fantasy. Roy's control is evident at those moments when his narrative of his past and more especially his African fantasy proceeds uninterrupted, when he 'stick[s] to the stork', 'evil incarnate', and when he successfully (because seamlessly and unconsciously) incorporates or subordinates material from his two real worlds (past and present) into that fantasy. More often, this material intrudes itself into Roy's fantasy, disrupting its coherence and threatening his control. As 'the control breaks down and the memories come back', Roy's 'refuge … becomes more precarious' (157). Roy's other refrain – 'it's coming back to me. It's all coming back. I wish it wasn't but it is' – signifies the vulnerability that literally spells the end of his hard-man status and signals the return of the repressed and with it his fantasy of total male control over his outer and inner realities.

Paradoxically, in order to deconstruct Roy's fantasies of total male control, Welsh had to write a tightly controlled novel that visualizes and spatializes for the reader the made-upness as well as the breaking-up of the hard-man persona as representative of Scottish identity in general. (In effect, Welsh deconstructs one Scottish myth the way James Macpherson constructed another, earlier on in his Ossian poems.) Welsh's interest in physical writing and its relationship to identity formation is evident in the novel's very first line, 'It. was. me. and. Jamieson', and in the use of fonts, type sizes, and page layout to refer to different times, places, realities and states of consciousness: hospital, mind, past, present, Scotland, Africa and 'Africa', memory, imagination. Typography and layout do not so much allow as force the reader to follow Roy as he rises (or more often is aroused, awoken from his reverie) toward consciousness or descends 'deeper' into fantasy or into the past (and toward 'truth') through a series of cinematic operations – montage sequences, split screens, jump cuts, cross cuts, and lap dissolves – to create an elaborate set of 'screen memories' to represent and repress.

Marabou Stork Nightmares is a literally claustrophobic novel, set entirely inside Roy's mind and hospital room. Even so, the novel ranges over an astonishing array of places and narratives. As a result, *Marabou Stork Nightmares* manages to be at once intensive and expansive, deeply personal and profoundly historical. The link between the personal and the historical was anticipated by Freud, who in *The Psychopathology of Everyday Life* noted that 'the way in which national traditions and the individual's childhood memories are formed might turn out to be entirely analogous' (140). Even as he uses Roy to explore 'the heroic male psyche as both a lost empire and a dark continent' (Schoene-Harwood 154) in terms of individual and national identity (de)formation and breakdown, Welsh uses decidedly contemporary means to facilitate a part of his audience connecting with the novel in a highly positive as well as largely post-national way. Thus, what is clearly psychological disintegration also offers access to identity re-formation. Although the means to this re-formation is inscribed in the novel in Roy's discovery of dance culture, it is embodied throughout *Marabou Stork Nightmares* in the various ways Welsh employs the DJ's tools of mixing, slipping, and scratching to create the print equivalent of dance culture in particular and the visual age in general. These means ironize Standard English, which Welsh has described as administrative, imperialist and anal, and they foreground dance culture's use of club technologies and reconfiguring of material as well as psychic space. To say, as Dominic Head does, that these techniques are 'gratuitously' deployed and inferior to Janice Galloway's 'more accomplished' use in *The Trick Is to Keep Breathing* is to misunderstand the ways in which *Marabou Stork Nightmares* represents an advance in the search Gavin Wallace describes in 'Voices in Empty Houses: The Novel of Damaged Identity': 'To find the cracked and strangled Scottish voice and lend it healing speech will take the Scottish novelist on a journey through a mental landscape disfigured by all the "horrors" of self-inflicted silences' (231).

Marabou Stork Nightmares is especially rich in its treatment of voice. Indeed, even though it all takes place inside Roy's head, *Marabou Stork Nightmares* may best be described the way Welsh described *Trainspotting*, as 'a bunch of voices shouting to be heard'. The use of multiple voices to represent 'the shattered identity of the Scots' has become, Fiona Oliver contends, 'a rich source of artistic expression' in contemporary Scottish fiction. David Borthwick views this differently, as a loss when measured against the communal voice and working-class solidarity of Grassic Gibbon's *Grey Granite*. If Oliver seems overly optimistic about these 'disparate voices' as a rich source of artistic expression, Borthwick seems a bit too gloomy (although understandably so) about the terrifying fragmentation which leaves Roy and others like him no recourse other than retreating into 'a private heaven'. Instead of escaping from the 'tartan monster' of the past, Welsh engages it. Roy may retreat, or try to retreat, into his private world, but the novel does not. The novel uses multiple voices and other forms of polyphony and intertextuality to expose and explore Roy, his African fantasy, the hard man and Scottish identity as constructs and myths. It does so in a way which, even as it derives from Gray's similar efforts in 'The Index of Plagiarisms' and 'The Ministry of Voices' sections of *Lanark* and *1982 Janine*, represents an advance on them because at once less cerebral than Gray's and more integral to Welsh's undermining of the hard man discourse (in the hard-boiled style of gritty realism).

Marabou Stork Nightmares is clearly linked to those earlier Scottish novels – *Lanark*, *1982 Janine*, and Iain Banks's *The Bridge* – in which the state of suspended animation in which the protagonist finds himself signifies 'the changeless and paralysed condition of Scotland' (Craig, *Modern* 132). This trope can be traced back even further to works such as Hugh MacDiarmid's *A Drunk Man Looks at a Thistle* and Robert Burns's 'Tam o' Shanter' which feature 'a bout of prolonged and disdainful self-examination, usually conducted in a moment of unusual stress or anxiety' (Ian A. Bell 228). James Kelman's *How late it was, how late* offers additional evidence of its appeal to Scottish writers: 'Ye wake in a corner and stay there hoping yer body will disappear ... but ye want to remember and face up to things, just something keeps ye from doing it' (1). Roy finds himself in much the same situation, in a hospital room rather than on a street but like Sammy oscillating between remembrance and repression, albeit in a more far-reaching, highly intertextual way. *Marabou Stork Nightmares* also draws on the familiar Scottish trope of the decrowning double, as well as Scottish fiction's and film's preoccupations with childhood and family. Roy's surname plays on 'strong' and 'strange' but also recalls one of the main characters, the schoolgirl Sandy Stranger, in what had been *the* Edinburgh novel until *Trainspotting* showed up, Muriel Sparks's *The Prime of Miss Jean Brodie*. His Christian name recalls Sir Walter Scott's elusive Rob Roy Macgregor, a connection impossible to miss in a year that saw the release of both Welsh's novel and the film *Rob Roy*, with its approving, tartanned-up depiction of hardened masculinity. Roy's concentration camp for bees alludes to Banks's *The Wasp Factory*. Like that novel's Old Saul, the elder Strang's Alsatians serve as the decrowning doubles of those faithful Scottish canines, Lassie and Greyfriars Bobby. The novel's 'Africa, my Africa' (and numerous other allusions) works the same way by parodying its source, in this case W. E. Henley's patriotic and often parodied poem, 'For England's Sake'. Late in the novel Welsh discloses the sources of Roy's African fantasy in the books he read in Manchester, another temporary refuge. *Marabou Stork Nightmares*' intertextuality also includes the Scottish fantasy tradition of J. M. Barrie, Arthur Conan Doyle and Robert Louis Stevenson, the African adventure stories of H. Rider Haggard and John Buchan, one of the Scots who helped run the British Empire (and whose stories include the kind of strong homoerotic element which Roy tries unsuccessfully to repress). Welsh also draws on the American fantasy tradition, including Frances Hodgson Burnett's *The Secret Garden* and L. Frank Baum's *The Wizard of Oz*.

Enid Blyton's children's fiction plays an especially important role in Welsh's novel and in the formation of a distinctly British character based on the English model. In reading and attempting to emulate Blyton's children, Roy, like the young Irvine Welsh, was learning to become British and more especially English, not Scottish. 'Trust, responsibility, and scrupulous fairness, combined with courage, resolve, decisiveness, determination, and physical prowess, were the idealized traits of the empire builders, and we see these qualities at their inception in Blyton's children' (Singh 218). Because Roy is barred (as Welsh himself was) from emulating Blyton's Famous Five as soon as he and his playmates venture out of Muirhouse into the surrounding middle-class neighbourhoods, Blyton's stories contribute to

Roy's sense of resentment and self-loathing. It is a sense in which matters of socio-economic class and national identity are separate yet intertwined. Indeed, it is hard not to think of *Marabou Stork Nightmares* as a vengeful parody of Blyton's *Magic Faraway Tree* series (1939–51) with its 'Land of Do-As-You-Please' and 'Land of Take-What-You-Want', which, interestingly, play a more overt role in Alan Moore and David Lloyd's comic-book series / graphic novel, *V for Vendetta* (1989–90). (The Hibs, incidentally, had their own Famous Five, from 1949 to 1955.)

Comic books satisfy Roy's desire for self-transformation and empowerment much better. Superboy and his loyal canine friend Krypto provide an ironically idealized version of Roy and the dog which savaged him. *The Fantastic Four* depicts a team of superheroes who act as a supportive family and contrast with the dysfunctional Strangs; they also anticipate Roy's involvement in the Capital City Service. Although the Four's Human Torch helps explain Roy's pyromania, it is Silver Surfer who looms largest in Roy's imagination. When he first appears, in *The Fantastic Four* series, Silver Surfer is the herald of Galactus, 'Devourer of Worlds', who sustains himself by consuming the essences of heavenly bodies. In his gleaming silver body, Silver Surfer is the hardest of hard men, but also something of a soft touch. As Norrin Radd he had agreed to become Galactus's herald in order to save his peaceful planet, Zenn La, from being devoured, and on Earth he is punished when he falls in love with Alicia Masters. The importance of comic books in *Marabou Stork Nightmares* extends further, however. In much the same way that the connection between Roy and the young gangster Pinky in Graham Greene's *Brighton Rock* comes via The Sex Pistols, the connection between *Marabou Stork Nightmares* and Gothic fiction (Petrie, *Contemporary* 135; Schoene-Harwood 154) comes via the dark comics (forerunners of graphic novels) which in turn recall cartoons and comic strips. Roy may be fearsome, but he is also ridiculous. This hard man of the scheme is the iconically Scottish Monarch of the Glen re-imagined as the comically bristling Thistleman belligerently proclaiming 'wha daur meddle wi' me' (see Riach 235–6, 238). Roy thinks of himself and his family as cartoon-like decrowning doubles of Oor Wullie and the Broons:

'The Strang look' was essentially a concave face starting at a prominent, pointed forehead, swinging in at a sharp angle towards large, dulled eyes and a small, squashed nose, down into thin, twisted lips and springing outwards to the tip of a large, jutting chin. A sort of retarded man-in-the-moon face. My additional crosses to bear: two large protruding ears which came from my otherwise normal-looking mother, invisible under her long, black hair. (20–1)

The novel's intertextual range extends still further. Roy's sister's name creates a link to colonialism via Rudyard Kipling's *Kim* (Kelly 114–18). The fact that the Strangs' youngest child, Elgin – whose name recalls the Scotsman Thomas Bruce, Earl of Elgin, of Elgin Marbles fame – suffers from severe autism and ends up institutionalized in a home for 'exceptional children' suggests the delusion at the centre of John Strang's imperial fantasy. Even as it contrasts with 'the actual and often brutal exploitation of colonial Africa', the elder Strang's fantasy 'shows just how alluring nostalgic fantasies of untrammelled power and superiority, like those facilitated by colonial Africa, are to many men' (Schoene-Harwood 153). That a novel set in the late 1970s to early 1990s should deal with the idea of empire from a decidedly postcolonial point of view is unsurprising given Scotland's situation during this same period. Beyond the nostalgic fantasy of an Africa concocted from adventure stories in which the hard man plays the part of hero and the rapist plays the central role in a series of rescue fantasies, lies the subtextual dark continent of the Scottish Discursive Unconscious, comprising national heroes Mungo Park and David Livingstone and the ignominious defeat of the Highland Brigade which occurred at Magersfontein on 10 May 1899, at the outset of the Boer War and which delivered a terrific blow to Scottish self-esteem (see also Kelly 117–18). *Marabou Stork Nightmares* is set during another period of conflict, when black South Africans were seeking to end apartheid and Scots (some anyway) were seeking a measure of independence for themselves. And it was published the year after South Africa rejoined the Commonwealth. Through Roy's African fantasy and the Strang family's brief immigrant sojourn, Welsh confronts Scotland's complex participation in the British Empire: in the one as self-proclaimed (and often self-deluded and self-aggrandizing) explorers, rescuers and missionaries, in the other as just a handful of the many working-class Scots who felt compelled to leave Scotland 'for promise of fulfilment' (Fry viii).

As Kelman's Sammy puts it, 'Ye go somewhere'. That John

Strang's South African dream of emigration comes to nothing is hardly surprising; like the Scotland of the Kailyard school and the Highland myths, it is, as Roy quickly realizes, 'romanticized bullshit'. So is Roy's African fantasy: '[Johannesburg] looked spectacular from the sky ... . Close up, downtown Johannesburg just looked like a large Muirhouse-in-the-sun to me' (61); 'Edinburgh to me represented serfdom. I realised that it was exactly the same situation as Johannesburg; the only difference was that the Kaffirs were white and called schemies or draftpaks. Back in Edinburgh, we would be Kaffirs; condemned to live out our lives in townships like Muirhouse or So-Wester-Hailes-To or Niddrie, self-contained camps with fuck all in them, miles fae the toon ... .' (80). And from the vantage point of the romanticized bullshit of his own African fantasy, Roy also hates returning to the real South Africa; that is the reason he denies so frantically the counter-view Bernard presents in his scabrously and scathingly funny poem entitled 'Doreen Starr's Other Cancer' which he reads to a comatose but nonetheless cognizant Roy.

John's South African dream ends as a result of his hard man ways. His drunken assault on a taxi-driver leads to a prison sentence and subsequent deportation. His elder brother Gordon's dream succeeds for the same reason: the former teddy boy who had taken pleasure in beating up hippies became 'a crusty old Boer' and successful businessman who, when he isn't sexually abusing Roy, extols him as 'a true Scotsman', 'a real Afrikaaner' (65). Just as Tom Devine has worked his way 'through the reefs of Highland self-pity and sentimentality, on which so many narratives have been wrecked, to the excruciating historical irony of the suffering experienced by the victims of the victims' (Kidd), Welsh covers similar ground in *Marabou Stork Nightmares*. However, as the publication of Arthur Herman's *How the Scots Invented the Modern World* (2001) and Michael Fry's *The Scottish Empire* (2002) demonstrate, old Scottish myths and mythmaking die hard and may be harder to eradicate than the Marabou stork.

South Africa is only one of John Strang's several thwarted dreams. Middle-class respectability and 'spawn[ing] some sort of master race' (144) are others. His escape to South Africa, like his wife Verity's earlier escape to Italy, comes to nothing. The family returns to Muirhouse, one floor up in the same block of maisonettes, which means one step down in the scheme's parody

of the social order. The family's downward trajectory is as much
genetic as socio-economic. Their future is literally written on
Roy's (as well as Kim's and Elgin's) body: 'I was the auld man's
double' (153). The cycle of failure is no less a part of the family's
history: 'me in the casuals and Kim perennially a few years behind
in her school work, now working at the baker's' and Elgin 'trapped
in a world of his own' and shopped out to the Corgi Venture for
Exceptional Young Men and therefore doubly 'exempt from this
torture' (30). For Roy the torture centres on his recurrent nightmare, worthy of Goya, of the Marabou stork devouring the head of
a flamingo. The nightmare represents the hard man's preying upon
any and all soft touches, which appears in so many forms in
Welsh's novel. Tony incestuously preys upon his mentally slow
sister Kim; Uncle Gordon preys upon eleven-year-old Roy; Roy,
Lexo and the others prey upon Kirsty; Verity viciously if only
verbally attacks Kirsty ('A fuckin slag's gaunny ruin my laddie's
life!'), and John gloats over Roy's acquittal as a triumph of British
justice. In preying upon Roy, the image of the stork devouring the
head of the flamingo suggests the seeming inescapability of his
condition – a condition which the novel invites us to understand in
all its complexity rather than to condemn out of hand.

Although Roy is certainly a chip off the paternal block in terms
of physical appearance, propensity for violence, and paranoia – in
effect, a hard man waiting to happen – he is also another mythic
Scottish type. He is the lad o' pairts who benefits, for a time, in a
non-exploitative way from the emigration experience and more
particularly from the educational opportunities South Africa
provides. 'On my eleventh birthday I could see possibilities. The
old man's piss up blew that away. It showed me I'd been a daft cunt
to ever have had these dreams' (77). Looking at his father, he sees
himself and is filled with a profound self-loathing that, as Cairns
Craig and others have pointed out, characterizes Scotland and
that, as Fiona Oliver has noted, has fuelled much contemporary
Scottish writing. It also fuels Roy's emergence as a hard man as he
seeks the power, respect and control he otherwise lacks but had
briefly experienced in South Africa, in school and especially with
Uncle Gordon. 'The funny thing was that it didn't really feel like
abuse at the time, it felt mildly funny and amusing watching
Gordon make a drooling tit of himself over me. I felt a sense of
power, a sense of attractiveness, and a sense of affirmation that I

hadn't previously experienced' (72). And it fuels his hunt for the stork, which he first saw on an outing to Kruger National Park, which entered his dreams that very night, and which now is the goal of his African fantasy, in which the stork is an oneiric figure comprising a complex set of displacements and condensations. In order to find and exterminate the stork, Roy and his companion and guide Sandy Jamieson must first meet Lochart Dawson who, like everything else in Roy's fantasy and in Welsh's novel, is a composite. Dawson combines something of the lawyer Donaldson, something more of Uncle Gordon and a great deal of the real-life Wallace Mercer, chairman and chief stockholder of the Hearts of Midlothian Football Club who in 1990 launched a bid to take over arch-rival Hibs. Dawson, owner of Jamboland, is willing to sponsor Roy and Sandy (as if they were a football club) because he wishes to acquire Emerald Park, which includes Lake Torto, the storks' habitat. The Marabou stork has no more place in the vast leisure complex Dawson has planned to attract tourists than football casuals like Roy and the rest of the Capital City Service crew have in a Scotland transformed into a huge theme park and in an Edinburgh rebranded as a centre for cultural tourism, where inadequate housing is less of a problem than having too few hotel rooms. Of the many connections between Dawson and Mercer, two are especially significant. One is the way Mercer's takeover bid was foiled, when fans banded together in a successful Hands Off Hibs campaign to save their team. The other is that agreeing to Dawson's sponsorship makes Roy complicit in the plan and therefore makes the purity of his quest as suspect as the real Roy's hardness. Complicating matters further, adding a layer of myth to the layers of fantasy surrounding a core of reality, is the fact that Lake Torto exists only in Roy's fantasy, not in the real Kruger National Park, and alludes appropriately enough to the terrifying Basque spirit known for abducting young people, then cutting them into pieces and eating them. A hard man – or spirit – indeed.

Welsh's handling of time, including actual events that can be accurately dated, contributes to the novel's transformation of individual psychology into national mythology. Welsh's friend and Rebel Inc founding editor Kevin Williamson has correctly pointed out that what *Marabou Stork Nightmares* records is the way the 'unofficial history' of Edinburgh in the late twentieth century 'affected working-class people in Edinburgh much more than anything that ever happened in the festival or when Edinburgh hosted the European summit or the vote for a Mickey Mouse parliament': 'AIDS, mass unemployment the rise of Hibs football casuals, the Hearts takeover, the closing of the docks, ecstasy and dance culture' (Redhead 159). This is a doubly useful distinction. First, Williamson's tone underscores the resentment that, along with guilt, fuels Roy's narrative. Roy's bitter insight, 'In Muirhouse nae cunt can hear you scream … . well, they can hear ye, they just dinnae give a fuck' (141), extends beyond the scheme to the situation of the working class and the underclass during the Thatcher-Major years, and the semi-comatose Roy in hospital. Second, Williamson's distinction makes unofficial history visible. The problem with this distinction is that it downplays the actual and rather extensive role that official history does play in the novel and in the Scottish Discursive Unconscious. Far from downplaying official history, *Marabou Stork Nightmares* foregrounds it from the very start in order to contest it. The novel in effect complicates history by seeing it as manufactured myth and in a way that goes well beyond allowing the hard man to present his version, as in McGrath's play, *The Hard Man*. The novel's two epigraphs underscore the need to read the novel within a broad historical context. One offers a sardonic look at the parts Scots played in the British Empire, the other is John Major's 'We should condemn more and understand less'. Together they serve as a shorthand which encourages the reader to accomplish what Roy hopes to avoid: remembering everything, however humiliating, however complicitous. The novel's silence on the failed 1979 referendum or the Falklands War or the Iron Lady's infamous May 1988 Sermon on the Mound or the Scots' Claim of Right two months later does not mean that these events do not loom large – as does the 1984–85 miners' strike which appears only indirectly, in John Strang's praising Thatcher for putting the 'unions in their place right enough' (83).

Unlike *Trainspotting*, which takes place in a more or less continuous present, *Marabou Stork Nightmares* creates a much more complex relationship between the individual and both the present and especially the past (both historical and mythical) that also distinguishes the novel from the straightforward causality and chronology that characterize the more usual realistic presentations of the hard man. Just as there are different levels of reality and consciousness in *Marabou Stork Nightmares*, there are different times as well. The most obvious are the time of the telling (1992 or 1993), the time(lessness) of Roy's African fantasy, and the biographical time from Roy's youth up until his suicide attempt, shortly after 24 September 1991. There are at least two other times at work in the novel: official history, or histories, from the mid-1970s through 1993, or more accurately 1995, when the novel was first published, and Scotland's earlier history, as far back as 1690, the year William of Orange defeated James Stuart at the Battle of the Boyne, a victory celebrated by Protestant Unionists each July.

Although there are very few specific dates in the novel, enough actual events are mentioned to establish an approximate chronology. Roy was probably born in the late 1960s; his father first mentions going to South Africa when Roy is eight or nine; the Strangs are in South Africa the year Zimbabwe-Rhodesia gains its independence (1979, which is also the year of the failed Scottish referendum); they return to Scotland when Roy is about twelve and just entering secondary school; he leaves school after completing his 'O' Levels (1987?) and takes a job at Scottish Spinsters; he joins the Hibs casuals, Capital City Service, soon after and meets Lexo the year Aberdeen signed Charles Nicholas (1988); the rape and trial probably occur in 1989 or 1990; Roy then flees Edinburgh for Manchester; he may already be there in June 1990, when Mercer makes his bid to take over Hibs FC (and in February 1991 when Gordon Modiak arranged the acid attack on his wife, Louise Duddy, who had left him after years of abuse, which left her blind and horribly disfigured). Back in Edinburgh, Roy attempts suicide while watching a videotape of the very recent 24 September 1991 Skol Cup semifinal match between Airdrie and Dunfermline in which Airdrie's Jimmy Sandison's being wrongly cited for a handball resulted in Dunfermline's winning the match and the right, as Roy puts it, to be fucked by Hibs in the final. According to John Strang, Roy has been in a coma for two years, putting the time of the narrating at 1993, the same year as John Major's 'we should condemn more and understand less' remark occasioned by the abduction and murder of two-year-old Jamie Bulger by ten-year-old Jon Venables and Robert Thomson. But John Strang also says that he has just voted in the general election – for the SNP as a way of protesting the poll tax – which puts the time of the narrating at 1992, the same year that the Zero Tolerance campaign was launched in Edinburgh, although the novel has the campaign in place two years earlier. Far from detracting from the novel's realism, the several (presumably unconscious) misdatings demonstrate how malleable history is and how dependent on the conjunction of memory and imagination that Hilary Mantel calls myth. And it is worth noting two other matters related to the novel's handling of time. One is that Roy's story not only coincides with Thatcher's reign, 1979–90; it also can be read as an ironic gloss on her famous 1987 'epitaph for the eighties': 'there is no such thing as society. There are individual men and women, and there are families'. *Marabou Stork Nightmares* also coincides with the enormous social and political unrest and change in South Africa (and elsewhere) that resulted in a new constitution, new elections, new government and a Truth and Reconciliation Commission – all of which forms the background against which Roy's story takes place. What, after all, is *Marabou Stork Nightmares* but an elaborate attempt both to seek and to evade truth and reconciliation? One other matter related to time needs to be mentioned here. This is the way the novel occasionally elides time in order to create causal relationships that exist aside from simple chronology. For example, several months separate Martine Fenwick's kb-ing Roy at a Christmas party from the gang rape of Kirsty, but in the novel, as in Roy's disordered mind, the one follows the other.

Given the disordered state of Roy's mind and of the Scottish Discursive Unconscious, one needs to ask what 'Kirsty's gory feminist vengeance' tells us about 'the inescapability of extreme masculinity', as Pat Kane put it in discussing the recent spate of New Lad / New Bastard Scottish stories and novels. Contrasting *Marabou Stork Nightmares* with Gray's 1982 *Janine*, Schoene-Harwood faults Welsh for taking a fatalistic stance which results in 'a total eradication of sexual differences. Woman is deprived of her potentially subversive heterogeneity and becomes a completely predictable image of man … . By denying Kirsty her womanly difference, Welsh denies himself the opportunity to conceive of an alternative, feminine response to violence, a woman's way out of the clockwork orange that is patriarchy' (156). There is ample evidence, both internal and external, to support Schoene-Harwood's reading of the novel. Within, one witnesses the cycles of violence, the sexual abuse of women and children, the transformations of the mama's boy Roy assaults in a school lavatory into 'a huge burly bastard with a real mouth and a big swagger' and more importantly of Kirsty into a female version of the hard man, and the Scottish legal system's self-perpetuating patriarchy and the Scottish male's capacity for rationalizing even his worst offences, as in Ozzy's claiming that Kirsty 'was lucky it wis cunts like us ... it might've been a fuckin psycho like that Yorkshire ripper cunt' (213). The system of perverted values that Roy represents is especially and ironically evident in the final image he sees before lapsing into coma, of the footballer, Jimmy Sandison – 'I'd never seen a man so shocked and outraged at such an obvious miscarriage of justice' (255). 'Never a man', Roy adds, 'But I once saw a woman who was worse, much worse'. Without *Marabou Stork Nightmares*, one sees the pervasive role revenge plays in Welsh's other fictions: for example, Davie Mitchell's on Alan Venter and Kelly on the English punters in *Trainspotting*; Gary's in 'The Shooter' and Boab's in 'The Granton Star Cause' (both in *The Acid House*), Rebecca's in 'Lorraine Goes to Livingston' and Samantha's in 'Fortune's Always Hiding' (both in *Ecstasy*), and in the play *You'll Have Had Your Hole* and in *Porno*. There is also what Welsh calls 'the most contentious element' of the novel: 'why bother sensitizing yourself when it's going to fuck you up even more?' (Christopher).

Kirsty's transformation from fearful, traumatized victim to fearless avenging angel is not surprising given (1) how thoroughly she has been abused, first by Lexo's crew, then by the Scottish legal system, and (2) her realization that the Zero Tolerance campaign has only a slim chance of success given the kind of rationalizing to which characters such as Ozzy are prone. (Concerning the Scottish legal system's continuing failure to deal adequately with sexual assaults, see Michael Howie and Angie Brown's 'Why Rapists Love Our Courts'.) What is surprising is the willingness of some critics to read Kirsty's transformation and the novel's ending so literally, and thus to fail to read each one as 'a completely predictable *image* of man' (as Schoene-Harwood calls Kirsty; emphasis added). This willingness is especially noticeable in Duncan Petrie's discussion of the novel's ending and what he believes it implies about Welsh's writing more generally: a 'predilection for graphic, and often cheap, shock beyond the more everyday banal brutality of scheme life ... . [which] sits uncomfortably alongside, and even undercuts, Welsh's ability to humanise his subjects, allowing a broad readership to empathise and understand the motives of complex characters like Mark Renton or Roy Strang' (*Contemporary* 95). The novel alerts readers early on to the unreliability of Roy's narration: 'Can I feel her [the nurse's] touch, or do I just think I can? Did I really hear my parents or was it all in my imagination? I know not and care less. All I have is the data I get. I don't care whether it is produced by my senses or my memory or my imagination. Where it comes from is less important than the fact that it *is*. The only reality is the images and texts' (16). Recall that Gray makes this kind of indecidability central to both *1982 Janine* and *Lanark*: 'Did Thaw really kill someone or was that another hallucination?' (351). Although Kirsty 'corrects' several of Roy's earlier accounts (of his role in the rape, of her supposedly snubbing him when in fact she says she even fancied him), the novel never makes clear, and never can make clear, whether Kirsty is physically present in the hospital room or not and whether what Roy hears is what she says and how much over-lap there may be between the real Kirsty and an imagined one. Kirsty is a real person who is nonetheless also, like Roy's African fantasy, an imagined construct, one that produces the novel's final image of Roy in Roy's hallucinating mind. That final image, after all, bears an uncanny resemblance to images that appeared earlier in the novel, his recurring marabou stork nightmare in particular: 'Ah kept seein the heid ah that flamingo in the stork's mooth and it was shouting oan ays tae help it, in a sad, sick voice' (152). And this image combines with others, of, for example, Churchill chomping on his cigar and Roy's recurrent complaint or fear that something is stuck in his throat. Just as the African fantasy is filled with Roy's rescue fantasies, it and Roy's larger narrative are filled with castra-tion fears beginning as early as page 6, escalating through the two women transformed in the *Butcher Boy*-like comic-book fantasia first into slags and then into giant preying mantises, 'lipstick smeared on their deadly pincher-like insect jaws' and culminating in the novel's conclusion.

'The persistence of the self-mutilating ethic' (Craig, *Modern*) of the fearful and the fearless reflects the impotence and castration that Tom Nairn, in *The Break-Up of Britain*, believed Scotland would continue to experience until it achieved independence. The self-mutilating ethic leads inevitably to *Marabou Stork Nightmares'* ending not because Welsh can imagine no other, but because Roy cannot. And Roy cannot because one component of the Scottish Discursive Unconscious, the hard man, is overwhelmed by another, Catholic/Calvinist guilt, as conscience in the form of an imagined, vengeful Kirsty preys on Roy in Welsh's brilliant updating of the Scottish Gothic tradition in slasher/female-revenge film and graphic novel terms. Having failed as hard man, Roy becomes everything he has feared: soft touch, easy prey, hysterical female, the madman in the hospital bed rather than the madwoman in the attic. Does a scenario such as this require that a real Kirsty physically emasculate the former hard man Roy Strang? No more than the collapsing of typographical differences in the novel's concluding chapter necessarily signals Roy's emerging from the polyphonic mists of memory, imagination and ambiguous sensory data to take, consciously if briefly, his place in the real world. It is just as plausible and in some ways more logical to believe that the collapsing of typographical differences signals quite the opposite: Roy's finally and completely losing the control he has tried so desperately to maintain and as a result either plunging into madness or rising, fearfully and reluctantly but uncontrollably into consciousness. Roy's struggle with his *two* worst fears – emasculation and awakening – literally and quite vividly demonstrate two larger points. First, as Ascherson says of Culloden, Glencoe and other mystified and mythified historical events, that 'the iconic wounds are the self-inflicted ones' (174). And second, as Judith Butler notes, that 'crafting a sexual position … always involves becoming haunted by what's excluded. And the more rigid the position, the greater the ghost, and the more threatening it is in some way' (online version). Thus the hallucinogenic, Hogg-like quality of the final pages, with their swirl of images, many of them comic-book images, scavenged from the rubbish heap of Roy's and Scotland's past, especially in the novel's penultimate paragraph in which Roy undergoes a hallucinogenic succession of transformations which turn the hard man into 'a comical scarecrow', 'an old man', and Captain Beaky. As the 1970s song put it,

> The bravest animals in the land are Captain Beaky and his band
> That's Timid Toad, Reckless Rat, Artful Owl and Batty Bat
> They march through the woodlands singing songs
> That tell how they have righted wrongs.

The allusion to Captain Beaky exists not as culmination but as part of the larger swirl of conflicting, even mutually excluding self-images drawn from the popular culture which together comprise Roy's alternately menacing and self-loathing character. In their composite complexity they provide a welcome alternative to and antidote for another, better-known image, also from 1995, of a tortured, indeed impaled William Wallace orgasmically crying out the word 'freedom', which far from contesting the hard man myth, perpetuates it, doing in effect what *Marabou Stork Nightmares* and many other contemporary Scottish novels refuse to do: 'to collaborate with a transcendental, totalizing and finally determining sense of national identity' (Ian A. Bell 226).

6

GLUE AND *PORNO*

Glue is Welsh's most expansive novel and also his most leisurely in terms of pace and development, especially after *Filth*'s relentless narrative onslaught. Described by its publisher as an 'epic and ambitious novel about friendship', *Glue* is also very much a mid-career, mid-life novel, written, Welsh said, with greater confidence than the earlier works ('"Glue"'). Yet, he maintained, his writing style is 'basically the same' and he is 'still a petulant brat' (Linklater). In calling *Glue* 'a return to form', his publisher was in effect acknowledging the battering Welsh's reputation had taken take since the publication of *Ecstasy* in 1996. Quite inadvertently, the publisher also called attention to the role form plays in this novel, one similar in certain respects to the structure of Welsh's earlier fiction, but quite different too. There was the loose, asymmetrical structure of *Trainspotting*, the layered narrative of *Marabou Stork Nightmares*, the alternating and parallel narratives of *The Acid House* and *Ecstasy*, and the nearly non-stop monologue rush of *Filth*, which the block-form of the table of contents foreshadows; form following function, *Filth* is structured as a claustrophobic box. *Glue* is differently organized. Each of its four parts is set at the beginning of a decade: 'round about 1970', '1980ish', 'it must have been 1990', 'approximately 2000', plus a three-page epilogue, 'Reprise: 2002'. The brief opening part (1970) is followed by two much longer ones of approximately equal length, then an even longer fourth section (typical of Welsh's much greater interest in now, not then). Instead of being divided as the first three parts are into four sections, each narrated by one of the four friends, the fourth part is divided into twenty sections which alternate between Edinburgh (Terry and Billy), Australia and airports and flights in between as Carl Ewart journeys home to see his dying father; the structure of this part reflects the dispersal of the characters since Gally's death as well as their reunion and Carl's homecoming.

In keeping with its occasionally self-reflexive nature, *Glue* at times comments on its own structuring principles, starting with the dedication (to eleven friends 'for sticking together even when falling apart') and especially in the sections narrated by Carl: mixing and 'tidyin up the debris' (275, 276). Even as it moves ahead in time, *Glue* includes a good deal of narrative fragmentation, over-lapping, backtracking and repetition. *Glue* provides the big picture in a series of personal close-ups which, even as they leave out a great deal, manage to create a sense of wholeness and continuity. The title underscores another of the novel's structuring principles. As the definition from *Chambers Dictionary* which precedes the rest of the novel and which forms part of its paratextual apparatus notes: 'glue: *gloo, n.* an impure gelatin got by bodily animal refuse, used as an adhesive'. *Glue* also alludes to Welsh's earliest drug experience, sniffing glue, as well as the punk fanzine, *Sniffin' Glue*. The definition also points to the characters' status as schemies (animal refuse) in the eyes of mainstream middle-class society. Friendship may be the chief adhesive in *Glue*, recalling, if unintentionally, the nineteenth-century term, adhesiveness, to refer to male friend-ships, but it coexists with and is dependent on other narrative adhesives: music, drugs, football, sex, neighbourhoods, codes of behaviour and the residue of Scotland's Catholic and Calvinist past in the form of nearly crippling guilt (or in Terry Lawson's case, its absence).

The novel's title also points to three kinds of social struc-tures: public (later private) housing, the family, and gender formation. The novel begins in 1970 with the Galloways moving into 'one of these new slum-clearance places' (probably Broomhouse) where at least one of the other three principal families live. As O'Hagan points out in *Our Fathers*, the postwar boom in public housing addressed real and long-standing needs, but the high ideals and even higher expectations (captured so well in *Glue*'s opening pages) were undermined by bad design, poor materials and corruption. As Richard Finlay explains in *Modern Scotland: 1914–2000*, instead of promoting equality, the new estates 'replicate[d] systems of hierarchy in which certain areas would be designated "good" places and others would be bad' (246). Unlike the old neighbourhoods they replaced, which had functioned as self-contained communities where residents could live, shop and socialize, the new estates lacked amenities, became breeding grounds for social pathologies, and led to a new social phenomenon: leaving the neighbourhood for all-night forays into the city. Paternalistic in its planning, the new housing also fostered the culture of dependency which the Thatcher government broke by encouraging (in effect requiring) private ownership, leaving the most vulnerable citizens in the worst housing. Worse still, the early emphasis on quantity of units rather than quality resulted in the structures quickly falling into irremediable disrepair which took a further psychological toll on its residents until many of these estates began to be razed in the early twenty-first century (Finlay 254–5).

Not only does *Glue* take up each of these issues; it does so from the inside, as they affected the people who lived in this housing over two decades: in a place and from a point of view and over a period of time that distinguishes *Glue* from O'Hagan's *Our Fathers*, Torrington's *Swing Hammer Swing*, Kelman's *How late it was, how late*, and Galloway's *The Trick Is to Keep Breathing* – and not just because these others are all set in or around Glasgow. In *Glue* the characters' fortunes are reflected in and to a high degree are dependent on the physical environment as a manifestation of the social, political, cultural and economic practices and policies. Thus the novel's trajectory: from the high hopes of the opening pages, symbolized by the large windows of the Galloways' new flat and the vista it affords, to the breakdown of the scheme (materially, socially and economically). Even after the younger generation (except briefly Terry) move out (and the novel moves with them), environment remains important. At a spacious, well-appointed house in Germany, Carl realizes that 'This environment makes life, human relations, so simple and easy. How shite and grubby and how long all this would have taken in a pub or at a party. We head off for a stroll together … .The bottom ay the gairden dips, and we look ower the trees, down tae the lake wi the mountains in the background. – Great view, eh? This is a beautiful part of the world. The best ever. Ah love it here, me'

(285). The view recalls iconographic images of the Scottish Highlands and with it the freedom (or *Braveheart* 'freedom') that Carl and the others are largely denied in their Scottish scheme. It is no less true, however, that Carl's German reverie must be read in a context which includes a high measure of self-loathing (the pubs, parties and schemes that he associates with Edinburgh) and the considerable wealth that makes the idyllic German setting possible. The context also includes the novel's overall (and autobiographically self-revealing) trajectory which transforms Edinburgh into a site of return and possibility (for the characters, especially Carl, but mostly for Welsh, whose one-line author's note on the book's half-title page reads, 'Irvine Welsh lives in London'). Ten years later, Carl's friend Terry is even more aware of the effect of environment on the Scottish psyche: 'The scheme, the government employment scheme, the dole office, the factory, the jail. Together they created a squalid stink of low expectation which could choke the life out of you if you let it' (456).

In a way, *Glue* is Welsh's further attempt to reverse the terms of John Major's admonishing Britons to 'condemn more and understand less'. To effect this reversal, Welsh focuses on four central characters, the relationships between them, the family structures in which they are nurtured (or not) and the social as well as narrative structures which either constrain or free them. Although developed over more pages and years than *Trainspotting*'s characters, the four are no less types than they are characters in the material sense. They are like postmodern versions of the four elements (earth, air, water and fire): Billy and sports, Gally and weapons, Carl and music, Terry and sex; Billy is taciturn, Gally unsure, Carl supportive, Terry self-centred and unambitious. Between their individuality and their being the schemie equivalent of the Fantastic Four, the characters are often paired in certain ways: the Lawson and Galloway households are fatherless, the Birrell and Ewart households are conventionally complete and supportive. Gally and Terry become wasters, Billy and Carl become reasonably successful, although not in ways their families would have imagined: one as a club-owner (although not as independent as he seems or would like to be), the other as a DJ. Terry and Gally marry and have children and fail as both husbands and fathers. They also have fewer choices than Billy and Carl. Where Gally and Terry smoulder with resentment, Billy and Carl channel it: 'it's no two schemies anymore, it's N-Sign the DJ and Business Birrell, the Boxer', Carl proclaims. Welsh's point is not that one must applaud Billy's and Carl's successes and condemn Gally's and Terry's failures. Rather, it is that one must understand the structures that make both possible. Billy's business success certainly derives from his hard work, but it also derives from chance: his being taken to a boxing match in June 1985 by his father, who himself lacked the ambition that enabled Billy to succeed as boxer and businessman, Duncan Ewart to succeed as shop steward, and Carl to succeed as a DJ.

Glue is clearly a book about men and about male bonding – the pun is unavoidable. Women play a decidedly subordinate role even when they are heads of household. *Glue* is a novel of fathers and sons and male friends and a novel about how boys become men in the small world Welsh describes: about their first fight, sex, album, drink, drugs, job, etc., about trying to make an impression on mates, girls, hard men, about trying to obey the law(s) of the father(s): the 'ten commandments' of Duncan Ewart, biological father to Carl, surrogate father to his friends. All of this sounds simple, but Welsh's treatment of masculinity manages to be at once exhaustive, insightful, serious, funny and strangely affecting. It is also a little risky in making a contribution to the Nick Hornby-genre of ladlit-lite in an effort to understand why his male characters remain boys well into their thirties. While Terry replicates his father's irresponsible masculinity, Carl adapts his father's love of Elvis Presley's music for a new generation in a way which satisfactorily resolves the larger oedipal crisis. Similarly, Willie Birrell's passivity seems to have contributed to his son's quiet competitiveness, which Billy channels far more successfully than Davie Galloway does, as Gally tries to deal with his father's frequent absences from home – absences that derive from his desire to provide for his family through the only way he knows, robbery. The return of Andy Galloway late in the novel, seen crying beside his son's grave, suggests Welsh's more or less sympathetic view of fathers in general in the novel, a far cry from the way they have been depicted in his earlier work. The sympathy is not unqualified, not even for the father who is dealt with most and most sympathetically. Duncan Ewart's 'ten commandments' for a post-Christian working-class Scot hardly offer an infallible guide for surrogate son Gally, whose efforts to follow them contribute to his downfall.

Although the death of Carl's mother is mentioned, it is the death of two men, his father Duncan and his friend Gally, that are emphasized. Gally commits suicide in front of his friends, leaping from George IV Bridge to the Cowgate. Whether he does this to prove his masculinity to his friends or to heap guilt upon them or simply to escape a life made intolerable by guilt and being HIV-positive is unclear. His death reminds the reader of the deaths of so many other young men in Welsh's fiction and of the suicides of people Welsh knew which led him to become involved in the Be Foundation, helping people prevent and deal with teenage suicide. Gally's suicide affects his friends (each of whom feels responsible in some way) centrifugally, dispersing them, leaving them unglued. Duncan's death has the opposite effect, drawing the living together, giving them the opportunity to talk about Gally's death, to piece together from their separate accounts something like the full story in a different kind of male bonding. (As Harry Gibson says, 'The men in *Glue* can talk, but they can't say much to each other', until now [Brown, 'Drama']).

Berthold Schoene provides an especially insightful reading of the novel in terms of the important change Welsh signals in the formation of male identity. Schoene contrasts the monologic mode of narration in *Filth* and the first three parts of *Glue* with 'the tumultuous kaleidoscope of spontaneously interweaving and unravelling narrative moments' of part four, which reflects a change in the way the three remaining friends 'relate to each other' ('Nervous'). 'Break[ing] the bonds of traditional masculinity', they forge a new, intensely personal form of male identity which corresponds to the freer attitude of the two young women introduced late in the novel who talk about and engage in sex more freely and without the hang-ups of the four friends or the Scottish women seen earlier in the novel or of American singer Katherine Joyner, also introduced in part four. In effect, *Glue* engages in a kind of urban renewal – traditional male consciousness-raising – in order to break down the paralysing 'homophobic fear of male-to-male bonding' which prevents the men from talking freely to one another. Schoene also nimbly connects the change in male identity formation with the newly reformed Scottish state ('Nervous' 142–3). Schoene's argument is persuasive but fails to address two

matters, one adequately, the other at all. The first is Schoene's
rejecting, in effect, Welsh's own assessment of *Glue*. Conceding
the obvious, that *Glue* is 'more upbeat, happier than *Filth*', Welsh
goes on to say, 'But I don't really believe it' (Redhead 145). The
proof of his disbelief is the novel's absurdly optimistic ending.
Schoene also fails to deal with the novel's at times no less absurdly
inappropriate language. Admittedly, some of the problem with
language results from Welsh's having become the victim of his
own success. What is fresh and vivid in the early books (the first
three in particular) seems somewhat jaded now, especially after
being so often imitated. More importantly, too much of the writing seems canned or a combination of the inept and the inapt:
'Billy retorted', Willie 'nodded sagely', 'Catarrh nodded in empa-
thetic agreement', 'Terry breathed in the damp, fetid air, its fusty
vapours tugging at his throat and crusting his lungs'. Irony here is
remarkably heavy-handed, nowhere more so than in Welsh's
version of Chekhov, with a crossbow substituted for the pistol
early in the novel going off near the end. Carl's thoughts on 'the
illusion of romance' are trite by any standard and especially so in
light of Renton's 'Choose Life' diatribe in *Trainspotting*. The
'shoom' and 'whoosh' meant to signify Carl's drugged state
suggest that Welsh himself is just going through the motions, as
in Billy's slightly earlier thoughts on 'how much the tendency to
ennoble glorious defeat was ingrained in the Scottish psyche'
(424). Stale language for equally stale ideas. Thus, although
Duncan Petrie is right to claim that in *Glue* 'Welsh engages more
forcefully [or at least more fully] than Spence [does in *The Magic
Flute*] with the broader social, economic and political changes
affecting Scotland', he is wrong to believe that *Glue* 'provides a
corrective to one of the central problems of Welsh's *Trainspotting*,
where the narrative trajectory had confirmed the unsustainability
of the social group' (*Contemporary* 180). Petrie is wrong not because
of what *Glue* says but because of the way the novel says it. The
weakness carries over to Welsh's next novel.

Porno was already well under way by the time Welsh appeared at
the 2001 Edinburgh Book Festival to read from and help publicize
Glue. The novel that was then in progress was even more expansive
than the 483-page book published exactly one year later, without
the 'bits' set in San Francisco (an important setting in Welsh's next
novel, *The Bedroom Secrets of the Master Chefs*) to which Welsh alluded

at the time. Welsh was then also working on the musical *Blackpool*, which like *Glue*, *Porno* and *Marabou Stork Nightmares*, involves a backward glance. (*Blackpool* involves two trips to Blackpool by the same characters, twenty years apart.) *Porno*'s reception was helped along when newspapers reported that, following complaints, Waterstone's had taken down window displays for the novel from its two Princes Street shops in Edinburgh. (Waterstone's claimed that the displays, featuring condoms and inflatable dolls, were about to be taken down anyway.) The display picked up on the book's suitably garish cover, in pink and red, with some yellow, white, black and blue lettering, with an inflatable sex doll featured front and back. One month later, Lisa Jardine, chairperson of the 2002 Man Booker Prize selection committee which criticized publishers for submitting so many 'pretentious, portentous, and pompous' novels, 'lamented the absence of *Porno* from the short-list'. The fault, she said, lay with the publisher for not submitting it, not with the committee, which had not seen it (Chris Gray; Tonkin). Although *Porno* was published late in the Booker cycle, Jardine's claim that the other judges 'had no idea it ever existed' begs credulity, given how heavily the novel was promoted. Interviews with the author appeared in all the British broadsheets, the menacing look on the face of the shaven-headed but now besuited Welsh in the photos which accompanied the interviews seemed less punkish put-on than a different kind of posing. Unlike the Man Booker committee, the Saltire Society not only knew of *Porno*'s existence but put Welsh's novel on that year's shortlist. The publicity included a great deal of speculation over a film version, with the original cast reprising their roles a decade later. Danny Boyle was enthusiastic, but Ewan McGregor quickly rejected the idea, claiming that the novel wasn't all that good. It was a view shared by many reviewers of a novel that drew a decidedly mixed response.

Like Welsh's other novels, *Porno* is rich with characters, or as previously noted, with character types. All of *Trainspotting*'s principal characters are back (other than Tommy). A decade later, Sick Boy's dreams of personal success have come to nothing, or less than nothing as he is reduced to a 'crummy bedsit' in Hackney so small that he hardly has room to hang his Armani suit and so ill-situated that he feels uneasy about taking women there for sex. Here two imperatives collide: the need to appear more successful than he is and the need to use others, particularly women. Ironically, his ambition takes him back to Leith and away from London (and his ex-wife, the Jewish princess he hoped would be this frog's ticket to success, as well as the son he despises for not showing signs of paternal ruthlessness nearly as much as he loathes his own ne'er-do-well father). When his Aunt Paula, hoping to pursue her own dream in the Spanish sun, offers him the Port Sunshine pub on very favourable terms, Sick Boy overcomes his initial disgust over this seedy local and sees the chance to realize his own fantasies of empowerment in rapidly gentrifying Leith. The ambitions of Sick Boy (now Simon David Williamson) and of Leith imply Welsh's distaste for this gentrification. Simon's loathing of Leithers – a form of self-loathing – does not preclude his presenting himself both as one of Thatcher's children and as a working-class hero with 'a punk vision' (483) who has more in common with Renton than with Begbie.

Where Simon can only see others as either the cause of his misfortunes or opportunities for exploitation, the Renton of *Porno* sees himself at fault. He exists at the point where Catholic and Calvinist guilt intersect and is motivated by the need to redeem (or better) himself. The Mephistophelean Simon speaks in a variety of voices. Adjusting voice to audience, he keeps his self-deluded self carefully hidden to everyone but the reader, who comes to inhabit that inner space, enjoying both the privileged position and a measure of ironic distance and moral superiority quite different than the sympathetic intimacy of *Trainspotting*. Renton speaks in a single voice, or in two forms of that single voice. One is in Standard English, the other occasionally drifting into dialect, in his speech to others or, more rarely still, in his internal discourse. Renton is once again Simon's opposite: 'a hypocrite, a winner who played at being a loser. Aye, a bright, upwardly mobile cunt who would one day fuck off' (382). He is, in other words, just what Simon wants to be. As Simon says, in language reminiscent of *Glue* but not of that novel's ethos: 'He's a traitor, a grass, a scab, a selfish egotist, he's everything that anyone who is working class needs to be in order to get on in the new capitalist order' (170). For Simon, this 'everything' does not include Mark's remorse, which is the reverse of Simon's resentment. Both remorse and resentment are fuelled by the characters' self-loathing and sensitivity to the judgment of others which drives them to improve themselves (each in his own way) and to incorporate the views of these others into their internal discourse (as in the line just quoted) in the form of Bakhtinian (dialogical) 'sideward glances'. Now that his relationship with Katia in Amsterdam has come to an end, Renton returns to Edinburgh to get on with his life and to make amends for past wrongs. His sense of responsibility especially annoys Simon when Renton delays his return in order to complete his business arrangements with his partner rather than 'leave Martin in the lurch' after seven years together.

The only person who lies beyond Renton's desire to make amends is Begbie, fresh from HMP Saughton where he served his sentence for killing Donnelly (who was first seen in *Trainspotting* following his release from prison). Begbie is as violent as ever, but curiously seems less menacing, the threat he poses less palpable. As with so much in this novel, he appears closer to the often comical cartoon figure of the film. Although suffering from severe headaches and even more severe paranoia, Begbie (as well as Simon) is in many ways like Boab Coyle ('The Granton Star Cause'). The cock of the Walk returns home to suffer a series of comic rejections: his mother doesn't have time to feed him, his business partner Lexo has turned their fencing operation into a restaurant, and he fails to reach orgasm with his new girlfriend Kate.

Spud is still himself, only more so, as incapable of change as Begbie, but in a passive mode. Spud is now married to Alison and has a son, but he is no better a husband and father than Begbie and Simon are, only, like Renton, more remorseful. Especially interesting is the fact that Begbie and Spud are not only the two central characters least able to change; they are also the two whose speech and thoughts are rendered in dialect. To his credit, Spud wants to better himself, for the sake of others as well as for his own. Unlike Begbie, he goes into rehab and does have a dream: to write a people's history of Leith. (Spud has apparently never heard of *Trainspotting*.)

The only major addition to the novel's cast of characters is Nicola (Nikki) Fuller-Smith, who shares narrating duties with Sick Boy, Renton, Spud and Begbie. Nikki is trying to escape from a saccharine English family that makes Dianne's parents, in *Trainspotting*, look less frighteningly bland than Renton then claimed. A student at Edinburgh University, first in literature and now (2002) in film, she is bored with her studies and with her present life ('the latest in the assembly line of [professor] Colin Addison's student shags'). Although beautiful, she too is filled with self-loathing (female, not schemie or Scottish) and an equally strong need to prove herself (as Renton, Spud, Sick Boy and, in his way, Begbie also do). Cringing and envious every time she sees or thinks about the childhood classmate who went on to become a world-class gymnast and celebrity, Nikki seeks success (as well as revenge) by becoming the star of the porn film that Sick Boy hopes to use to realize his ambition. The film, *Seven Rides for Seven Brothers*, also allows Nikki to put the film studies that she already finds boring to practical use, to step out of the underworld of the massage parlour where she works giving inexpert handjobs, and *épater le bourgeois*, namely her family. It also allows her to move out of the narrowly individualistic and competitive environments of the university and the massage parlour and into the more collaborative environment of filmmaking. (Simon's attempt to turn collaboration into individual success for himself will ultimately backfire in yet another instance of comedic poetic justice in Welsh's work.) Having from the start of his career been accused of writing ladlit of a misogynistic kind for the *Loaded* crowd, Welsh seems with Nikki (as with Charlene late in *Glue*) to be trying to make amends and to prove that he can 'do' women. That the result is not successful is doubly damning given how large a role Nikki plays in the novel and its narration.

More successful is the novel's cast of supporting characters. (It is worth noting however that, with the exception of Dianne, the line between major and minor characters is much more clearly defined in *Porno* than in *Trainspotting*.) The desperate middle-aged professor Colin Addison; Melanie, left by a boyfriend with debts and a son; Nikki's nineteen-year-old flatmate, a sweet, priggish feminist named Lauren; Begbie's second murder victim, the paedophile/rapist Gary Chisholm; Simon's Aunt Paula, who moves out of Leith and Port Sunshine to a new life in Alicante (which may or may not last, and which may be based more on wishful thinking than on the possibility of a permanent relationship with her Spanish boyfriend). Several of these secondary characters are borrowed: Juice Terry, Rab Birrell, Billy Birrell and Carl Ewart / N-Sign from *Glue* (Rab's stag party serves to establish *Porno*'s time frame relative to *Glue*); Conrad Donaldson from *Marabou Stork Nightmares* and *Filth*; Larry Wylie from 'A Soft Touch', Alison, Gav

Temperley, Seeker, Second Prize, Mikey Forrester, Nelly, Lexo, Leslie from *Trainspotting*; Kate from 'Elspeth's Boyfriend'; Dode, Spud's taciturn uncle in *Trainspotting*, is his loquacious, Latin-spouting cousin now: a security guard who claims to be an engineer, he combines two Scottish archetypes, the lad o' pairts and would-be emigrant.

Welsh's handling of his titular subject is nearly as varied as his cast of characters. Although generally relegated to the realm of the subliterary and dealt with aesthetically the way that Catherine Mackinnon and Andrea Dworkin dealt with the same subject sociologically, psychologically, legally and ethically, pornography has increasingly come to be treated much more objectively and sympathetically by many writers, filmmakers and scholars. Susan Sontag wrote her 1967 essay 'The Pornographic Imagination' in order to elucidate both the similarities and the differences between pornography as conventionally understood and the kind of porn that rises to the level of 'art'. Novels by John McGahern, Martin Amis and Ian McEwan have dealt with pornography and A. L. Kennedy's *Original Bliss* and Alasdair Gray's *Something Leather* have used pornography to illuminate Scottish identity, as in a way does David Mackenzie's NC 17 film *Young Adam* (2003), adapted from a novel by Alexander Trocchi, who supported himself and his heroin habit by writing pornographic novels for Olympia Press.

Porno arrived at a time when pornography and the pornographic imagination were seemingly ubiquitous. Simon agrees: 'porn is mainstream now' (347); 'pornography sneezes and popular culture catches a cold. People want sex, violence, food, pets, DIY and humiliation. Let's give them the fuckin lot. Look at humiliation television, look at the papers and the mags, look at the class system, the jealousy, the bitterness that oozes out of our culture: in Britain we want to see people get fucked … ' (179). Welsh made the same points in the many interviews used to publicize *Porno*. Just as he came to write *Trainspotting* as a result of returning to Edinburgh and seeing so many of his friends either addicted or HIV-positive or dead, the idea for *Porno* came after returning a decade later to find his friends making DIY porn as if it were a new form of karaoke, with inexpensive digital cameras doing for porn what decks did for DJs. As interviewer Sally Vincent explains: 'first he knew of it, he sauntered into one of the old Edinburgh dives to see a few old mates, expecting to find the place as he'd left it, the punters all popping Es and bopping around in a sweat haze, and found himself the only man with clothes on in the middle of some kind of huge, gonzo sex orgy. It seemed that while his back was turned, everyone he knew had gone through a process of disinhibition that had passed him by'. Welsh's surprise seems at once disconcertingly disingenuous and strangely sincere. After all, how can so uninhibited an author be shocked at the 'disinhibition' of others, unless it is the phenomenon's having passed him by that surprised him, or his discovering in his shock the trace of his own 'provincial moral squeamishness' (to borrow F. Scott Fitzgerald's phrase). In an interview published four days before the novel's release, Welsh strikes a decidedly moralistic note that some may find at odds with the novel's seemingly easy handling of sex. Sounding like the self-appointed guardian of public morality, or perhaps a parody of one, Welsh told Nicholas Christian that the 'new novel had been driven by a horror at what he felt was a public willingness to tolerate pornography. The novel should be seen as a work that is against pornography and the "over-sexualisation" of society'. Welsh's comment notwithstanding, the novel's treatment of porn is remarkably varied and even-handed. Porn both empowers women and exploits them, privileges men and the male gaze while at the same time turning pricks into props. Porn democratizes artistic production by extending punk's DIY aesthetic while at the same time being a rule-bound form (as rule-bound as one of Rebecca Navarro's Regency romances) employing a stultifyingly limited repertoire of sexual and camera positions. Porn is, like drugs, a regulated yet widely available substance which nominally exists outside the mainstream economy yet, as Frank Rich points out, constitutes a far larger part of that economy than many believe. Also, as both Welsh and Rich note, porn exists within the mainstream culture in disguised form: Rich's ads and MTV, Welsh's gymnasts.

That *Porno* is overtly critical of the commodification process which pornography now represents is obvious, particularly in Simon's litany of the qualities that a working-class individual must possess in order to prosper in the local and global economy. These are qualities quite different from and at odds with Duncan Ewart's ten commandments and quite visible in the gentrification of Leith which Welsh criticizes in the novel and elsewhere. The critical element is also visible in student/sex-worker Nikki's remark, 'If you really want to see how capitalism operates, never mind Adam Smith's pin factory, this [the sauna where she works] is the place to study'. And not just the sauna. *Porno* deals briefly with the links between the sex and drug trades and at greater length with the economics of filmmaking (production, distribution and market-ing) and the larger making of a 'product'. (Coincidentally, soon after *Porno* was published, a glossy entitled *Product*, billed as 'the essential Scottish culture magazine', was launched to promote Scottish writers, filmmakers, artists and other cultural – not sex – workers.) Renton segues from thinking about using cocaine to thinking about consumption in general: 'People consume shite that does them no good at all, often just because they can. It's naïve to expect drugs tae be exempt from the laws of modern consumer capitalism. Especially when, as a product, they best help define it' (408). But it is Simon who is most obsessed with and consumed by consumer capitalism, as his rant on the relation between porn and consumerism in general demonstrates. Men need porn, he says, not because they are men but 'because we're consumers. Because those are things we like, things we intrinsically feel or have been conned into believing will give us value, release, satisfaction. We value them so we need to at least have the illusion of their avail-ability. For tits and arse read coke, crisps, speedboats, cars, houses, computers, designer labels, replica shirts. That's why advertising and pornography are similar; they sell the illusion of availability and the non-consequence of consumption' (450). Nikki however finds Simon's 'conversation' 'boring' and walks away – always a danger for the ranter or the writer, for Irvine Welsh no less than for Simon David Williamson.

Porno is not just a novel about porn and consumerism. It is also a consumer object whose aesthetic qualities are part of its appeal, part of Simon's 'illusion of availability' and 'non-consequence of consumption'. These qualities include paratextual elements such as the novel's distinctive, parodically 'shocking' as well as lurid cover and dust-jacket. (*Porno* is the first Welsh novel to be issued in the US in both clothbound and paperback editions, the former serving as guarantor of the novel's and its author's elevated status and the increased wealth of his ageing fanbase.) They also include the numerous interviews Welsh gave as part of the publicity effort surrounding the novel's release. The aesthetic qualities include the novel's structure and the quality of the writing. The novel begins in much the same high-energy way that *Trainspotting* does. Welsh's parodies of film porn are quite expert in capturing both the representation of sex and more especially the process by which that representation is manufactured. Welsh proves hilariously adept at depicting the narrative and *coitus interruptus* of porn filmmaking and in exposing, as it were, the absurdly regimented and claustrophobically reductive narrative grammar of this most obsessively taxonomic film genre. This is especially the case in the scene involving a reverse anal cowgirl shot, which ends when Simon's unknowing barmaid comes up to announce the arrival of a news photographer and Melanie suddenly drops her full weight on Terry, rupturing his penis. This in turn leads to the discovery of the film's male star, the shy, well-endowed Curtis, straight out of *Boogie Nights*. Differently effective is Welsh's handling of Simon's voice, or more specifically the way he adapts his voice to his audience.

More often, the writing is rather flat, leading Tom Lappin to punningly call *Porno* 'a flaccid read'. While some of the 'bad' writing may be generously judged as parodic, much is either inappropriate or Bulwer-Lytton bad. The dialect with which Welsh had to reacquaint himself in writing *Porno* posed a special problem which Welsh solved by greatly limiting its use to Spud and Begbie, only rarely (and inconsistently) using it with Renton and Simon. The latter strategy signifies how far both characters, like their author, have moved from their roots in Leith (their returns notwithstanding). It also suggests how much more user-friendly *Porno* is than *Trainspotting* and how much *Porno* sounds/reads like one of Welsh's imitators, Helen Walsh, for example, whose descriptions of sex in *Brass* are similarly clichéd. Welsh, once a mocker of pretentious styles (Gifford, 'Clever' 8), has himself become stylistically pretentious. And, in having every one of the five narrators endlessly explain themselves to themselves and others, he has become sententious too.

Not only does Welsh over-write and over-explain; he over-structures the novel too. As we have seen, his earlier novels and many of his stories follow one of two basic formats: stories which develop using alternating narratives and those that develop serially, with visual effects (typography, page design) often used in the former to help create the feel of a DJ mix and the synesthetic atmosphere of the club experience. *Porno*, perhaps in response to *Glue*'s having been 'character-based' and therefore having taken what Welsh considered a 'wastefully' long time to write, is tightly structured in a double sense, one effective, one not. Like *Trainspotting*, *Porno* comprises multiple, alternating narratives, but in a way that is, like the dialect, much more user-friendly. *Porno* is also divided into three parts, each subdivided according to narrator easily distinguishable both by voice and by the kind of section title assigned to each narrator. Simon's are consecutively numbered 'Scams' (starting with 'Scam # 18,732'), Nikki's are brief elliptical quotes from that section (' ... the attachments ... '), Spud's are single words or simple phrases ('Counselling'), Renton's are consecutively numbered 'Whores of Amsterdam' (starting with 'Pt 1'), and Begbie's are all in capital letters ('OOTSIDE'). Simon and Nikki dominate the novel, 22 sections and over 140 pages each. However, not only does Simon's relative power (and importance) imperceptibly wane in the long middle part (as does Nikki's); Spud's, Begbie's and Rents's grows, with Rents (the novel's dark horse) increasing still more in part three.

Within the larger structure are a number of important substructures. One involves the making of *Seven Rides for Seven Brothers*, a parodically pornographic (as well as backstage) version of the well-known film musical. A second borrows the basic structure of 'A Soft Touch' and 'The Granton Star Cause'. The reader finds pleasure in the comic blows to masculine self-esteem inflicted on and suffered by Begbie, Spud and Simon (but not Renton, who in *Porno* is even less self-consciously sensitive about his male ego than he is in *Trainspotting*). A third substructure is the scam, a fourth is making it (in all its forms: sexual, economic, etc.: Simon's business ventures, Spud's people's history of Leith, Nikki's proving herself, Renton's moving on, Dianne's completing her thesis), and a fifth is revenge (and its opposite, making amends, associated with Spud and to a greater extent Mark). In their different ways, Begbie and Simon are obsessed with avenging themselves, with Simon deftly making Begbie a part of his own ingenious plan to exact his pound of flesh from Renton for stealing the £16,000 ten years earlier. His scheming character ensures that Simon is always plotting, his every move calculated. Unfortunately, so is Welsh's novel, in which (to cite just one example) Spud's cat plays the part that Gally's crossbow does in *Glue*: the Chekhovian pistol scene in the first act that must go off in the third. *Porno* in fact resembles Dianne's thesis, in both its rigid organization and wooden language (150). Simply put (and borrowing an idea Welsh includes in the novel), *Porno* is overly Apollonian and insufficiently Dionysian. It is made too much in the scheming Simon's image and too little in the naturally priapic Juice Terry's.

In this context, *Porno*'s epigraph, 'Without cruelty there is no festival', from Nietzsche's *Genealogy of Morals*, proves especially apropos. It points to the will to power and to master–slave moralities; to resentment as a powerful motivating factor, along with guilt and shame; to the pleasure taken in being cruel and to the origin of this pleasure in an economic (rather than moral) imbalance. The creditor is given the pleasure of discharging his power on the powerless debtor without any guilt or shame attached to this act, punishment and cruelty merely serving as the means for securing repayment. As Simon puts it, 'Renton is getting paid back with interest' (138). Begbie feels the same way, even as Simon makes Franco his unwitting tool. More importantly, neither Simon nor Begbie is particularly interested in the actual monetary debt; it is Renton's betrayal that they resent and to which they respond. Later in the novel Simon invokes the other side of Nietzsche's equation. *Seven Rides*, he claims, is not primarily about making money; it is about 'self-actualisation' and gaining respect. It is therefore very much tied to the slave's feeling of resentment: about showing his social, economic, and cultural masters what the working-class individual can do. (Welsh's drawing his epigraph from Nietzsche rather than from, say, Paul Reekie or Iggy Pop accomplishes much the same goal.) This 'doing' exists solely in terms set by the masters and needs to be read, as Nietzsche himself indicated, in economic terms. Thus the other significance of the epigraph, one presumably unintended by the author but manifest in the novel nonetheless. This is not the linkage between carnival and resentment that Michael Andre Bernstein emphasizes, but instead, as Bakhtin understood, the fate of carnival and the carnivalesque once cut off from their roots in authentic folk culture. This fate entails the withering and hardening of carnival and the carnivalesque into the merely literary and the purely personal of bourgeois capitalist culture, while losing along the way their power to subvert and renew (Bakhtin, *Rabelais* 36–7; *Problems* 130–2). In Welsh's case, this culture is not the authentic folk culture of the Middle Ages but the authentic subculture of *Trainspotting*. Thus the kind of progress measured in late-capitalist terms from *Trainspotting* to *Porno*, from

Iggy Pop's 'Lust for Life' as used in the film *Trainspotting* to using the same song to hawk Carnival Line cruises, from The Sex Pistols' 'God Save the Queen' as sneering punk anthem to the playing of the same song at the Queen's Golden Jubilee.

Porno's ending replays *Trainspotting*'s, adjusted for inflation (£60,000 instead of £16,000). Instead of *Trainspotting*'s portrait of the ex-addict as a young emigrant, we have a group shot of Renton, Dianne and Nikki gleefully (not fearfully) heading off to America (not Amsterdam). An ellipsis serves as *Porno*'s too-clever-by-half final word suggesting the unlikely possibility of yet another sequel in which Welsh may recycle the San Francisco sections deleted from *Porno* (unless he already has in *The Bedroom Secrets of the Master Chefs*). Despite its weaknesses, readers can take pleasure in *Porno*'s ending because they take pleasure in Simon's pain: the pain without which, as Nietzsche understood, there is no festival. However, in the midst of the carnivalesque laughter, readers will detect an elegiac undertone. This elegiac quality, which Kevin Williamson and John King address in their reviews, derives from what several characters, Spud in particular, feel in seeing Leith succumb to the twin forces of gentrification and corporate interests. The nostalgia manifests itself in another, deeper way which, although less overtly present in the narrative, is actually more pervasive and palpable. This is the way that the Leith of *Porno* seems a far more abstract place than the Leith of *Trainspotting*, as if in its very texture the novel agrees with Renton when he says that home is not Leith or Amsterdam or any material place at all; rather, it is 'where the heart is'. Just as the novel's long-windedness may be said to measure Welsh's reluctance to leave Old Leith behind, *Porno*'s language measures the distance Welsh has travelled from Edinburgh's mean streets to a no-place that can be anyplace. This is a language once so deeply rooted in Leith as to put all of Edinburgh on the postmodern literary map. Doing so eventually transformed Edinburgh into the 'Inspiring Capital' of Scottish cultural tourism and Welsh himself into the author of *Glue, Porno,* and now *The Bedroom Secrets of the Master Chefs*, about 'a hard-drinking, womanizing environmental health officer who travels from Leith to San Francisco to find the father he has never known and understand the self-destructive compulsions that cripple him' (Turpin). 'It does feel different in a lot of ways', Welsh has said of the new novel. 'It's not quite so heavy on the vernacular, and the characters are kind of middle-class, but more in that classless space that a lot of guys who have made good find themselves in. It's an uncomfortable space that they are trying to make their own' (O'Hagan). This is a space that leaves little room for the disruptive energies of Welsh's earlier, truly carnivalesque fiction. One can hardly begrudge Welsh for moving on, out and up, but neither can one fail to notice that what he condemns in Leith, Welsh enjoys abroad, 'living in a posh redevelopment of an "old scummy street" in Dublin' (English). Welsh is, of course, in a very real if unintended way partly responsible for Edinburgh's and now Leith's phoenix-like rise from its own cultural and economic ashes – so much so that it is difficult not to hear in his continued railing against the political and cultural elite a subtext of self-blame and guilt. It is this guilty recognition of having 'given it all away' (435) that gives this long-winded work a poignancy which much of Welsh's earlier writing (*Trainspotting* excepted) gave the appearance of studiously avoiding.

As noted earlier, the Welsh backlash which began with the publication of *Ecstasy* in 1996 had far more to do with reviewers' and the larger literary culture's unexamined assumptions than it did Welsh's writing. Reviewers who had praised Welsh for reinvigorating the British novel in 1993 became critical as the Welsh phenomenon took hold and the British novel started to look as if it were being remade in Welsh's image and in terms of popular (especially visual) culture rather than according to the standards of the literary novel. The largely negative response to Welsh's most recent novel, *The Bedroom Secrets of the Master Chefs*, on the other hand, coming exactly one decade after *Ecstasy*, has been well deserved. The irony here is that *Bedroom Secrets* is not only Welsh's least successful novel; it is also his most conventionally literary. *Ecstasy* was criticized for departing from standards that really did not apply. *Bedroom Secrets* has been damned for failing to be the kind of literary novel Welsh in fact wanted it to be. Reviewers who appear to have read the novel the most closely have been the most scathing in their assessment of the novel and its author: 'If words could be scraped from the pages of a novel into the garbage, those contained between the covers of Irvine Welsh's latest offering deserve to be consigned there, along with the remnants of their author's literary reputation' (Mark Austin in the *Daily Yomiuri*, Japan's leading newspaper); 'Those howls of rage of his early years have turned to the empty baying of a dog. Take him away' (Neel

Mukherjee in *The Times* of London); 'Although it fails at every imaginable level – metaphysical, ethical, technical, thematic – it is at the stylistic level, the level of the sentence, that Welsh's ['extraordinarily bad new'] novel is most wanting' (Robert Macfarlane in the *New York Times Book Review*). Of the handful of reviewers who wrote favourably of Welsh's novel, Deborah Orr was the most enthusiastic, so much so as to make one wonder if she were being more satiric than sincere, parrying Welsh's egregiously bad writing with exorbitant praise every bit as parodic in its way as John Crace was in his 'Dr Jekyll and Mr Hyde' send-up of *Bedroom Secrets* (*Guardian* 31 August 2006) or Lorne Jackson in her review: 'Welsh was once revered as the guru oav the switched oan generation. Nae mare. These days he's more like a faulty light-switch – plenty of shocks, but nae real power'.('Nae kiddin pal, this fella's goon an lost the plot').

The Bedroom Secrets of the Master Chefs will survive the negative reviews because the Welsh phenomenon has entered a new stage. Published four years after *Porno* and written over more than three years, *Bedroom Secrets* was not so much a greatly anticipated literary event as just another instance of Welsh being in the news because he has become newsworthy in a way quite different than he had been in the 1990s. Although residing in Dublin, the newly remarried Welsh has become increasingly seen by the press as one of Edinburgh's literary elder statesman (Rankin and McCall Smith being the other two). The premiere of Welsh and Dean Cavanagh's play *Babylon Heights* about the making of the *Wizard of Oz* was widely covered (though barely reviewed), along with a protest by the Restricted Growth Association over the play's treatment of its characters, the actors who played Munchkins in the *Wizard of Oz* film. Casting and planned filming of *Ecstasy* and *Wedding Belles* proved newsworthy, and a remark about Conservative Party leader David Cameron being no worse than Tony Blair was also widely reported as evidence that Welsh had himself turned Tory. In numerous interviews, Welsh looked back, ruefully, on his heroin use in the 1980s and spoke of art as an alternative to drugs and of his having grown older, wiser and comfortable with his life as a man of leisure who has done 'well out of Thatcherism'. Welsh's reading from the novel at the Edinburgh Book Festival the following month resulted in one member of the audience accusing Welsh of misogyny – an allegation also much bruited in the news. (Welsh seems to have chosen to read this rather unrepresentative scene because of its shock value.) The coverage helped make *Bedroom Secrets* Welsh's oddest bestseller – odd not because of the negative reviews (Welsh had gotten those before) but because the long-anticipated novel seemed so incidental, as if it were just one more event (like the One City book and the Keane music video) in this new stage in the Irvine Welsh phenomenon in which, instead of a succession of peaks, there was a more or less constant flow.

That said and the justified criticism of the negative reviews notwithstanding, *The Bedroom Secrets of the Master Chefs* does deserve attention for several other reasons. One is that its failure is especially surprising given how well-suited its subject matter is to Welsh's pulp instincts and practices. Twenty-five year-old housing officer Danny Skinner takes an instant dislike to new co-worker Brian Kibby, on whom he then unwittingly puts a curse which enables Skinner to drink all he wants while having Kibby suffer all the ill effects, from hangovers to near-fatal medical consequences. The curse's course runs parallel to Skinner's dual quests: to discover his father's identity and to become a better person by resolving the Jekyll and Hyde conflict within himself. There are several flashes of brilliance, such as the ending, which rises to the graphic novel occasion, and this passage: 'Scotland: the recipe for disaster. Take a cut of Calvinist repression, sprinkle on some Catholic guilt, add lots of alcohol and cook in a cold, dark, grey oven for three-hundred-odd years. Garnish with gaudy, ludicrous plaid. Serve with chivs on the side' (267). Unfortunately, most often *Bedroom Secrets* takes the bad writing of *Porno* a step further, with Welsh, like Danny Skinner's clothing, 'scream[ing] at ideas beyond his station', and the author himself, like Brian Kibby, 'invit[ing] humiliation'. At times the bad writing is suited to a particular character and seems part of a general plan which Welsh foregrounds in the description of the Old Boys, an Edinburgh punk band, which Skinner locates on the internet. 'They sang highly reactionary songs about social decline' and 'extolled the virtues of wartime Britain' in a deadpan style. 'The Old Boys themselves never gave the game away, though several critics were pushed too far by the inflammatory and racist single 'Compulsory Repatriation'. … Perhaps due to the frustration that nobody really got them, they started to parody themselves, with attendant declining returns' (282–3). If *Bedroom Secrets* is meant to be parodic, then the parody here is neither homage nor critique, merely pale imitation. And if the style is meant to be ironic, then one would have to say that Welsh was also being ironic in comments made to interviewers around the same time, which resemble the novel both in style and substance (see, for example, 'I Can't Live Without'). The dropping of product names (Volvic, Stella Artois, 'quality Bordeaux purchased from Valvone & Crolla') may bespeak a character's pretensions, but far more interesting, and worrisome, is Welsh's calling *Bedroom Secrets* 'a treatise on hate' whose literary pedigree includes Hogg's *Private Memoirs*, Oscar Wilde's *Dorian Gray*, Stevenson's *Jekyll and Hyde*, even a touch of Shakespeare's *Macbeth*. The equivalent of the dropping of product names, Welsh's efforts to establish *Bedroom Secrets*' literary pedigree underscores how, like the Old Boys, he has become unwittingly self-parodic. What had previously seemed authentic, natural and subversive has become deliberate and deferential as the former literary Kasper Hauser suffers a fatal dose of the anxiety of influence. The search for the father may be, as Skinner's San Francisco girlfriend says, 'an over-rated quest to be sure' (262). Nonetheless, it underscores Welsh's efforts in all his fiction, particularly the work published since devolution, to understand his own divided identity: between then and now, between being nobody and being a celebrity, between literary Kasper Hauser and autodidact, and between serving as the point of intersection for 'a bunch of voices shouting to be heard' and becoming a monological celebrity. Welsh is right: 'All that duality stuff … . It's a massive theme in Scottish literature' (Page). Although he has called Skinner (the wastrel) and Kibby (the nerd) his alter-egos, the characters Welsh resembles most are the ones closest to his own age, including Skinner's mother Bev, who still thinks of herself as a punk even though she is really a small businesswoman, and Alain De Fretais, the grotesquely fat celebrity chef whom Skinner for a while thinks may be his father and whom he eventually murders. Alain De Fretais really is (or was) Alan Frazer of Gilmerton: another local boy who, like Skinner, Kibby, and Welsh, wanted both 'to belong' *and* 'to be somebody'. But 'to belong' to what exactly, especially in a novel all dressed up in *faux* literary style but with nowhere really to go?

Ironically enough, and, as even a cursory check of headlines in the *Scotsman* and *Scotland on Sunday* indicate, 'Scotland's latest image makeover' notwithstanding, the social problems addressed with such unstudied brilliance and in vital contact with sub- and popular culture in the early work remain as real in 2006 as they were in 1993: the pathological masculinity, disaffected youth, heroin addiction, dependency in all its forms in 'a nation still divided by poverty and inequality' where, thanks to the class divide, 'now it's even harder for the poor to get on'. This is a Scotland where a *Trainspotting* is again needed but where it may no longer be possible.

PART III
Criticism and Contexts

7

OTHER WRITINGS

'My attitude to writing is, fuck it, I'll have a go'. Never having
expected to write a book, let alone have one published, Welsh
'never became too precious about the media [he] wrote in'
(Introduction, *Acid* screenplay viii). Where most 'writers' work
within a fairly narrow range, with the different genres and media
hierarchically arranged and with the most 'literary' writers also
confining themselves the most narrowly, Welsh has been as
promiscuous literarily as his characters are sexually. Welsh's
demystification of writing and the writer proves a complex signifier, however. It serves as the sign of the authenticity of Welsh's
voice (which transcends genre and media) and as the point on
which youth culture (literate and postliterate) fixes a gaze more
often directed towards visual culture. It also serves as a brand
name, marketable, consumable, profitable, and as the (former)
schemie's way of making his presence known, his (representative) voice heard: an individual act within (initially even against)
the consumer culture which nonetheless has wider social, political and economic implications. It is a way which has greatly benefited Welsh, of course, as well as those for whom he speaks and

the actors, directors and others who have acted or adapted his words.

Many of the stories Welsh hurriedly wrote to meet the demand following the success of *Trainspotting* and *The Acid House* deserve to be more widely available, although not, one hopes, in a retrospective (and retrograde) 'collected stories'. 'The Rosewell Incident', in *Children of Albion Rovers*, edited by Kevin Williamson, may be the best and certainly is the most ambitious. Welsh's satiric gaze alights upon everyone equally, from the casuals who cannot think let alone act beyond their provincial turf battles to the alien youth Tazak whose first line is the Begbie-ish 'Well, we pay these cunts a visit the night. See what thir up tae, eh'. 'The Rosewell Incident' cleverly and efficiently encompasses Scots' UFO sightings, the mystery surrounding Rosslyn Chapel, Scottish defeatism and provincialism, the middle-class obsession with the 'authenticity' of Welsh's voice, and the Criminal Justice Act, with its efforts to police the repetitive beat generation rather than address underlying causes of dissent. 'The Best Brand of Football' in *A Book of Two Halves* (1996), edited by Nicholas Royle, follows Welsh's other preferred organizational method: event following event in an accumulation of like-minded episodes, from morning to night. 'A Fault on the Line' in *Acid Plaid*, edited by Harry Ritchie, is much more compact and blackly humorous. It is essentially a shaggy-dog story told in grotesque realism / adult comic-book style about a monstrously self-centred, misogynistic Scot whose obsession with football trumps everything, including beer, and everyone, including his wife and children. Welsh's contributions to these anthologies are noteworthy for another reason. His reputation and notoriety helped raise the profile (and profitability) of contemporary Scottish fiction writers and of the small Scottish magazines and presses that had published their work. In this, it is synergy more than Caledonian anti-syzergy that is at play. This is more the case with *Children of Albion Rovers*, published by Rebel Inc, than with *Acid Plaid*, published by London-based Bloomsbury, and in the UK than in the US where 'The Rosewell Incident' was excerpted in the decidedly artsy, book-size *Open City* #5 as part of the marketing for *Children of Albion Rovers*, distributed in the US by Penguin. ('Eurotrash' appeared in *Open City* #3 as part of Norton's marketing of *The Acid House* and 'Another Lost Continent', from *Marabou Stork Nightmares*, appeared in the similarly artsy American literary magazine *Grand Street*.) The conjunction of the retrospective and the prospective, of an emerging Scottish fiction and its commercial potential in the global marketplace, is also apparent in *Ahead of Its Time* (Vintage 1998) which includes old and new work by writers associated with Duncan McLean's Edinburgh-based Clocktower Press. The cover hitches the fortunes of all the writers and of the collection as a whole to Welsh: the garish purple and yellow front, with its blood-red thistle, alludes to *The Acid House, Marabou Stork Nightmares, Ecstasy* and *The Irvine Welsh Omnibus*.

The problematic relationship between subcultural community and cultural commodification, between the new fiction and the new marketing, is also apparent in *Disco Biscuits: New Fiction from the Chemical Generation*, edited by Sarah Champion (Sceptre, 1997), *Intoxication: An Anthology of Stimulant-Based Writing*, edited by Toni Davidson (Serpent's Tail, 1998) and *Vox 'n' Roll: Fiction for the Twenty-First Century*, edited by Richard Thomas (Serpent's Tail, 2000). 'The State of the Party', previously serialized in five instalments in *The Face*, is another of Welsh's day-in-the-life stories, this time of three friends. One of the three dies of a drug overdose, then is literally dragged to a party by his unsuspecting friends, and physically assaulted by thugs who resent his not speaking when spoken to. More significant than the story itself is its initial appearance in *The Face* and the launching and marketing of *Disco Biscuits* by means of a national clubbing tour modelled on the launch of *Ecstasy*. Easy to dismiss as exploitive and opportunistic, *Disco Biscuits* represents the changing nature of both the clubbing scene and the literary marketplace as well as the intersection of disaffected youth and consumer culture. 'Victor Spoils' (*Intoxication*) focuses on Gav Temperley from *Trainspotting*, sometime after the novel's conclusion and after Gav has decided to keep the kind of council job that Welsh's success as a writer enabled him to leave behind in 1995. The E's he consumes do not save Gav from being a boring nine-to-five drudge or a dismal lover. In fact, his consumption of the drug only confirms his status as yet another of the wasters who populate Welsh's fiction, three of them in 'Victor Spoils' alone. *Vox 'n' Roll* is a collection of stories by writers who have participated in the Vox 'n' Roll readings at Filthy McNasty's Bar & Whiskey Café in Islington, North London. The collection in a sense closes the circle that the Beat-inspired pub- and later club-readings began: going from club-reading to club-launch to publishing the readings.

Welsh's contribution is not the verse-story he read at the café in September 1999, 'Voodoo Nightmare as Fat Fucker Overheats at Rave', which he subsequently contributed to the BBC for its *Book of the Future*, 'the UK's first democratically elected book', with proceeds going to Comic Relief. Instead, he contributed 'Elspeth's Boyfriend', narrated by Begbie and set shortly after the time of *Porno*. Like all the stories discussed thus far, 'Elspeth's Boyfriend' is comedy – but, comedy mixed with menace. Begbie's monstrous egotism is more troubling than the husband's in 'A Fault on the Line' precisely because the story is less grotesque and more conventionally realistic than 'Fault'.

Welsh's contributions to Nick Hornby's *Speaking with the Angel* (Penguin, 2000) and to the two 'Weekenders' collections, *Travels in the Heart of Africa* (Ebury, 2001) and *Adventures in Calcutta* (Ebury, 2004) are noteworthy for a different reason. Where the causes Welsh supported by contributing and lending his name to anthologies such as *Ahead of Its Time* and *Disco Biscuits* were contemporary Scottish fiction and youth culture, the cause now is charity, raising consciousness of and money for a school for autistic children, for Calcutta's poor and for Sudanese refugees. 'Catholic Guilt (You Know You Love It)', from *Speaking with the Angel*, which also includes stories by celebrated authors Zadie Smith, Dave Eggers, Helen Fielding. Melissa Bank, Roddy Doyle, Patrick Marber, and Hornby and one non-literary celebrity, Colin Firth, elaborates on a theme found in *Glue* in which Davie Galloway rejects all thought of having sex with Terry Lawson's sister because she looks too much like his friend. In the much funnier story, the main character is a strident homophobe who, because he had been sexually abused by a priest when he was young, has repressed his homosexual desires until he dies while having sex with his best friend's twin sister. The punishment meted out for his sin of homophobia (Welsh's carnivalesque inversion of the Catholic Church's prohibition against homosexuality) is to force him to bugger his friends until he repents. One good punchline begets another: the homophobe refuses to repent so that he can continue to engage in gay sex, which he now realizes he enjoys. The two 'Weekenders' collections combine fiction and non-fiction, again from (mainly) well-known writers, about Calcutta and the Sudan. The two stories, 'Contamination' and 'Reality Orientation' are not just the longest (by far) in the collections; they are melodramatic, largely humourless, certainly overwritten in *faux* 'African' and 'Indian' English, and dismayingly, if understandably, written from the outside (while pretending in each case to offer an inside look). In the two 'Weekenders' stories, Welsh dispenses with the qualities that made his writing interesting in order to play all too earnestly the part of recognized 'writer'. The cost is seen not just in the heavy-handed language but in the insistent plotting and the loss of spontaneity and authenticity of these (and other late) works as well.

A similar shift is noticeable in the non-fiction Welsh has written since the late 1990s. The list of published non-fiction begins in 1991 with two letters to the *Scotsman* (18 October 1991: 14 and 25 October 1991: 16) concerning Trevor Griffiths' play *Comedians* at Edinburgh's Royal Lyceum Theatre. Like Welsh's early fiction, these letters and much of the early non-fiction meet the criterion Welsh set for himself: he wrote them because he had something to say. Although most of the non-fiction pieces that followed were solicited and may best be categorized as 'occasional', they nonetheless 'speak' for Welsh in ways that much of the later *ex-cathedra* non-fiction does not. There is a passionate identification with and seemingly sincere effort to use his own success to further the work and careers of writers, artists and others with whom he strongly identifies or is in some way personally connected, including photographer Nick Waplington, director Peter Mullan, writer/editor/activist Kevin Williamson, DJ Annie Nightingale, former Edinburgh schemie turned Bay City Roller Les McKeown, Calton Athletic founder David Bryce, and others. The *Guardian* tried to play up Welsh's bad-boy image for a 16 January 1999 article: 'She's pregnant and he's got his fist raised. Guess who's the victim? Wrong. Irvine Welsh will smack the next person who accuses him of stereotyping'. But the article itself is less combative and much more reflective than *Guardian* readers familiar with *Trainspotting, Filth* and *You'll Have Had Your Hole* might have expected. The same is true of Welsh's articles for the *Guardian* a few months before and after, on Graham Cumington's play *Pain*, about to open at Edinburgh's Traverse Theatre, and, on the eve of the England–Scotland football match, on the changing nature of the rivalry. 'Why I Hate Theatre', in *The Stage*, is understandably more combative given the hostile reception accorded Welsh's play *You'll Have Had Your Hole*. The earlier Welsh gave way to one less vernacular and impassioned, more refined and restrained, less like the poet laureate of the chemical generation and more like the grand old man of youth culture and member in good standing of the literary establishment. He began writing thoughtful and generally appreciative but decidedly bland book reviews (of Arthur Herman's *Scottish Enlightenment: The Scots Invention of the Modern World*, James Kelman's *You Have to Be Careful in the Land of the Free*, Alasdair Gray's *The Ends of Our Tethers*, James Meek's *The People's Act of Love*, Craig Clevenger's *The Contortionist's Handbook*, William McIlvanney's *Weekend*, and Patrick McCabe's *Winterworld*. He was one of 'five great writers' sent out to review a great restaurant for the *Guardian* ('Literary Lunch', 12 October 2003). *The Times* asked him, upon the release of Michael Winterbottom's film 24 *Hour Party* (2002), to look back on the 1976–92 Manchester club scene. The *Scotsman* and the *Guardian* asked him about new books he would recommend, while in 2005 the *Independent* asked him about his 'secret life' and later his 'cultural life'. 'I'm always watching films and I love French cinema. There's nothing better than sitting watching a classic movie at the French Institute and discussing it over almond croissants and coffee, or a glass of nice red wine' (Cripps) is dismayingly representative and perhaps best understood from the perspective of Frantz Fanon's *Black Skin, White Masks*. (To understand just how representative the sentence just quoted is, read the article Welsh wrote two months earlier for the *Guardian* on violence in Scotland ['A New Report']) or Welsh's article – more a bit of whitemailing – in the 5 March 2006 *Observer* on his trip to Greenland.)

Welsh's transformation nicely dovetailed with the *Daily Telegraph*'s as Britain's bestselling daily broadsheet sought to increase its market share by appealing to younger readers (the average age of its readers having been in the mid-50s). Running from 3 March through 21 July 2003 and written while Welsh taught for a semester at Columbia College in Chicago, where he met Beth Quinn, a student, whom he married in July 2005, his weekly columns are decidedly personal but only occasionally either risky or illuminating of himself or America. (The series title, 'From America', evoked Alistair Cooke's preeminently English 'Letter from America' for BBC radio and the 1987 hit single 'Letter from America' by the Leith duo, The Proclaimers.) For the most part, Welsh takes on innocuous topics such as the Chicago winter, American soccer, baseball, Tartan Day and St Patrick's Day parades, horse-racing, America's pet fetish, victim culture, the obesity epidemic, with predictable results. He mainly writes from (and about) Chicago, but he also travels, for example, to Los Angeles which he had visited twenty years earlier under very different circumstances, not as a celebrity staying at a luxurious hotel but an impoverished youth just trying, as he wrote in 'Eurotrash', to get by. Even more interesting is the 14 April 2003 column on the Prague Writers Festival, where he met Arundhati Roy ('Absinthe'). What appears to have struck Welsh was not just the powerful presence and political activism of this physically diminutive writer, who having written just one novel, the Booker Prize-winning *The God of Small Things*, chose not to write any other fiction. Rather, it was Roy's using her considerable reputation and celebrity to focus attention on local problems in her own area of India and to become an eloquent and effective spokesperson for global issues, from the environment and poverty to peace. Where Welsh spoke occasionally against the yuppification of Leith and of the failure of the City of Edinburgh to treat its poorest residents fairly, spending lavishly on the MTV Europe awards ceremony, for example, but not on the poor, Roy dedicated herself to political activism. Where Welsh had said he would write only as long as he had something to say but now claims to be addicted to writing, she wrote the one novel she felt compelled to write, and then turned away from fiction, leaving that novel to stand alone and speak for itself. At least in part, Welsh's admiration suggests a commendable, if very Scottish (Catholic and Calvinist) guilty recognition of having (not unlike Bruce Robertson) betrayed his working-class origin. It is this sense of betrayal that energizes the filth and fury of his early work, its black humour and grotesque realism, and that makes his arrival at LA's tony Chateau Marmont a sign of both his success and his drifting into hollow celebrity, the hedonism promoted by *Loaded* and *The Face* fuelled now by his *Daily Telegraph* column. The irreverence of *Trainspotting* and *A Visitor's Guide to Edinburgh* (written with Kevin Williamson) suited Welsh better. Launched at the 1993 Edinburgh Festival where Welsh was being hailed for *Trainspotting*, the *Guide* was decidedly punkish in its DIY look, satiric content and mocking cover with the Edinburgh icon, Greyfriars Bobby, hypodermic jutting from its paw, cleverly recalling the poster for The Sex Pistols' 'Who Killed Bambi?', a safety pin in the smiling fawn's ear.

The *Guide* was too little read to have much effect on the Welsh phenomenon. Harry Gibson's stage version of *Trainspotting* was far more influential, especially in keeping Welsh in the news and in doing for British theatre what Welsh's book did for the British novel. The play premiered at Glasgow's Mayfest, where it was directed by Ian Brown in 1994. It was restaged at the Citizens, directed this time by Gibson, in March 1995, before moving to London, first at the small Bush Theatre (dir. Brown, April 1995), then at the much larger Ambassadors in the West End in December, with national tours in 1995 and again in 1996. By then, *Trainspotting* had won the *Sunday Times* award for best new play, at the Regional Theatre Awards ceremony. In addition to setting off a flurry of stage adaptations of Welsh's works and of other Scottish novels, including Banks's *The Bridge*, Galloway's *The Trick Is to Keep Breathing*, and Gray's *Lanark*, the play's success created an important link between traditional theatre and carnivalesque club culture. That link was more apparent in the intimacy of the Bush than at the larger Ambassadors as well as in the version of the script published in 1996 (with *Headstate*), than that of the 'sanitized' New York City production published in 4 *Play*.

The other stage adaptations of Welsh's work included in 4 *Play* had much less of an impact on the Welsh phenomenon as well as on British theatre. With a set more elaborate than the one used for similar effect in the first production of Arthur Miller's *Death of a Salesman*, Gibson's *Marabou Stork Nightmares* is a much more ambitious and expensive adaptation and as a result has only been staged twice, at Glasgow's Citizens (March 1996) and in Leicester (September 1996). Gibson's adaptation of *Filth*, which premiered at the Citizens (September 1999), before going to London, fared much better, in part because it lent itself to a much more spartan mode of dramatic presentation and in part because of the perfect casting of Tam Dean Burn as the furious, paranoid-schizophrenic monologist, Bruce Robertson. Neither Burn's charged performance nor Gibson's deft adaptation was enough to save the play. Keith Wyatt's *Ecstasy*, essentially a dramatization of the novella 'The Undefeated', was first performed in two Canadian nightclubs in 1999 and again at the 2000 Edinburgh Fringe, and Gibson's adaptation of *Glue* was performed at the Citizens, 3–8 December 2001. (Gibson's adaptation of *Porno* has not yet been staged or published; John Paul McGroarty's version, designed as a radio play, was performed in June 2006 at the Leith Dockers Club as part of the Leith Festival.)

Welsh's connection with *Headstate* was quite different. Even before *Trainspotting* was published, Welsh had been working with Boilerhouse Theatre Company on a piece which, while attributed to Welsh, was in fact 'devised' by nine people and as such evidences Welsh's early interest in collaboration. Designed as a 'pre-club night' and a 'piece of physical theatre' (the theatrical equivalent of Welsh's interest in physical writing), *Headstate* is not actually a play, although it has been judged as such by theatre critics and found wanting. The dialogue is oftentimes melodramatic and banal, and certainly evidences the pitfalls of writing by committee. However, dialogue is far less important than performance in, and the experience of, *Headstate*. This experience includes setting, or rather space/venue, and the place Welsh and the other devisers expected *Headstate* would occupy in the audience's larger evening, in which a night at the theatre is prelude rather than culmination and in which the seemingly banal views expressed by the characters (again types) speak quite directly of and to clubbers caught between high expectations and post-rave and -club burnout. The language which is foregrounded on the page is less apparent in performance, in which it functions more like the lyrics of the songs that Welsh heard Annie Nightingale play on her radio show. Premiered on 18 October 1994 in Aberdeen before opening at Glasgow's Tramway the following night, *Headstate* was also staged in a converted church at the 1996 Edinburgh Fringe and then was featured at the July 1997 Greenwich and Docklands Festival where, as Linda Gardiner noted in an otherwise withering (and uncomprehending) review, the lighthouse venue re-created 'the atmosphere … of a tightly controlled rave'. Although *Headstate* is not overtly political, context, in the form of the 1994 Criminal Justice Act which sought to regulate and constrain club and rave culture, in effect makes it so.

Welsh's one solo attempt at playwriting received scathing notices, which, even if largely deserved, had the unfortunate effect of making plausible the claims of those who sought an end to the Welsh phenomenon and the fin-de-millennium British culture it represented in these critics' eyes. Even in its revised form, *You'll Have Had Your Hole* at London's Astoria 2 (directed by Ian Brown), following its disastrous premiere at the West Yorkshire Playhouse in Leeds, received hostile reviews. The fact that the bad notices from the Leeds production were used to advertise 'this calculatingly nasty stage play' in London particularly incensed theatre critics. Willy Maley tried to put *You'll Have Had Your Hole* in the context of contemporary Scottish theatre's shift from politics to popular culture (in Welsh's case, club culture) for which the Astoria 2 setting (the LA Club) was more suitable than the West Yorkshire Playhouse. Jack Conrad, writing in the *Weekly Worker*, was more attentive to Welsh's handling of class and highly critical of the way a 'bourgeois press could only see nihilistic drug-taking, rape, cynical manipulation and torture [and] … could only hear swearing and abuse'.

Welsh's foray into playwriting may not have been successful, but it is typical of his willingness to work in different media and in collaborative environments. These collaborations go as far back his work with Boilerhouse on *Headstate*. In 1996 he and Primal Scream released the single 'The Big Man and the Scream Team Meet the Barmy Army Uptown' in support of Scotland in their match against England at Wembley, and in 1998 he scripted the group's music video *If They Move, Kill 'Em*. In 1997 Welsh's band Hibbee Nation released 'Life of Dance' and 'The Key to the House of Love'. He also wrote lyrics for Kris Needs, wrote and produced a fifteen-minute film to accompany Gene's EP 'Is It Over?' (2001), and provided the original idea for a promotional film for the Trash Can Sinatras. He worked with Harry Gibson on the musical *Blackpool* (Edinburgh, 2002) and with Dean Cavanagh on both *Dose* for the Wales Comes Clean campaign promoting safe sex (BBC Wales, 2003), and the play *Babylon Heights* (2006) and the television drama *Wedding Belles* (2007). Welsh's involvement in the making of *The Acid House* was more extensive even if Welsh's scripts are little more than transcriptions. More faithful to the fiction than *Trainspotting* and less commercial, *The Acid House* is '100 percent pure' and 'uncut', as the advertising put it, in more than one sense.

'The Granton Star Cause' premiered at the 1996 Edinburgh Film Festival the same year that the play *Trainspotting* was back in Edinburgh and *Headstate* was staged as part of the Edinburgh Fringe. That was also the month that *Ecstasy* was published and a half-year after the film *Trainspotting*'s release. 'Granton Star Cause' was first screened on Channel 4 one year later, amidst controversy over its depiction of God as a mean-spirited drunk. The full film premiered at the Roxy in Brixton, South London on 12 December

1998 and went into general release on 1 January 1999 and in the US two months later. As with *You'll Have Had Your Hole*, much of the hostility had less to do with the film's weaknesses than with reviewers' incomprehension. Paul McGuigan's direction and Andrew Hulme's editing create cinematic equivalents of Welsh's own visual style, itself influenced by elements of youth culture (album covers, fanzines, comic books, graphic novels). Equally important, the Welsh-influenced soundtrack augments image and dialogue. This is especially noticeable where the film draws on Welsh's contacts in the music scene: Nick Cave's dirge-like version of versions of Glen Campbell's 'By the Time I Get to Phoenix' and the stunning use of 'Precious Maybe', a song Beth Orton composed for *Acid House*. Orton's plaintive voice and lyrics work in counterpoint to the scene of Katriona coming home drunk and fighting with Johnny. All diegetic sounds dying away, the scene plays itself out silently and to devastating effect against Orton's music. Where the story is blackly humorous, a shaggy-dog story about the softest of soft touches, whose every attempt to get a little self-respect leads to a pratfall, the filmed version teases out a depth lost on most readers but nonetheless present in Welsh's story.

Welsh has subsequently worked more extensively in film. Along with Jimmy McGovern and fourteen strikers and their wives, he helped write *Dockers* (aired on Channel 4 in 1999) about the 28-month-long dockers' strike in Liverpool. A few months later he began planning *The Lottery*, to star Gary McCormack (a friend from Leith who plays Larry in 'A Soft Touch'), *Gold Coast Showman*, with Paul Vasili, about Arthur Wharton, the first black footballer, and *Hang the DJ*, with Cavanagh. As part of 4 Way Films, founded in 1999 by Stuart Cosgrove, Robert Carlyle, and Antonia Bird, Welsh has written scripts for *Meat Trade* (a cross between Burke and Hare and *Dirty Pretty Things*), *Hotel California*, based on the true story of two British youths who escaped from Thailand to avoid prison terms for drug possession, and *Soul Crew*, about the notorious Cardiff gang of football casuals, and he plans to direct a film version of Alan Warner's *The Man Who Walked*. (Welsh earned his first director credit in 2006 for the music video of Keane's 'Atlantic'.) Filming began in June 2006 on the television mini-series *Wedding Belles*, scripted by Welsh and following the lives of four female friends from Edinburgh who have drug habits. With their small budgets, and their focus on mainly local subjects rather than the global marketplace, these films provide a welcome alternative to Welsh's later fiction with its increasingly mainstream feel. So do adaptations – planned and realized – of some of Welsh's other fiction: Cavanagh's *Filth* screenplay, Alex Usbourne's long-planned adaptation of 'A Smart Cunt' as 'Some Weird Sin', Roger Paul, Peter Cummings and Kyle Leydier's 'Bad Blood' from *Trainspotting*, screened at the 2005 Tribeca Film Festival and starring Alan Cumming, and Canadian filmmaker Rob Heydon's *Ecstasy*, an adaptation of Welsh's novella 'The Undefeated', which began filming in 2006. The local also looms large in Welsh's proposed social history of Edinburgh chip shops, his efforts on behalf of fellow Scot Kenny Richey, who faces execution in the United States for a murder he apparently did not commit, and long-time friend and music promoter Ernesto Leal, who faces deportation, and in Welsh's most unusual collaboration, on a project he initiated to benefit OneCity Trust, which promotes social inclusion. The resulting book, *One City*, comprises three loosely linked stories, all set in Edinburgh, by Welsh ('Murrayfield, You're Having a Laugh', which Welsh read at the 2004 Edinburgh Book Festival), Ian Rankin, and Alexander McCall Smith, with an introduction by J. K. Rowling.

Looking back at the Leith of *Trainspotting*, Mary Moriarty, owner of the Port O' Leith bar, said in May 2005, 'It was horrendous but that period is gone and this [Tim Bell's *Trainspotting* tour] is like a history tour' (Lister). Eight months later, the tenth anniversary tour of Harry Gibson's stage adaptation of *Trainspotting* kicked off in Glasgow on 9 January with brief stops around the UK and with a cast who were mainly in their teens when the novel first appeared. What the juxtaposition of the two tours suggests is pretty much what Welsh's two attempts to rework *Trainspotting* suggest (ten years on in *Porno*, from a female perspective in *Wedding Belles*): that even as his readers look forward to the release of Welsh's next book, the story collection *If You Liked School, You'll Love Work*, *Trainspotting* and the Irvine Welsh phenomenon it set in motion have come, like Dublin-based Welsh himself, if not to the end of *the* line, then to the end of *a* line: to the end, certainly, of an era. No longer making history, they are history.

8

CRITICAL RECEPTION

The critical response to Irvine Welsh's writing does more than establish the strengths and weaknesses of individual works and the progress of his career. It also registers the origin and development of the Irvine Welsh phenomenon.

The critical response to *Trainspotting* was highly and almost uniformly enthusiastic. Alan Chadwick's early notice (quoted earlier) announced the arrival of a major new talent who, as Catherine Lockerbie, the *Scotsman*'s literary editor, noted, 'writes of the underside of the capital with a vengeance'. The fact that Welsh was seen not just as a new writer, but as a new Scottish writer, contributed to his appeal both north and south of the border. Reviewers stressed the novel's language as well as its unconventional structure, its connection to Kelman's fiction and its preoccupation with various forms of dependency. In arguably the most interesting and insightful of the reviews, Jenny Turner emphasized *Trainspotting*'s intense and intensely physical Scottishness (especially the Scottish drive to self-destruction), as well as the 'shockingly close emotional engagement' and 'a dread and mirthless sort of wit beyond wit'. Harry Gibson's stage adaptation contributed to the novel's and its author's critical acclaim. As Charles Spencer said of the first London production, 'It's the power of Welsh's language that makes the nightmare so vivid' and at times so funny. Reviewers of the novel outside the UK, especially in the US, were similarly enthusiastic even though the Scottish context was often lost on them. Coming late to Welsh, many knew of his growing reputation in Britain but responded to *Trainspotting* in relation to the film version just then being released, especially the controversy surrounding the film's depiction of drugs.

Published in the UK just seven months after *Trainspotting*, *The Acid House* greatly furthered Welsh's reputation. While some reviewers found his attempts at satire and his Alasdair Gray-like typographical experiments unconvincing, others commended Welsh for his ventriloquism and his comic but compassionate depiction of the lives of his working-class characters. And while some commented on his narrow range, others saw Welsh 'pushing the limits of his versatility'. Welsh's second novel raised what was to become a persistent concern: the tendency to value shock over substance. Despite reservations about Welsh's depiction of a brutal gang rape, *Marabou Stork Nightmares* was largely praised for its ambitiousness, its intricate structure, and for its 'powerful investigation of a life gone bad, written in a demanding and insistent prose that gives no quarter' (Polk). 'Feminists will read this book and find no better depiction of rape and its consequences, and sociologists will cite this novel for its depiction of life in the projects' (Merikangas). 'Irvine Welsh may become one of the most significant writers in Britain', Nick Hornby predicted. 'He writes with style, imagination, wit and force, and in a voice which those alienated by much current fiction clearly want to hear'. 'Style, wit, imagination and force' were lacking in Welsh's next book, at least according to many reviewers. Although a handful of reviewers spoke well if not enthusiastically of *Ecstasy*, most felt the novellas were superficial at best, silly at worst, clumsily told, proof that he had either written himself into a rut or exhausted entirely his small stock of material and literary means. *Filth* did little to dispel doubts, least of all following the backlash that *Ecstasy* began and only a few months after the disastrous reception afforded Welsh's play *You'll Have Had Your Hole*. Many felt Welsh was becoming repetitive and therefore boring or was succumbing to the *bêtes noires* of sensationalism and sentimentality. A few judged Welsh's handling of voice particularly effective, even if the novel's most visible feature, the typographic tapeworm, was not.

His first book in three years, *Glue* was read by many as an advance in terms of characterization, plotting, and possessing a social, psychological and imaginative depth and breadth missing from his earlier work. However, *Glue* was also criticized for being lazily written and 'depressingly monotonous' and conventional. 'Whereas *Trainspotting* dared to open up working-class cultural experience in order to show the fractured realities of a Scotland on the brink of devolution, *Glue* – or Trainspotting: The Return – is so wide of its audience, so out of political focus as to cancel out any possibility of transgressiveness … ' (McAvoy).

Porno, the much-anticipated sequel to *Trainspotting*, received a decidedly mixed response. John Burnside saw *Porno* as proof of Welsh's continuing growth: 'Welsh is as funny as ever – and the writing is just as energetic – but his vision is more poignant, more essentially tragic with each new book'. John King and Kevin Williamson located the source of *Porno*'s power in Welsh's treatment of his native Leith and the corrosive effects of gentrification and globalization on it. At the opposite extreme are those who find in *Porno* not Old Leith's endgame, but Welsh's. In the latest in a long line of sour assessments of Welsh's work, Tom Lappin sees in *Porno* 'pitiable evidence of a past-it writer failing to recapture his literary libido'. Focusing on characters a full generation younger than himself, *The Bedroom Secrets of the Master Chefs* plays a variation on Lappin's theme. Here the libidinous excesses of Welsh's early work are replaced by Welsh's most concerted effort to write in a more conventionally 'literary' style which the majority of reviewers found wanting. (For details, see the end of Chapter 7.)

Academic critics have in general been much less disapproving of, or at least less judgmental about Welsh's work. Not surprisingly, much of the criticism has dealt with *Trainspotting*. Robert Morace's *Irvine Welsh's 'Trainspotting': A Reader's Guide* analyses the novel as well as discussing Welsh, the novel's reception and stage and screen adaptations. Patricia Horton's '*Trainspotting*: A Topography of the Masculine Abject' considers the novel in relation to Scotland's need for 'a new story'. Where Horton finds 'the real strength of the novel … in its emphasis on the diversity and multiplicity of the working-class community', Andrew Monnickendam sees *Trainspotting* signalling the switch from working class to underclass at the end of the nationalist era. Several essays focus on the novel's language. Contrasting Kelman's modernism with Welsh's postmodern approach, Drew Milne contends that Welsh's critique of Scottish nationalism represents a new Scottish self-confidence but also notes that Welsh uses 'wit to deflect attention from its own responsibility for producing a relentlessly sour and self-destructive cynicism'. Nicholas M. Williams discerns the roots of Welsh's authenticity in 'the combination of Scots narration and disreputable subject matter'; stripping away the pretensions of high art while 'resist[ing] the transparency of much novelistic discourse', Welsh links language to the body. In 'Ghosts in Sunny Leith', Alan Freeman locates 'the key to the power of Welsh's utterance' in his 'pulling apart of the conventions of realism' in order to de-stabilize language and identity and to make adaptability the key to identity formation. Alan Riach ('Unnatural Scene') discusses the various ways Welsh's fiction, particularly *Trainspotting*, departs from realism: its greater physicality, energy, subjectivity, 'sympathetic engagement and moral judgement'. Although she deals specifically with the film, Bonnie Blackwell finds in *Trainspotting* 'an intricate proposal for the resacralization of language outside exhausted narrative templates'. Two essays focus on the novel's unconventional structure. Jennifer M. Jeffers uses Deleuze's concept of the rhizome to understand the ways *Trainspotting* resists consistency and universalization. Marina Mackay examines the way first-person narration is deployed to resist 'the anthropological activity of observing and recording' that the novel seems to perform.

Other critics focus on Welsh's handling of Scottish identity. Robin Spittal discusses the various ways *Trainspotting* challenges and inverts aspects of Scottishness even as it risks 'being subsumed into the global image of Scotland the brand' and thus becoming a new Scottish icon. Linking *Trainspotting* and novels by A. L. Kennedy and Janice Galloway, Fiona Oliver hears the voice of 'a dissatisfied generation of young Scots concerned with confronting and articulating the implications of colonization to lost identity – both cultural and personal'. Drawing on Deleuze and Guattari, Jeffrey Karnicky finds *Trainspotting* resisting 'traditional notions' and inventing 'novel subjectivities'. Looking at much the same question from the perspective of postcolonial theory, Grant Farred sees *Trainspotting* 'deal[ing] a deathblow' to the nation-state and positing the European Union as the only possible future for Renton and for Scotland. Looking at Welsh's depiction of failing cities and failing bodies, Gill Jamieson contends that space in general and the body in particular 'underpin [Welsh's] attempts to renegotiate ideas of community, identity and nationality'. Examining *Trainspotting* in relation to commodity culture, Christoph Lindner compares Welsh's novel unfavourably with the nineteenth-century novels of Mrs Gaskell. More usefully, Claire Squires treats *Trainspotting* as an example, rather than as a critique, of consumer culture, comparing publishers to drug-dealers, pushing not just books but nationality as a marketing concept ('Trainspotting'). Dominic Head and Elspeth Findlay each discuss Trainspotting as part of, rather than apart from, the middle class, while William Stephenson argues that 'Welsh's work is as much about consumerism and spirituality as it is about drugs' and that it involves 'a dual critique of late capitalism and house culture that exposes the problematic connection between them'.

Trainspotting's success in translation and on stage and screen has resulted in a number of important studies. Michael Gardiner examines how cultural contexts (Cool Britannia and British subcultures) affected the translation of Trainspotting and Marabou Stork Nightmares into Japanese as much as the inherent difficulties of Welsh's vernacular. Iain Galbraith and Martin Bruggemeier and Horst W. Drescher consider the difficulty of translating Trainspotting into German (Galbraith for a German stage production); Murielle Chan-Chu and Martin Bowman discuss Belgian-French and Canadian-French versions of the play, and Eduardo Barros-Grela a Spanish translation of the novel. Bert Cardullo briefly and Derek Paget at much greater length examine adapting the novel for the screen. Because the film has come to influence how the novel is read and remembered, a number of studies of the film alone are worth mentioning here. Jürgen Neubauer's 'Critical Media Literacy and the Representation of Youth in Trainspotting' examines the film version as a popular event, as a subcultural critique of consumer society and as a part of that culture. Martin Stollery provides a good overview of the film qua film and on its representation of youth culture (drawing heavily on Karen Lury's 'Here and Then: Space, Place and Nostalgia in British Youth Culture'). Building on his earlier 'Transnational Trainspotting', Murray Smith offers an excellent as well as comprehensive reading in his short book in the British Film Institute's 'Modern Classics' series. In Literature, Politics and Culture in Postwar Britain, Alan Sinfield carefully distinguishes the novel with its 'repudiation of mainstream culture, in the interest of a national, class and generational specificity', from the film which he castigates for diminishing or removing altogether 'most of the challenging aspects'. Analysing 'the rhetoric of the posthuman bodies of heroin addicts', Christine L. Harold concludes that the film 'epitomizes the permeable, fluctuating nature of the physical body and thus highlights the limitations of critical approaches grounded in moral judgment and linear reason'.

A number of essays deal partly or entirely with *Marabou Stork Nightmares*. Ellen-Raïsa Jackson and Willy Maley contend that although postcolonial studies cannot fully explain Welsh's second novel, they can help us understand 'cruces of complicity' in systems of race and class. Contrasting Grassic Gibbons's *Grey Granite* and *Marabou Stork Nightmares*, David Borthwick sees in the latter 'no communal voice whatsoever that can express working-class experience in a holistic way' and no desire on the characters' part for solidarity. David Leon Higdon discusses the highly 'circumscribed', individualistic way revenge functions in Welsh's work. Zoe Strachan, Stefan Herbrechter and especially Berthold Schoene-Harwood illuminate Welsh's treatment of masculinity, in terms of both changing masculine roles (Herbrechter) and the ways in which the crisis of masculinity reflects the crisis in Scottish national identity (Schoene-Harwood), while Carole Jones 'explores the ... movement from glorious to inglorious male victimhood' in William McIlvanney and Irvine Welsh, from 'the heroic masculinity of *Docherty* to the toxic masculinity of *Marabou Stork Nightmares*'. Matthew Hart reads *Glue* and Bill Buford's *Among the Thugs* as 'texts trapped between national and "post-national" interpretive and structural imperatives' and argues that 'the strength of Welsh's fiction ... is its study of the formation and deformation of tribal groups, as familial, musical and pharmacological subcultures come to dominate – and now find some accommodation – in their struggle with (and within) traditional allegiances of class and nation'. Duncan Petrie reads *Glue* and Alan Spence's *The Magic Flute* as recent examples of a favourite Scottish form, narratives of childhood, crediting Welsh with 'engag[ing] more forcefully with the broader social, economic and political changes affecting Scotland'.

Willy Maley makes good use of Deleuze and Guattari's theory of minority discourse and the damage that a dominant culture inflicts on minority cultures in his essay on Welsh's short fiction, and Anne Donovan uses 'Where the Debris Meets the Sea' to 'argue that as Scottish teachers we cannot ignore the greatness and variety of work being published in our country, nor its relevance to young people'. Dominic Drumgoole (briefly) and Willy Maley (more fully) make the case for Welsh's positive, carnivalesque effect on Scottish and British theatre.

Now that Andrew Crumey's especially useful online essay is no longer available, the best overviews of Welsh's work are James F. Ketcham's entry in the *Dictionary of Literary Biography* (vol. 271), Christie L. March's *Rewriting Scotland*, Peter Childs's *Contemporary Novelists: British Fiction Since 1970* and his entry for the online *Literary Encyclopedia* (www.LitEncy.com). For placing Welsh in the contexts of contemporary British and Scottish fiction, see *Scottish Literature*, ed. Douglas Gifford, et al., Peter Childs's 'The English Heritage Industry' and David Goldie's 'The Scottish New Wave'. Robert Crawford's five-page discussion of *Trainspotting* at the end of the second edition of *Devolving English Literature* provides an excellent starting point for further analysis. Nearly as brief and even more important is Cairns Craig's discussion of *Trainspotting* in *The Modern Scottish Novel* in relation to 'the dialectic of the fearful and the fearless' which he finds characteristic of Scottish fiction generally and of the novels written between the two referendums more particularly. Finally and most obviously, Aaron Kelly's *Irvine Welsh* is well researched and, even if his analyses occasionally become too remote to be convincing ('God's spitefully arbitrary decision to transform Boab into a fly itself provides an allegory of the estrangements of human identity under late capitalism and our seeming incapacity to comprehend the profound and systematic changes taking place under globalization even as, paradoxically, capitalism's routine seems more dully repetitive and constant than ever'), Kelly does a commendable job fleshing out the background of Welsh's fiction. Regrettably, Kelly receives only passing mention in the present study, which was conceived and largely written before his work was published.

BIBLIOGRAPHY

IRVINE WELSH: MAJOR WORKS

The Acid House. 1994. New York: Norton, 1995.
The Acid House: A Screenplay. London: Methuen, 1999.
The Bedroom Secrets of the Master Chefs. New York: Norton, 2006.
Ecstasy. London: Jonathan Cape, 1996.
Filth. London: Jonathan Cape, 1998.
Glue. London: Jonathan Cape, 2001.
The Irvine Welsh Omnibus. London: Jonathan Cape / Secker & Warburg, 1997.
Marabou Stork Nightmares. 1995. New York: Norton, 1996.
Porno. London: Jonathan Cape, 2002.
Trainspotting. 1993. New York: Norton, 1996.
'Trainspotting' and 'Headstate'. London: Minerva, 1996.
You'll Have Had Your Hole. London: Methuen, 1998.

OTHER WORKS CITED

Amidon, Stephen. 'Nothing to Rave About.' *Sunday Times*. (27 July 1997): 2.
Arlidge, John. 'The Dynamic Trio Take Film Honours to Scotland.' *Independent on Sunday*. (11 February 1996): 8.
——. 'Return of the Angry Young Men.' *Observer*. (23 June 1996): 14.
Ascherson, Neal. *Stone Voices: The Search for Scotland*. New York: Hill and Wang, 2002.
Aukin, David. 'It Was Logical to Create FilmFour.' *Guardian*. (12 July 2002): 2.
Austin, Mark. 'Welsh's New Novel Hard to Swallow.' *Daily Yomiuri*. (9 September 2006): n. pag. <www.yomiuri.co.jp/dy/features/book/20060909TDY22003.html>
Bakhtin, Mikhail. *Problems of Dostoevsky's Poetics*. Trans. and ed. Caryl Emerson. Minneapolis, MN: U of Minnesota P, 1984.
——. *Rabelais and His World*. Trans. Hélène Iswolsky. Bloomington, IN: Indiana UP, 1984.
Barnes, Hugh. 'Review of *The Acid House*.' *Independent on Sunday*. (3 April 94): 31.
Barros-Grela, Eduardo. 'El tratamiento de lexicografía ficticia en la traducción de narrativa.' *Espéculo: Revista de Estudios Literarios*. 23 (March–June 2003): n. pag.

Bassnett, Susan, ed. *Studying British Cultures: An Introduction*. London: Routledge, 1997.

Bearn, Emily. 'Chips Are Everything.' *Independent*. (24 August 2003): 4.

Beckett, Andy. 'Irvine Welsh: The Ecstasy and the Agony.' *Guardian*. (25 July 1998): 6.

_____. 'Raving with an MBA.' *Independent on Sunday*. (23 April 1995): n. pag.

Bell, Eleanor, and Gavin Miller, eds. *Scotland in Theory: Reflections on Culture and Literature*. Amsterdam: Rodopi, 2004.

Bell, Ian. 'Review of *Trainspotting*.' *Observer*. (15 August 1993): 47.

Bell, Ian A. 'Imagine Living There: Form and Ideology in Contemporary Scottish Fiction.' Ed. K. D. M. Snell. *The Regional Novel in Britain and Ireland*. Cambridge: Cambridge UP, 1998. 217–33.

Berman, Jennifer. 'Irvine Welsh.' *BOMB*. 56 (Summer 1996): 56–61.

Bernstein, Michael Andre. *Bitter Carnival: Ressentiment and the Abject Hero*. Princeton, NJ: Princeton UP, 1992.

Bing, Jonathan. ' "Trainspotting": Can It Repeat U.K. Success?' *Publishers Weekly*. (13 May 1996): 28.

Birch, Helen. 'Meeting God Down the Pub.' *Independent*. (16 April 1994): 29.

Black, Allan. 'Irvine Welsh.' *San Francisco Review of Books*. 20 (July–August 1995): 30–1.

Blackwell, Bonnie. 'The Society for the Prevention of Cruelty to Narrative.' *College Literature*. 31 (Winter 2004): 1–26.

Boddy, Kasia. 'Scotland.' Ed. John Sturrock. *The Oxford Guide to Contemporary Writing*. New York: Oxford UP, 1996. 361–76.

——. 'Scottish Fighting Men: Big and Wee.' Bell and Miller 183–96.

Boehnke, Dietmar. 'Double Refraction: Rewriting the Canon in Contemporary Scottish Literature.' Eds. Susana Onega, and Christian Gutlesen. *Refracting the Canon in Contemporary British Literature and Film*. Amsterdam: Rodopi, 2004. 53–68.

Borthwick, David. 'From *Grey Granite* to Urban Grit: A Revolution in Urban Perspectives.' The Association of Scottish Literary Studies, 2001. N. pag. <www.arts.gla.ac.uk/ScotLit/ASLS/Urban_Grit.html>

Bowman, Martin. '*Trainspotting* in Montreal: The Dramatic Version.' *International Journal of Scottish Theatre*. 1 (2000): n. pag.

Bradbury, Malcolm. *The Modern British Novel*. New York: Penguin, 1993.

Brantlinger, Patrick. *Fictions of State: Culture and Credit in Britain, 1694–1994*. Ithaca, NY: Cornell UP, 1996.

Bresnark, Robin. 'Irvine Welsh.' *Melody Maker*. (16 January 1999): 12.

Brooks, Xan. *Choose Life: Ewan McGregor and the British Film Revival*. London: Chameleon, 1998.

Brown, Mark. 'Drama in a Different Class.' *Scotsman*. (2 December 2001): 9.

Brown, Mick. 'Generation.' *Telegraph Magazine*. (5 July 1995): n. pag.

Bruggemeier, Martin, and Horst W. Drescher. 'A Subculture and Its Characterization in Irvine Welsh's *Trainspotting*.' *Anglistik & Englischunterricht*. 63 (Winter 2000): 135–50.

Burnside, John. 'Warped Factor: Ten.' *Times*. (17–23 August 2002): Play 15.

Butler, Judith. 'Gender as Performance: An Interview with Judith Butler for *Radical Philosophy*.' Eds. L. Segal, and K. Woodward. *Identity and Difference*. Milton Keynes: Open University P, 1997. 235–8. Also at N. pag. <www.theory.org.uk/ctr-butl.htm>

Calder, Angus. 'By the Waters of Leith I Sat Down and Wept: Reflections on Scottish Identity.' Ritchie 218–38.

Cardullo, Bert. 'Fiction into Film, or Bringing Welsh to a Boyle.' *Literature/Film Quarterly*. 25 (1997): 158–62.

Carey, John. 'Introduction.' *The Joke and Its Relation to the Unconscious*, by Sigmund Freud. New York: Penguin, 2002. vii–xxviii.

Cavenett, Wendy. 'A Star Is Bored.' *Independent*. (11 July 1998): 20.

Chadwick, Alan. 'Fear and Lothian.' *Herald* (Glasgow). (31 July 1993): Weekender 6.

——. 'Welsh and the Agony of Ecstasy.' *Sunday Times*. (19 May 1996): 3.

Chan-Chu, Murielle. '*Trainspotting* au théâtre: une adaptation culturelle. *Post-Scriptum*. 3 (2004): n. pag. <www.post-scriptum.org/index.htm>

Childs, Peter. *Contemporary Novelists: British Fiction Since 1970*. London: Palgrave Macmillan, 2005.

——. 'The English Heritage Industry and Other Trends in the Novel at the Millennium.' Shaffer 210–24.

Christian, Nicholas. 'Irvine Welsh Attacks Edinburgh's "Domineering Middle-Class Culture".' *Scotland on Sunday*. (25 August 2002): 3.

Christopher, James. 'Blood on the Tracks.' *Time Out*. (12–19 April 1995): 18–29.

Coe, Jonathan. 'Where Angels Fear to Tread.' *Sunday Times*. (10 March 1994): sec. 7, 13.

Cohen, William A., and Ryan Johnson, eds. *Filth: Dirt, Disgust, and Modern Life*. Minneapolis, MN: U of Minnesota P, 2005.

Conrad, Jack. 'Moralism and Morality.' *Weekly Worker*. (4 February 1999): n. pag. <www.cpgb.org.uk/worker/274/moralism.html>

Cowley, Jason. 'Prickly Flower of Scotland.' *Times*. (13 March 1997): 33.

Crace, John. 'Books: The Digested Read.' *Guardian*. (31 July 2006): 36.

Craig, Cairns. *The Modern Scottish Novel: Narrative and Narration*. Edinburgh: Edinburgh UP, 1999.

——. 'Scotland and the Regional Novel.' Snell 221–56.

Craig, Carol. *The Scots' Crisis of Confidence*. Edinburgh: Mainstream, 2003.

Crawford, Robert. 'Defining Scotland.' Bassnett 83–96.

——. *Devolving English Literature*. 2nd ed. Edinburgh: Edinburgh UP, 2000.

——. ed. *The Scottish Invention of English Literature*. Cambridge: Cambridge UP, 1998.

Cripps, Charlotte. 'Cultural Life: Irvine Welsh Novelist.' *Independent*. (9 December 2005): 2.

Crumey, Andrew. 'Big-hitters Promise Dazzling Chapter for the Book Festival.' *Scotland on Sunday*. (19 June 2005): 2.

Deerin, Chris. 'SNP in "Racist" Leaflet Storm.' *Daily Mail*. (20 September 1996): 11.

Devine, Tom. *The Scottish Nation: 1700–2000*. London: Lane/Penguin, 1999.

Devine, Tom, and Paddy Logue, eds. *Being Scottish: Personal Reflections on Scottish Identity Today*. Edinburgh: Mainstream, 2002.

Donovan, Anne. 'Contemporary Scottish Fiction in the Upper School.' Ed. Alan MacGillivray. *Teaching Scottish Literature: Curriculum and Classroom Applications*. Edinburgh: Edinburgh UP, 1997. 108–14.

Downer, Lesley. 'The Beats of Scotland.' *New York Times Magazine*. (31 March 1996): 42–5.

Drumgoole, Dominic. *The Full Room: An A–Z of Contemporary Playwriting*. London: Methuen, 2000.

Eagleton, Terry. *The Idea of Culture*. Oxford: Blackwell, 2000.

Easthope, Anthony. 'But What Is Cultural Studies?' Bassnett 3–18.

Ellis, Carolyne. 'The Author's Author: Who Do the Novelists Really Rate?' *Guardian*. (26 October 1998): 17.

English, Shirley. 'What Is It with Yuppies and Water?' *The Times*. (16 July 2005): 37.

Farquarson, Kenny. 'Through the Eye of a Needle.' *Scotland on Sunday*. (8 August 1993): n. pag.

Farred, Grant. 'Wankerdom: *Trainspotting* as a Rejection of the Post-colonial?' *SAQ*. 103 (2004): 218–26.

Findlay, Elspeth. 'The Bourgeois Values of Irvine Welsh.' *Cencrastus*. 71 (2002): 5–6.

Finlay, Richard J. *Modern Scotland 1914–2000*. London: Profile, 2004.

Freeman, Alan. 'Ghosts in Sunny Leith: Irvine Welsh's *Trainspotting*.' Ed. Susanne Hagermann. *Studies in Scottish Fiction: 1945 to the Present*. Frankfurt-am-Main: Peter Lang, 1996. 251–62.

Freud, Sigmund. *The Joke and Its Relation to the Unconscious*. Trans. Joyce Crick. New York: Penguin, 2002.

——. *The Psychopathology of Everyday Life*. Trans. Anthea Bell. New York: Penguin, 2002.

Fry, Michael. *The Scottish Empire*. East Lothian: Tuckwell, 2001.

Frye, Northrup. *Anatomy of Criticism: Four Essays.* 1957. Princeton, NJ: Princeton UP, 1971.

Galbraith, Iain. 'Finding Fucking Words: A German Stage Milieu for Irvine Welsh's *Trainspotting.*' *Southfields.* 5 (1998): 53–68.

Gardiner, Linda. 'Elegy for Edinburgh.' *Nation.* (20/27 August 2001): 25–6, 28.

Gardiner, Michael. 'British Territory: Irvine Welsh in British and Japanese.' *Textual Practice.* 17 (2003): 101–17.

Genette, Gérard. *Narrative Discourse.* Oxford: Blackwell, 1980.

Gifford, Douglas. 'Clever Books and Sad People.' *Books in Scotland.* 54 (Autumn 1996): 1–8.

——. 'The Lion in Winter.' *Books in Scotland.* 51 (Autumn 1994): 6–14.

——. 'Lonely Quests and Enchanted Woods.' *Books in Scotland.* 49 (Spring 1994): 19–25.

Gifford, Douglas, Sarah Dunnigan, and Alan Macgillivray, eds. *Scottish Literature in English and Scots.* Edinburgh: Edinburgh UP, 2002.

Gilbert, Pamela K. 'Medieval Mapping: The Thames, the Body, and Our Mutual Friend.' Cohen and Johnson 78–102.

Goldie, David. 'The Scottish New Wave.' Shaffer 526–37.

Gordon, Giles. 'Pandering to the English View of Scotland the Depraved.' *Scotsman.* (13 June 1997): 19.

Gow, Carol. '*Trainspotting* is Less Dangerous than Ignorance.' *THES.* (22 March 1996): 26.

Grant, Iain. 'Dealing Out the Capital Punishment: Irvine Welsh.' *Sunday Times.* (5 September 1993): SC 14.

Gray, Alasdair. *1982 Janine.* 1984. Edinburgh: Canongate, 2003.

——. *Lanark.* 1981. Edinburgh: Canongate, 2002.

Gray, Chris. 'Judges Drop Favourites from Booker Shortlist.' *Independent.* (25 September 2002): 5.

Hagemann, Susanne. 'Introduction.' *Studies in Scottish Fiction: 1945 to the Present.* Frankfurt-am-Main: Peter Lang, 1996. 7–15.

Hallam, Julia. 'Film, Class and National Identity: Reimagining Communities in the Age of Devolution.' Eds. Justine Ashby, and Andrew Higson. *British Cinema, Past and Present.* London: Routledge, 2000. 261–73.

Harold, Christine L. 'The Rhetorical Function of the Abject Body: Transgressive Corporeality in *Trainspotting.*' *JAC.* 20 (2000): 865–87.

Hart, Matthew. 'Solvent Abuse. Irvine Welsh and Scotland.' *Postmodern Culture.* 12 (2002): n. pag. <http://muse.jhs.edu/journals/pmc/v012/12.2hart.html>

Haywood, Ian. *Working-Class Fiction: From Chartism to "Trainspotting".* Plymouth: Northcote, 1997.

Head, Dominic. *The Cambridge Introduction to Modern British Fiction, 1950–2000*. Cambridge: Cambridge UP, 2002.

Herbrechter, Stefan. 'From *Trainspotting* to *Filth*: Masculinity and Cultural Politics in Irvine Welsh's Writings.' Eds. Russell West, and Frank Lay. *Subverting Masculinity: Hegemonic and Alternating Versions of Masculinity in Contemporary Culture*. Amsterdam: Rodopi, 2000. 109–27.

Herman, Arthur. *How the Scots Invented the Modern World*. New York: Three Rivers, 2001.

Higdon, David Leon. ' "Wild Justice" in the Works of Irvine Welsh.' *Studies in Scottish Literature*. 33–34 (2004): 421–34.

Hill, John, Martin McLoone, and Paul Hainsworth, eds. *Border Crossing: Film in Ireland, Britain and Europe*. Belfast: Institute of Irish Studies in association with the U of Ulster and the British Film Institute, 1994.

Hodge, John, ed. *Trainspotting* and *Shallow Grave*. London: Faber and Faber, 1996.

Home, Colette Douglas. '48-Hour Rule That Can Give Families a Chance.' *Daily Mail*. (15 November 1996): 9.

Hornby, Nick. 'Chibs with Everything.' *TLS*. (28 April 1995): 23.

Horton, Patricia. '*Trainspotting*: A Topography of the Masculine Abject.' *English: A Journal of the English Association*. 50 (2001): 219–34.

Howard, Gerald. 'Hanging with the Scottish Homeboys.' N. pag. <www.wwnorton.com/irvinewelsh/scots.htm>

Howie, Michael, and Angie Brown. 'Why Rapists Love Our Courts.' *Scotsman*. (9 December 2005): 2.

Innes, Charlotte. 'A Little Drug'll Do Ya.' *Los Angeles Times*. (18 August 1996): Book Review 1.

Ishiguro, Kazuo. *The Remains of the Day*. 1989. New York: Vintage, 1990.

'It's Generational and Geographical.' *Scotsman*. (26 February 1994): n. pag.

Jackson, Ellen-Raïsa, and Willy Maley. 'Birds of a Feather?: A Postcolonial Reading of Irvine Welsh's *Marabou Stork Nightmares*.' *Revista Canaria de Estudios Ingleses*. 41 (November 2000): 187–96.

Jackson, Lorne. 'Nae kiddin pal, this fella's goon an lost the plot.' *Sunday Mercury* (Birmingham). (20 August 2006): 3.

Jameson, Fredric. *Postmodernism, or, the Logic of Late Capitalism*. Durham, NC: Duke UP, 1991.

Jamieson, Gill. 'Fixing the City: Arterial and Other Spaces in Irvine Welsh's Fiction.' Eds. G. Norquay, and G. Smyth. *Space and Place*. Liverpool: John Moores UP, 1997. 217–26.

Jeffers, Jennifer M. 'Rhizome National Identity: "Scatlin's Psychic Defence" in *Trainspotting*.' *Journal of Narrative Theory*. 35 (Winter 2005): 88–111.

Jeffries, Brett. 'Britart Has Stolen the Shock Tactics of the Avant-Garde but Ignored the Subversive Agenda.' *New Statesman*. (20 March 1998): 42–3.

Jones, Carole. 'White Men on Their Backs: the Representation of the White Male as Victim in William McIlvanney's *Docherty* and Irvine Welsh's *Marabou Stork Nightmares*.' *International Journal of Scottish Literature*. 1 (Autumn 2006): n. pag. <www.ijsl.stir.ac.uk/issue1/jones.htm>

Jones, Thomas. 'Thought-Quenching.' *London Review of Books*. (7 January 1999): 32–3.

Jury, Louise. 'Millions More Flock to Flicks.' *Independent*. (22 June 1996): 3.

Kakutani, Michiko. 'Slumming.' *New York Times Magazine*. (26 May 1996): 16.

Kane, Pat. 'Fatal Knowledge of an Inescapable Masculinity.' *Scotland on Sunday*. (16 July 1995): 12.

Karnicky, Jeffrey. 'Irvine Welsh's Novel Subjectivities.' *Social Text*. 21 (Fall 2003): 135–54.

Kelly, Aaron. *Irvine Welsh*. Manchester: Manchester UP, 2005.

Kennedy, A. L. 'Scots to the Death.' *New York Times*. (20 July 1996): 19.

Kerr, Euan. 'Interview with Welsh.' *Morning Edition*. National Public Radio (26 July 1996).

Ketcham, James M. 'Irvine Welsh.' Ed. Merritt Modeley. *British and Irish Novelists Since 1960*. Dictionary of Literary Biography, Vol. 271. Detroit: Gale, 2003. 350–8.

Kidd, Colin. 'Victims of the Victims.' *TLS*. (24 October 2003): 4–6.

King, John. 'The Boys Are Back in Town.' *New Statesman*. (2 September 2002): 36–7.

Kirby, Terry. 'Irvine Welsh Is Criticised by Scots Author over Portrayal of Homeland.' *Independent*. (8 January 2004): 12.

Lappin, Tom. 'Brain Rotting.' *Scotsman*. (24 August 2002): 6.

LaSalle, Mick. ' "Trainspotting" Needs a Fix.' *San Francisco Chronicle*. (26 July 1996): D1.

Lasdun, James. 'A Smart Cunt.' *Village Voice*. (23 July 1996): 74.

Lawson, Terry. 'Hey, Hey We're the Junkies.' *New Orleans Times-Picayune*. (2 August 1996): L24.

Lea, Daniel, and Berthold Schoene, eds. *Posting the Male: Masculinities in Post-war and Contemporary British Literature*. Amsterdam: Rodopi, 2003.

Lefebvre, Henri. 1974. *The Production of Space*. Oxford: Blackwell, 1991.

Lindner, Christoph. *Fictions of Commodity Culture*. Aldershot: Ashgate, 2003.

Linklater, Alexander. 'I Am Still a Petulant Brat Showing Off.' *Evening Standard*. (24 April 2001): 29.

——. 'Irvine Welsh: He Sells Millions of Books by Writing about Human Degradation in a Scottish Phonetic Vernacular. Is This Britain's Strangest Literary Phenomenon?' *Prospect*. 63 (May 2001): n. pag. <www.prospect-magazine.co.uk/printarticle.php?id=3564&category=135&issue=514&author=>

Lister, David. 'Literary Walks Turn Down Darker Paths.' *The Times*. (3 May 2005): 8.

Lockerbie, Catherine. 'Pure Dead Demotic.' *Scotsman*. (14 August 1993): n. pag.

Lury, Karen. 'Here and Then: Space, Place and Nostalgia in British Youth Cinema.' Murphy 100–8.

Lyon, David. *Postmodernity*. 2nd ed. Minneapolis, MN: U of Minnesota P, 1999.

Macaulay, Ronald K. S. *Extremely Common Eloquence: Constructing Scottish Identity Through Narration*. Amsterdam: Rodopi, 2005.

Macdonald, Kevin. 'Postcards from the Edge.' *Independent on Sunday*. (28 January 1996): Arts 18. Rpt. 'Afterword – An Interview with Irvine Welsh.' Hodge 117–21.

Macfarlane, Robert. 'Pain Spotting.' *New York Times Book Review*. (20 August 2006): 19.

Mackay, Marina. '*Marabou Stork Nightmares*: Irvine Welsh's Anthropological Vision.' *National Identities*. 5 (November 2003): 269–81.

MacNab, Geoffrey. 'That Shrinking Feeling.' *Sight and Sound*. (October 2002): 18–25.

Maley, Willy. 'Subversion and Squirrility in Irvine Welsh's Shorter Fiction.' Eds. Dermot Cavanagh, and Tim Kirk. *Subversion and Squirrility: Popular Discourse in Europe from 1500 to the Present*. Aldershot: Ashgate, 2000. 190–204.

——. 'You'll Have Had Your Theatre.' *Spike Magazine*. N. pag. <www.spikemagazine.com/0199welshplay.htm>

Mantel, Hilary. 'No Passes or Documents Are Needed: The Writer at Home in Europe.' Ed. Zachary Leader. *On Modern Fiction*. New York: Oxford UP, 2002. 93–106.

March, Christie L. *Rewriting Scotland: Welsh, McLean, Warner, Banks, Galloway, and Kennedy*. Manchester: Manchester UP, 2002.

Massie, Allan. 'Still a Chance for Scots Culture to Flower.' *Sunday Times*. (2 January 2000): 14.

McArthur, Colin. '*Braveheart* and the Scottish Aesthetic Dementia.' Ed. Tony Barta. *Screening the Past: Film and the Representation of History*. Westport, CT: Praeger, 1998. 167–87.

——. '*Brigadoon*', '*Braveheart* and the Scots: Distortions of Scotland in Hollywood Cinema*. London: I. B. Tauris, 2003.

——. 'The Cultural Necessity of a Poor Celtic Cinema.' Hill et al. 112–25.

McAvoy, Joe. 'Scheme Dreams.' *Scotsman*. (28 April 2001): 6.

McCormick, Neil. 'Too Much Junkie Business?' *Daily Telegraph*. (15 February 1996): n. pag.

McCrone, David. *Understanding Scotland: The Sociology of a Nation*. 2nd ed. London: Routledge, 2001.

McGavin, Patrick Z. '"Trainspotting" Author "Stumbled into Writing".' *Chicago Tribune*. (30 July 1996): 52.

McIlvanney, Liam. 'Divided We Stand: Scotlands For Ever.' *TLS*. (21 April 2000): 25.

———. 'The Politics of Narrative in the Postwar Scottish Novel.' Ed. Zachary Leader. *On Modern Fiction*. New York: Oxford UP, 2002. 181–208.

McIntyre, Steve. 'Vanishing Point: Feature Film Production in a Small Country.' Hill et al. 88–111.

McKay, Alastair. 'Sunday Morning, Amsterdam.' *Scotsman*. (25 July 1998): Weekend 6.

McLean, Duncan, ed. *Ahead of Its Time: A Clocktower Press Anthology*. London: Vintage, 1998.

McLeod, John. *Beginning Postcolonialism*. Manchester: Manchester UP, 2000.

McMenanin, Tony. 'Porno Star.' *Maxim Online*. (22 October 2002): n. pag. <www.maximonline.com/entertainment/articles/article_4883.html>

McWilliam, Candia. 'Books of the Year.' *Independent on Sunday*. (1 December 1996): 32.

Merikangas, James R. 'Review of *Marabou Stork Nightmares*.' *American Journal of Psychiatry*. 153 (December 1996): 1641–2.

Mikhail, Kate. 'In the Front Row.' *Observer*. (31 March 2002): 16.

Milne, Drew. 'The Fiction of James Kelman and Irvine Welsh: Accents, Speech and Writing.' Eds. Richard J. Lane, Rod Mengham, and Philip Tew. *Contemporary British Fiction*. Cambridge: Polity, 2003. 158–73.

Molloy, Deidre. 'Scotland the Brave.' *Guardian*. (12 November 1995): 8.

Monk, Claire. 'Men in the 90s.' Murphy 156–66.

———. 'Underbelly UK: The 1990s Underclass Film, Masculinity and the Ideologies of "New Britain".' Eds. Justine Ashby, and Andrew Higson. *British Cinema, Past and Present*. London: Routledge, 2000. 274–87.

Monnickendam, Andrew. 'Literary Voices and the Projection of Cultural Failure in Modern Scottish Literature.' Eds. Ton Hoenselaars, and Marius Buning. *English Literature and Other Languages*. Amsterdam: Rodopi, 1999. 231–42.

Monteith, Sharon, Jenny Newman, and Pat Wheeler. *Contemporary British and Irish Literature: An Introduction through Interviews*. London: Arnold, 2004.

Morace, Robert A. *Irvine Welsh's 'Trainspotting': A Reader's Guide*. New York: Continuum, 2001.

Moran, Joe. *Star Authors: Literary Celebrity in America*. London: Pluto, 2000.

Morton, Tom. 'Remotely Civilised.' *Scotsman*. (20 November 1996): n. pag.

Mount, Ferdinand. *Mind the Gap: Class in Britain Now*. London: Short, 2004.

Mukherjee, Neel. 'Dangerous Food Poison.' *The Times on Line*. (29 July 2006): n. pag. <www.timesonline.co.uk/article/0,,23109–2288450.html>

Murphy, Robert, ed. *British Cinema of the 90s*. London: BFI, 2000.

Nehring, Neil. *Flowers in the Dustbin: Culture, Anarchy and Postwar England*. Ann Arbor, MI: U of Michigan P, 1993.

Neubauer, Jürgen. 'Critical Media Literacy and the Representation of Youth in *Trainspotting*.' *Anglistik & Englischunterricht*. 63 (2000): 151–69.

Norris, Frank. *McTeague: A Story of San Francisco*. New York: Doubleday & McClure, 1899.

Novick, Jed. 'Sticking to Your Roots.' *Insight.co.uk*. (May 2001): n. pag. <www.nigelberman.co.uk/feature1_may.htm>

O'Hagan, Andrew. *Our Fathers*. London: Faber and Faber, 1999.

O'Hagan, Sean. 'I'd Rather Look at the Hills Than Get Wasted.' *Observer*. (4 December 2005): 3.

Oliver, Fiona. 'The Self-Debasement of Scotland's Postcolonial Bodies.' *SPAN*. 42–43 (April and October 1996): 114–21.

'On Language.' *Scotsman*. (25 July 1998): Weekend 6.

Orr, Deborah. 'Chips (and Chivs) with Everything.' *Independent*. (4 August 2006): 22.

Orr, John. *Contemporary Cinema*. Edinburgh: Edinburgh UP, 1998.

Page, Benedicte. 'Irvine Welsh: A Walk on the Wilde Side.' *Bookseller*. (15 June 2006): n. pag. <www.thebookseller.com/?pid=2&did=19887>

Paget, Derek. ' "Speaking Out": The Transformations of *Trainspotting*.' Eds. Deborah Cartmell, and Imelda Whelehan. *Adaptations: From Text to Screen, Screen to Text*. London: Routledge, 1999. 128–40.

Petrie, Duncan. *Contemporary Scottish Fictions: Film, Television and the Novel*. Edinburgh: Edinburgh UP, 2004.

——. *Screening Scotland*. London: BFI, 2000.

Plain, Gill. 'Hard Nuts to Crack: Devolving Masculinity in Contemporary Scottish Fiction.' Lea and Schoene 55–68.

Polk, James. 'Bird of Prey.' *New York Times Book Review*. (11 February 1996): 10.

Porlock, Harvey. 'Boyfriend? Wet Patch?' *Sunday Times*. (9 June 1996): sec. 7, 2.

'The Power of Scotland.' *Scotland on Sunday*. (14 April 2002): 1–3.

Punter, David. 'Fictional Maps of Britain.' Bassnett 65–80.

Qureshi, Yakub, and Aidan Smith. 'Iconic Film "Sent UK Industry Off Rails".' *Scotsman*. (11 July 2004): 6.

Rankin, Ian. 'Review of *Filth*.' *London Evening Standard*. (27 July 1998): 48.

Rawsthorn, Alice. 'Small Budget Movie with Big Ambitions.' *Financial Times*. (27 January 1996): 5.

Redhead, Steve. *Repetitive Beat Generation*. Edinburgh: Rebel Inc, 2000.

Reynolds, Simon. 'Angel with a Dirty Mind.' *VLS*. (15 September 1998): 8–11, 127.

Reynolds, Simon. *Energy Flash: Journey through Rave Music and Dance Culture*. London: Picador, 1998.

Riach, Alan. *Representing Scotland in Literature, Popular Culture, and Iconography: The Masks of a Modern Nation*. Basingstoke and New York: Palgrave Macmillan, 2004.

——. 'The Unnatural Scene: The Fiction of Irvine Welsh.' Eds. James Acheson, and Sarah C. E. Ross. *The Contemporary British Novel*. Edinburgh: Edinburgh UP, 2005. 35–47.

Rich, Frank. 'Naked Capitalists.' *New York Times Magazine*. (20 May 2001): 50–6, 80, 82, 92.

Ritchie, Harry, ed. *Acid Plaid: New Scottish Writing*. London: Bloomsbury, 1996.

Romero, Dennis. 'Adding a Little Grit to Modern Novels.' *Los Angeles Times*. (26 June 1996): E1, E8.

Russell, Guy. 'The Cult Now Arriving.' *New Statesman*. (23 February 1996): 48.

Ryan, Ray. *Ireland and Scotland: Literature and Culture, State and Nation, 1966–2000*. Oxford: Oxford UP, 2002.

Schoene, Berthold. 'Nervous Men, Mobile Nation: Masculinity and Psychopathology in Irvine Welsh's *Filth* and *Glue*.' Bell and Miller 121–45.

Schoene-Harwood, Berthold. *Writing Men: Literary Masculinities from Frankenstein to the New Man*. Edinburgh: Edinburgh UP, 2000.

Self, Will. 'Carry On Up the Hypodermic.' *Observer*. (11 February 1996): 6.

Shaffer, Brian W., ed. *A Companion to the British and Irish Novel 1945–2000*. Oxford: Blackwell, 2005.

Sillars, Jane. 'Drama, Devolution and Dominant Representations.' Smith et al. 246–54.

Sinfield, Alan. *Literature, Politics and Culture in Postwar Britain*. London: Athlone P, 1997.

Singh, Rashna B. *Goodly Is Our Heritage: Children's Literature, Empire and the Certitude of Character*. Lanham, MD: Scarecrow, 2004.

Skinner, John. 'Contemporary Scottish Novelists and the Stepmother Tongue.' Eds. Ton Hoenselaars, and Marius Buning. *English Literature and Other Languages*. Amsterdam: Rodopi, 1999. 211–20.

Smith, Andrew. 'How To Get Rave.' *Sunday Times*. (14 February 1996): n. pag.

——. 'Irvine Changes Trains; Interview.' *Sunday Times*. (1 February 1998): 6.

Smith, Casper Llewellyn. 'Club Culture Spreads the Word.' *Daily Telegraph*. (1 June 1996): n. pag.

——. 'The Credible Voice of Rave Culture.' *Daily Telegraph*. (22 April 1995): n. pag.

Smith, Chris. *Creative Britain*. London: Faber and Faber, 1998.

Smith, Donald. *Storytelling Scotland: A Nation in Narrative*. Edinburgh: Polygon, 2001.

Smith, L. C. 'Welcome to the Acid House.' *Spin*. (August 1996): 22.

Smith, Murray. *Trainspotting*. London: BFI, 2002.

——. 'Transnational *Trainspotting*.' Smith et al. 219–27.

Smith, Murray, Jane Stokes, and Anna Reading, eds. *The Media in Britain: Current Debate and Developments*. London: Macmillan (now Palgrave Macmillan), 1999.

Smith, Peter J. 'Edinburgh: Catching Up with a City in Transition.' *New York Times Magazine*. (26 September 1999): 26–8, 30, 32.

Snell, K. D. M., ed. *The Regional Novel in Britain and Ireland*. Cambridge: Cambridge UP, 1998.

Spencer, Charles. 'Nightmare City.' *Daily Telegraph*. (4 April 1995): n. pag.

Spittal, Robin. '*Trainspotting* – A New Scottish Icon?' *Études Écossaises* 5 (1998): 195–205.

Spring, Ian. 'Image and Text: Fiction on Film.' Eds. Gavin Wallace, and Randall Stevenson. *The Scottish Novel Since the Seventies*. Edinburgh: Edinburgh UP, 1993. 206–16.

Squires, Claire. 'Novelistic Production and the Publishing Industry in Britain and Ireland.' Shaffer 177–93.

——. '*Trainspotting* and Publishing, or Converting the Smack into Hard Cash.' *Edinburgh Review*. 101 (1999): 50–6.

Stam, Robert. 'The Dialogics of Adaptation.' Ed. James Naremore. *Film Adaptation*. New Brunswick, NJ: Rutgers UP, 2000. 54–78.

Stephenson, William. 'Scoring Ecstasy: MDMA, Consumerism and Spirituality in the Early Fiction of Irvine Welsh.' *Journal for Culture Research*. 7 (2003): 147–63.

Stollery, Martin. *Trainspotting*. London: York P, 2000.

Strachan, Zoe. 'Queerspotting.' *Spike Magazine*. N. pag. <www.spikemagazine.com/0599queerspotting.htm>

Street, Sarah. *Transatlantic Crossings: British Films in the USA*. New York: Continuum, 2002.

Thompson, Ben. 'The Interview: Irvine Welsh.' *Independent on Sunday*. (2 June 1996): Real Life 2.

Todd, Richard. *Consuming Fictions: The Booker Prize and Fiction in Britain Today*. London: Bloomsbury, 1996.

Toibin, Colm, ed. *The Penguin Book of Irish Fiction*. New York: Penguin, 1999.

Tonkin, Boyd. 'Who'd Be a Booker Judge?' *Independent*. (21 January 2005): 12.

Trocchi, Alexander. *Cain's Book*. 1960. New York: Grove P, 1992.

Turner, Jenny. 'Love's Chemistry.' *Guardian*. (31 May 1996): G2: 17.

——. 'Sick Boys.' *London Review of Books*. (2 December 1993): 10.

Turpin, Adrian. 'These Will Be Huge – Cows Included.' *Sunday Times*. (1 January 2006): 6.

Vincent, Sally. 'Everybody's Doing It.' *Guardian*. (10 August 2002): 32.

Wallace, Gavin. 'Voices in Empty Houses: The Novel of Damaged Identity.' Eds. Gavin Wallace, and Randall Stevenson. *The Scottish Novel Since the Seventies*. Edinburgh: Edinburgh UP, 1993. 217–31.

Walsh, John. 'The Not-so-shady Past of Irvine Welsh.' *Independent*. (15 April 1995): Weekend 25.

Watson, Neil. 'Hollywood UK.' Murphy 80–7.

Welsh, Irvine. 'Absinthe Makes Sense of a Crazy World.' *Daily Telegraph*. (14 April 2003): n. pag.

——. 'The Best Brand of Football.' Ed. Nicholas Royle. *A Book of Two Halves: New Football Stories*. London: Gollancz, 1996. 25–39.

——. 'Catholic Guilt (You Know You Love It).' Ed. Nick Hornby. *Speaking with the Angel: Original Stories*. London: Penguin, 2000. 185–206.

——. 'Contamination: A Novella in Regress.' *The Weekenders: Travels in the Heart of Africa*. London: Ebury P, 2001. 125–268.

——. 'Dreaming of a White Christmas.' Ed. Duncan McLean. *Ahead of Its Time: A Clocktower Press Anthology*. London: Vintage, 1998. 191–204.

——. 'Drugs and the Theatre, Darlings.' Welsh. *Trainspotting' and 'Head-state'*. 1–10.

——. 'Elspeth's Boyfriend.' Ed. Richard Thomas. *Vox ' n' Roll: Fiction for the 21st Century*. London: Serpent's Tail, 2000. 217–34.

——. 'A Fault on the Line.' Ritchie 48–54.

——. *4 Play*. London: Vintage, 2001.

——. ' "Glue".' *Liveonline*. Washingtonpost.com. N.pag. <http://discuss.washingtonpost.com/wp-srv/zforum/01/author_welsh060601.html>

——. 'I Can't Live Without … Writer Irvine Welsh Reveals a Few of His Favourite Things.' *Mail on Sunday*. (20 August 2006): 9.

——. 'It's Hurting. But It Ain't Working.' *Guardian*. (25 November 1998): T12.

——. 'A New Report Claims Scotland Has a Higher Murder Rate Than America.' *Guardian*. (20 October 2005): G2: 8.

——. 'Reality Orientation.' Ed. Andrew O'Hagan. *The Weekenders: Adventures in Calcutta*. London: Ebury P, 2004. 155–261.

——. 'The Rosewell Incident.' Ed. Kevin Williamson. *Children of Albion Rovers*. Edinburgh: Rebel Inc, 1997. 171–228.

——. 'A Scottish George Best of Literature.' Eds. Allan Campbell, and Tim Niel. *A Life in Pieces: Reflections on Alexander Trocchi*. Edinburgh: Rebel Inc, 1997. 17–19.

——. 'She's Pregnant and He's Got His Fist Raised.' *Guardian*. (16 January 1999): 4.

——. 'The State of the Party.' Ed. Sarah Champion. *Disco Biscuits: New Fiction from the Chemical Generation*. London: Sceptre, 1997. 29–62.

——. 'Victor Spoils.' Ed. Toni Davidson. *Intoxication: An Anthology of Stimulant-Based Writing*. London: Serpent's Tail, 1998. 150–78.

——. 'Why I Hate Theatre.' *The Stage*. (4 February 1999): 8.

——, and Dean Cavanagh. *Babylon Heights*. New York: W. W. Norton, 2006.

——, Alexander McCall Smith, and Ian Rankin. *One City*. Intro. J. K. Rowling. Edinburgh: Polygon, 2006.

——, and Kevin Williamson. *A Visitor's Guide to Edinburgh*. Edinburgh: Rebel Inc, 1993.

Westbrook, Caroline. 'First Class Return.' *Empire*. 81 (March 1996): 90–107.

Whyte, Christopher. 'Masculinities in Contemporary Scottish Fiction.' *Forum for Modern Language Studies*. 34 (1998): 274–85.

Whyte, Hamish, and Janice Galloway, eds. *Scream, if You Want to Go Faster*. New Writing Scotland 9. Aberdeen: Association for Scottish Literary Studies, 1991.

'Will It Last This Time?' *Economist*. 345 (11 October 1997): 108–9.

Williams, Nicholas M. 'The Dialect of Authenticity: The Case of Irvine Welsh's *Trainspotting*.' Eds. Ton Hoenselaars, and Marius Buning. *English Literature and Other Languages*. Amsterdam: Rodopi, 1999. 221–30.

Williamson, Kevin. 'Welcome Home.' *Sunday Times*. (18 August 2002): Écosse 1.

Young, Elizabeth. 'Blood on the Tracks.' *Guardian*. (15 August 1993): Edinburgh supp.: 8.

——. 'The Long Slow Demise of Our Literary Culture.' *New Statesman*. (12 July 1999): 51.